THE ROUGH GUIDE

Website

Directory

There are more than two hundred Rough Guide
travel, phrasebook and music titles, covering
destinations from Amsterdam to Zimbabwe,
languages from Czech to Vietnamese, and musics
from World to Opera and Jazz

ROUGH
GUIDES

www.roughguides.com

Rough Guide Credits

Text editors: Andrew Dickson, Orla Duane
Series editor: Mark Ellingham
Production: Michelle Draycott, Helen Prior
Graphics Assistant: Peter Buckley

Publishing Information

This first edition published October 2001 by
Rough Guides Ltd, 62–70 Shorts Gardens, London WC2H 9AH.

Distributed by the Penguin Group

Penguin Books Ltd, 80 Strand, London WC2R 0RL
Penguin Putnam, Inc., 375 Hudson Street, New York 10014, USA
Penguin Books Australia Ltd, 487 Maroondah Highway,
PO Box 257, Ringwood, Victoria 3134, Australia
Penguin Books Canada Ltd, 10 Alcorn Avenue,
Toronto, Ontario, Canada M4V 1E4
Penguin Books (NZ) Ltd, 182–190 Wairau Road,
Auckland 10, New Zealand

Printed and bound by Omnia Books Ltd, Glasgow

Dear Gilles,

Good Luck in Paisley

THE ROUGH GUIDE

this should help you

Website

now that you don't

Directory

have me as your internet chum!

written by

Angus J Kennedy & Peter Shapiro

All the very best,

Contents

Contents

Contents

Contents

part one

Introduction

Find it
without losing your mind

Barring total deforestation of the world, it would be physically impossible to list, let alone review, every Website currently floating around the ether; in fact, this book lists less than one-tenth of one percent of all the information available on the World Wide Web. Therefore, the art of **finding something** pinned up on the world's biggest scrapboard is, without doubt, **the most valuable skill** you can glean from your time online. If you know how to use the Net to find an answer to almost anything quickly and comprehensively, you'd have to consider yourself not only useful but pretty saleable too. Most people, including many Net veterans, simply **bumble their way around**. Yet it's a remarkably basic skill to master. So read this section, then get online and start investigating. Within an hour or two you'll be milking the Net for all it's worth. It might turn out to be the best investment you'll ever make!

Find it

How it works

The Net is massive. Just the Web alone houses well over two billion pages of text, and many millions more are added daily. So you'll need some serious help if you want to find something. Thankfully, there's a wide selection of search tools to make the task relatively painless. The job usually entails keying your **search terms** into a form on a Web page and waiting a few seconds for the results.

Over the next few pages we'll introduce you to **search tools** that can locate almost anything: on the Web; linked to from the Web; or archived into an online Web database, such as email addresses, phone numbers, program locations, newsgroup articles and news clippings. Of course, first it has to be put online and granted public access. So just because you can access US government servers doesn't mean you'll find a file on DEA Operative Presley's whereabouts.

Your weapons

There are three main types of Web search tools: **search engines**, **hand-built subject directories** and **search agents**. Apart from the odd newspaper archive, they're usually free. Because they're so useful and popular, there was a trend towards tacking other services onto the side and building themselves into so-called **portals**, **communities** and **hubs**. More recently, that trend has begun to reverse with the launch of several skeletal search tools free of fancy overheads. Irrespective of which you use, ignore the quantity of froufrou and concentrate on the quality of the results. The next few pages discuss each category in detail and show you how to torture them for answers.

Search engines

The best way to find just about anything online is to start with a **search engine**. The good thing about search engines is they can search through the **actual contents** of Web pages (and file servers), and not just descriptions. The better search engines can rifle through **billions of Web pages** in a fraction of a second. You simply go to the search engine's Website and submit **keywords**, or search terms, into a simple form. It will query its database and, almost instantly, return a list of results or "**hits**". For example, if you were to search on the expression "Rough Guide Website Directory", here's what might come up on top:

1. Welcome to the Rough Guide Website Directory
The Rough Guide Website Directory is the ultimate guide to the World Wide Web, complete with a 2500+ site directory.
www.roughguides.com/web/index.html/

In this case the top line tells us the name of the page or site, followed by a description excerpted from the page and then the page's address. If it suits, click on the link to visit the site.

Tip: don't just click on a result, and then hit the Back button if it's no good. Instead, run down the list and open the most promising candidates in new browser windows. It will save you tons of time. Do this by holding down the **Shift key** as you click.

The reason it's so quick is **you're not searching the Web live**. You're merely searching a database of Web page extracts stored on the search engine's server. This database is compiled by a program that periodically "crawls" around the Web looking for new or changed pages. Because of the sheer size of the Net and a few factors relating to site design, it's not possible for the crawlers to find every site, let alone every word on every page. Nor is it possible to keep the database completely up-to-date.

That means you can't literally "search the Web" – you can only search a snapshot taken by a search engine. So, naturally, different search engines will give you different results depending on how much of the Web they've found, how often they update, how much text they extract from each page and how well they actually work.

So, which search engine?

There are dozens of search engines, but only a few are worth trying. In fact, you'll rarely need more than one. But since you'll be using it often, make sure it's up to speed. You'll want the **biggest**, **freshest**, **database**. You'll want to **fine-tune your search** with extra commands. And you'll want the most hits you can get on one page with the most **relevant results on top**. Right now, that's **Google.**

Google http://www.google.com

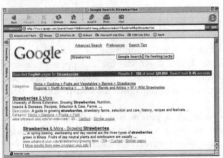

This completely free service has an uncanny knack of getting it right in the first few hits, both from within its search engine database and its association with the **Open Directory**. It also provides local cache access to pages that have disappeared since its crawl or are otherwise unavailable. Click on "cached" to see how this works. Use it when you can't get a link to load.

If Google falls short, try **All the Web** and **AltaVista**. They're also big, fast, clutter-free and can deliver a long page of relevant hits. Next up is **Northern Light**, which is worth a shot. It's also big, but not so fast or user-friendly despite its curious system of organizing hits into folders.

All the Web http://www.alltheweb.com

AltaVista http://www.av.com

Northern Light http://www.nlsearch.com

As for the rest? Just because an engine isn't the biggest or best doesn't mean it's worthless. Even the smallest engines can find unique hits. Still, unless you're after extra hits, you're unlikely to need them. Of course, they might improve:

Excite http://www.excite.com

HotBot http://www.hotbot.com

Lycos http://www.lycos.com

If you notice some engines give identical or very similar results it might be because they share technologies. **AOL**, **HotBot** and **MSN**, for example, currently use the **Inktomi** system.

But if you seriously need **more results**, rather than visit several engines in turn, query them simultaneously using an agent such as **Copernic**. You can tell how each engine ranks from the results. For more detailed analysis, see:

Search Engine Watch http://www.searchenginewatch.com

Search Engine World http://www.searchengineworld.com

Search Engine Showdown http://www.searchenginesshowdown.com

Search Lore http://www.searchlore.org

They keep tabs on all the finer details such as who owns what, how they work and who's currently biggest. Essential reading for budding Webmasters.

Limitations

Search engines aren't the be-all and end-all of what's on the Web. **They're only as good as their most recent findings**, which might be just a small proportion of what's actually there and possibly months old. So just because you can't find it through a Web search doesn't mean it doesn't exist. If you're after something brand-new, they're not always the best choice. You might be better off searching **Usenet** (see p.20) or a news service.

How to use a search engine

OK, get this right and you'll find anything. The trick is to think up a **search term** that's unique enough to get rid of junk results but broad enough not to miss anything useful. It will depend entirely on the subject, so be prepared to think laterally!

One search won't fit all – read the instructions

Although most search forms look alike, the mechanisms behind them differ. That means you might have to adjust your search terms slightly, depending on the engine, to get the best results. The same applies to online stores, encyclopedias, newspaper archives and anything else you can search. It also means some engines work better than others.

While the easiest way to learn is to dive straight in, at some point pause and read the instructions. You should find a link to a FAQ, Search Tips or Help section on the front page. The main things to glean are how to **create a phrase,** how to **search on multiple phrases** and how to **exclude certain words.** A few minutes' study could save hours of weeding through poor results.

A typical search

Let's start with a complex example. Suppose we want to search for something on one of the esteemed authors, *Angus Kennedy*. Let's see how you'd do it in **All the Web**.

If you were to enter:

angus kennedy

it would return all pages that contain "angus" **or** "kennedy" **or both**. That means there'd be lots of pages about Angus cattle and JFK. We don't want to sift through those, so let's make sure the pages contain **both words**. In Raging Search, and most other search engines, you can use a **plus sign (+)** to state that the page **must contain a word**. So let's try:

+angus +kennedy

That's better. All the pages now contain both words. Unfortunately, though, there's no guarantee that they'll be next to each other. What we really want is to **treat them as a phrase**. A simple way to do this is to enclose the words within quotes, like this:

"angus kennedy"

Now we've captured all instances of Angus Kennedy as a phrase, but since it's **a person's name**, we should look for *Kennedy, Angus* as well. So let's try:

"angus kennedy" "kennedy, angus"

As with the first example, we now catch pages with **either or both phrases**. Now suppose we want to narrow it down further and exclude some irrelevant results, for example others with the same name. Our target writes books about French literature, so let's start by getting rid of that pesky Rough Guide author. To **exclude a term**, place a minus sign (-) in front. So let's ditch him:

"angus kennedy" "kennedy, angus" - "rough guide"

That's about all you need to know in most instances. These rules should work in most engines, as well as the search forms on individual sites. However, there are exceptions.

Variations - such as Google

Google makes searching easier by including all the search terms. Which means you don't have to add the **+** sign. So searching on: *angus kennedy* would search for pages containing "angus" **AND** "kennedy." If you want to search for pages containing either, do two separate searches or use the Boolean operator "OR": *angus OR kennedy*.

Many engines also have a **dropdown menu** with the options of "any of the words", "all the words" or "the exact phrase". If the meaning of that isn't instantly obvious, try it.

To tune your searches further, look for an "advanced search option," or refer to the instructions. Observe how the engine interprets **capitals**, dashes between words, brackets, wild cards, truncations and the **Boolean** operators such as AND, OR, NEAR and NOT.

In particular, watch out for **stop words**. These are words that are normally ignored. In Google, for example, single letters are ignored unless you place a "**+**" sign in front of them. So to search for Angus J Kennedy, you'd enter: *"angus +j kennedy"*

Tip

You'll be using your favourite engines often, so drop their addresses onto your browser Links bar. But rather than save the front page, favour the one with advanced options. At All the Web, for example, click on "Advanced search" to bring up an assortment of tuning boxes, including the friendlier **100 hits per page** option. At Google and Raging Search, click on "Preferences" and "Customize" respectively to increase the default number of hits per page. You can then save the front page, as your preferences will be stored in your cookies.

Translations

If your results include foreign language sites, Google and Altavista can roughly translate them into English or another preference. Just click on "translate".

Can't find it?

If search engines can't find something it doesn't mean it's not on the Web. It just means their trawlers haven't visited that site yet. So you'll have to turn to another, maybe fresher source. Read on.

Subject directories

It's sometimes more useful to browse a range of sites within a topic or region rather than throw darts into the entire Web. For this you should turn to a **subject directory**. These aren't compiled by trawling the Web, **they're put together by human beings**. Everything is neatly filed under various categories, like a phone directory or library, making it easy for you to drill down to what you're after. This is particularly useful if you're looking for a listing of services in an area such as your home town.

You usually have the choice of browsing directories by **subject group** and sometimes by other criteria such as **entry date or rating**. Often you can search the directory itself through a form rather like a search engine. Unlike search engines, directories don't keep the contents of Web pages but instead record titles, categories, and sometimes comments or reviews, so adjust your search strategy accordingly. Start with broad terms and work down until you hit the reviews.

General directories

The Internet doesn't have an official directory, but it does have

several broadly focused directories that will help you on your way to most subject areas. The best **general directories** are:

About.com http://www.about.com

Open Directory http://dmoz.org

Yahoo http://www.yahoo.co.uk

Yahoo is the closest the Net has to a central directory. If the Web has seven wonders, it would probably be the first. Apart from the massive site directory it also has loads of added extras such as national and metropolitan directories, regional TV listings, weather reports, kids' guides, seniors' guides, yellow pages, sport scores – plus outstanding news and financial services. You should spend at least one session online exploring its reaches. Chances are you'll be back there every day.

The Open Directory is a relatively recent project, compiled by about 37,000 volunteers and served through several sites including Google. While it lacks Yahoo's armada of added services, its directory is better maintained in many areas. It pays to look at both.

About.com deserves a special mention, because unlike most broad directories its topics are presented by expert guides. This makes it an excellent jumping-off point if you need a helping hand. If you like this approach, **Suite101** (http://www. suite101.com) attempts the same tack.

There's no shortage of alternatives which might prove useful if the above fail, such as:

AltaVista http://www.av.com
Excite http://www.excite.com
LookSmart http://www.looksmart.com
Lycos http://www.lycos.com

But broad subject directories aren't always the best at digging up everything within a category or giving you expert guidance. For that you need a specialist directory – or, as the suits call them, **vortals**.

Specialists

Whatever your interest, you can bet your favourite finger it will have several dedicated sites and another that keeps track of them all. Such **specialized directories** are a boon for finding new, esoteric or local interest pages – ones that the major directories overlook. How do you find a specialist directory? You could go straight to Google with a very specific search, but in this case it would make more sense to seek a helping hand. Try **About.com** first. It maintains specialist directories on most common interests. Next, try Yahoo and the Open Directory. If there's more than a couple of Web directories on the subject they'll put them in their own section. You might also glean something from consulting a directory that specializes in listing specialist directories such as:

Complete Planet http://www.completeplanet.com
Directory Guide http://www.directoryguide.com
GoGettem http://www.gogettem.com
Search Bug http://www.searchbug.com
Search Engine Guide http://www.searchengineguide.com
Search IQ http://www.searchiq.com
Webdata http://www.webdata.com

Specialist sites often maintain a **mailing list** to keep you

posted with news and, in some cases, run **discussion lists** or **bulletin boards** so you can discuss issues with other visitors. If you feel you can contribute to the site, email the Webmaster. That's how the Web community works. Of course, you'll find thousands of specialist sites all through the pages that follow.

Search agents

Search agents, or **searchbots**, gather information live from a limited number of sites – to find new information, compare prices or stock, or combine the results from several search engines, for example. **Shopping agents** (p.281) like PriceWatch and Shopper.com scan online stores for the best deals.

Metasearch sites that query multiple search engines and directories simultaneously, such as Metacrawler, Vivisimo, Dogpile, Mamma and Ixquick, are close to useless. You'll get better results in less time by going directly to Google.

You'll find the same goes for the bewildering layers of **search aids** built into Internet Explorer and Windows. Click on IE's **Search** button, or **Search (Find) on the Internet** from the Windows Start menu, and a search form will appear on the left-hand side of your browser. Click **Customize** to choose from an impressive array of search engines, directories, email databases, maps and more. It looks promising, but again you'll probably get better value at the source. Only use Apple's metasearch agent, **Sherlock**, if you feel you need a handicap.

But all is not lost. For serious research, try **Copernic** (http://www.copernic.com). It's a free standalone program that can query hundreds of search engines, directories, Usenet archives, shops and email databases at once. It filters out the duplicates, displays the results on a single page in your browser and even retrieves them automatically for offline browsing.

There are also dozens of ways to monitor search engines, individual sites and newsgroups for changes. For example, **Spyonit** (http://www.spyonit.com) can notify you by email, pager, SMS or ICQ whenever your search term comes up on an auction, TV listing, directory or search engine. And **Tracerlock** (http://www.tracerlock.com) will let you know when your keywords come up on AltaVista, Usenet or the online personals.

For more on searchbots, see BotSpot (http://bots.internet. com).

Lists, picks & weblogs

If you're merely browsing for pleasure rather than looking for something in particular, you might like to try the sites dedicated to listing, ranking or reporting sites that are new, "cool" or popular. They come in many guises, from the top 100 busiest sites in various categories to daily doses of extreme weirdness. **Weblogs** ("blogs") are generally kept like diaries, with daily postings on whatever's attracted the author's interest over the last

24 hours. To find hundreds, run a search on "Weblog" at Dmoz.org. For some light entertainment, shuffle through the following selection:

100 Hot Websites
http://www.100hot.com
http://www.hitwise.com
Attempts to rank the hundred most visited Websites each week, overall or by category, in several countries.

Cruel Site of the Day
http://www.cruel.com
Something horrid daily.

Losers.org
http://www.losers.org
A list you don't want to make.

MemePool
http://www.memepool.com
Daily Weblog from multiple authors, archived by subject. A great source of interesting links.

Netsurfer Digest
http://www.netsurf.com/nsd/
Subscribe to receive weekly site updates and reviews.

Portal of Evil
http://www.portalofevil.com
At least three guaranteed jaw-droppers from the Web's outer limits daily. Not for the squeamish.

Useless Pages
http://www.go2net.com/useless/
http://www.worstoftheweb.com
The sludge festering at the bottom of the Net.

Yahoo's picks
http://www.yahoo.com/picks/
http://dir.yahoo.com/new/
What's new and cool, according to the staff of the world's biggest Web directory.

Finding stuff

Although a general search engine or directory might not instantly strike gold, they'll often point you in the right direction. As you get more familiar with the run of the Net, you'll gravitate toward specialist sites and directories that index more than just Web pages, add their own content and shine in specific areas. What's best depends largely on what you're after. When you find a useful site, **store it in your Favorites or Bookmarks**, so you can return. Here's how to:

Find someone's email address

Not as simple as you might think. When you're given an email address it's private unless you instruct someone to list it in a directory or make it public in some other way. So if you're looking for a long-lost friend's email address, there's no guarantee you'll find it. Nevertheless, it's worth trying the **email directories**. The biggest directories are:

Bigfoot http://www.bigfoot.com

Find it

Internet Address Finder http://www.iaf.net

WhoWhere http://www.whowhere.com

Yahoo PeopleSearch http://people.yahoo.com

These get most of their data from Usenet postings and visitors, so while they're not in any way comprehensive, they're pretty vast databases – and growing by the day. If these fail, try searching on your quarry's full name in a search engine or Deja.com. Alternatively, if you know where they work, search their company's Web pages, or (an old standby of detective agencies) **ring up and ask**. For other tips, see:

FAQ on finding email addresses: http://www.qucis.queen su.ca/FAQs/email/finding.html/

Yahoo's email search directory: http://dir.yahoo.com/Reference/ Phone_Numbers_and_Addresses/Email_Addresses/

ICQ email directory: http://www.icq.com/search/email.html/

Find local information

You'll sometimes want to find sites that cater to a very specific region. Say for example you want to look up film screenings across your city or select a honeymoon suite in Tamanrasset. Although it might seem logical to use a local search engine to find local sites or information, it's often not the most efficient method. Always start your searches with Google and then move on if that fails: most small local search engines simply aren't very good. Directories, however, can be another matter. Try Yahoo and the Open Directory and see what's listed in the region. Don't make it too narrow as it might be filed under the country, state or province rather than the town or suburb. Then drill down from the broad region into your area of interest. These should lead you to the major specialist directories in your area of interest. For a directory of regional directories, see:

Search Engine Colossus http://www.searchenginecolossus.com

Find a local business or phone number

While online residential and business telephone directories can be kept more up-to-date than their paper equivalents, they're not usually as easy to browse. Apart from the phone companies', offerings you'll also find a raft of private directories in competition. Some even deliver a book as well. If you haven't been exposed to their advertising, don't expect too much. Investigate a few of the following major services and see what they offer, and keep your eye out for advertisements in your local press. They should come looking for you, not vice versa.

192 Enquiries http://www.192enquiries.com

192.com http://www.192.com

BT PhoneNet http://www.bt.com/phonenetuk/

Scoot http://www.scoot.co.uk

Yellow Pages http://www.yell.co.uk

To find a phone number in almost any country:

World Pages International Directories http://www.worldpages.com/global/

Find answers to the most common questions

Where else would you look for answers to the most Frequently Asked Questions than the repository for Usenet FAQs? If the answer's not in http://www.faqs.org try Usenet itself. For more information on using Usenet, see *The Rough Guide to the Internet*.

Find out what others think on Usenet

You want to, but you don't know how. You want one, but you don't know which one. You have one, but you can't get it to work. You want more than just a second opinion. You want a forum on the subject. That's Usenet.

There's no better place to find opinions and personal experiences than Usenet, but it's a lot of text to scan. Although it's sorted into subject bundles, if you had to find every instance of discussion about something it could take days. And if it was tossed around more than a couple of weeks ago, the thread might have expired.

With **Google Groups** (http://groups.google.com), though, not only can you scan close to all Usenet now, but you can get a fair chunk of its history as well. You can pursue entire threads and profile each contributor. Which means you can follow a whole discussion, as well as check out who's who and how well they're respected. And on top of that you can identify which groups are most likely to discuss something and then join the group. You'll get to the bottom of even the most obscure subject.

However, since moving over from Deja.com, the archive has become a little less friendly to navigate. It would pay to read the Help page.

Find computer help

Enter a couple of unique phrases from your error or computer problem into Google Groups. Try both the Usenet and Web searches. If your question isn't answered in the archives, join a relevant newsgroup and post it there.

Find games, hints, and cheats

Try one of the big games sites such as the **Games Domain** (http://www.gamesdomain.com), **Gamespot** (http://www.gamespot.com), or **Happy Puppy** (http://www.happypuppy.com), or search through Usenet as explained above. Stuck on a level? Look for a walkthrough or ask in Usenet.

Find a product review or an online shop

See Shopping (p.280).

Find product support

Whenever you buy anything substantial, see if the company has a Website offering **follow-up support** and **product news**. If it's not on the accompanying literature, try putting its name between www and .com and if that doesn't work, look it up in any of the search directories.

Most companies offer some kind of online product support and registration, but if you want advice from other users, go to Usenet.

Find the latest news, weather, finance, sport, etc

Apart from hundreds of newspapers and magazines, the Net carries several large **news-clipping archives** assembled from all sorts of sources. Naturally there's an overwhelming amount of technology news, but there's also an increasing amount of services dedicated to what you would normally find on newsstands – and it's often fresher on the Net. They occasionally charge, though usually only for the archives. For pointers, check under News, Fashion, Finance, Weather and so forth. The best place to start would be **Moreover** (http://www.moreover.com), where you can search or browse headlines from over 1500 newsfeeds and then link to the story. **Yahoo Daily News** (http://dailynews.yahoo.com) is also good.

Find out about a film or TV show

See Film (p.115) or Television (p.305) or try the entertainment section of any major directory for leads to specialist sites. The **Internet Movie Database**, for example, is exceptionally comprehensive and linked to Amazon in case you're tempted to order the video.

Find the latest software

See Computing and Tech News (p.85).

Find health support

Start by searching the Web. Try Yahoo for listings of organizations and so forth, and then Google for mentions on Web pages. Chances are they'll refer you to useful mailing lists and discussion groups. If not, try Google Groups to see if, and in which groups, it's being discussed on Usenet. Ultimately, though, you'd like to join a mailing list.

Find a mailing list

The best place to find mailing lists is through a well-worded Web search (that includes "mailing list" and the topic), or through the small list directories at:

PAML http://www.paml.net
Meta List http://www.meta-list.net
List Universe http://www.list-universe.com
Liszt http://www.liszt.com

If that's not satisfactory, try Google Groups and check the FAQs from groups with hits.

Find something you've forgotten

Don't give up if you can't remember where you saw that hot tip last week. Just open Internet Explorer's History and search the cache. So long as it hasn't been deleted, you should even be able to recall it offline.

Find advice

If all else fails – and that's pretty unlikely – you can always turn to someone else for help. Use Deja.com or Google Groups to find the most appropriate newsgroup(s). Summarize your quest in the subject heading, keep it concise, post, and you should get an answer or three within a few days. Alternatively, try a mailing list or one of the free "expert" advice services such as:

Abuzz http://www.abuzz.com
AllExperts http://www.allexperts.com
AskMe.com http://www.askme.com

Finding the right Web address

You're sure to come across a **Web link or address that won't work**. It's common and usually not too hard to get around. Many of the addresses in this book will be wrong by the time you try them. Not because we're hopeless – they just change. That's the way of the Net. The most useful thing we can do is show you how to find their new homes.

Error codes

When something goes wrong, your browser will **display a page with an error message** – or nothing will happen no matter what you try. To identify the source of the problem, get familiar with the types of errors. Different browsers and servers will return different error messages, but they'll indicate the same things. As an exercise, identify the following.

Incorrect host name

When the address points to a nonexistent host, your browser should return a page headed "Cannot find server" and reading "The page cannot be displayed." Test this by keying: http://www.rufgide.com

Illegal domain name

If you specify an **illegal host name** or **protocol**, your browser should tell you. Try this out by keying http://wwwrufguide and then http:/www.ibm.com (noting the single slash before the www). Internet Explorer should automatically detect the latter error, and correct it.

File not found – 404 error

If the **file has moved**, **changed name** or you've overlooked **capitalization**, the server will tell you the file doesn't exist, or send you back to the front page. It differs between servers. Test this by keying a valid address with a bogus path, such as: http://www.bbc.com/bogus/ and http://www.cnn.com/bogus/

Busy host or host refuses entry

Occasionally you won't succeed because the server is either **overloaded with traffic** or it's temporarily or permanently **off-limits**. This sometimes happens when a site is heavily promoted or makes the news. It's a bit hard to test, but you'll come across it sooner or later. You might find foreign sites less busy when the locals are sleeping.

When nothing works

Now that you're on speaking terms with your browser, you're set to troubleshoot that problem address. First check your **connection**. Try another site, like: http://www.yahoo.com

If that works, you know it's not your connection. If you can't connect to any Website, **close and then reopen your browser**. It might only be a software glitch. Otherwise, it's most likely a problem with your Net connection or proxy server (if you're using one).

Check your mail. If that fails, log off then back on. Check it again. If your mailer connects and reports your mail status normally, you know that the connection between you and your ISP is OK. But there still could be a problem between it and the Net or with your proxy server. Check you have the right proxy settings and if so, disable them. If it still doesn't work, **ring your ISP** and see if there's a problem at their end or diagnose it yourself.

To do this, test a known host – say www.yahoo.com – with a **network tool** such as **Ping**, **TraceRoute** or **NetMedic**. If this fails, either your provider's connection to the Net is down or there's a problem with your **Domain Name Server**. Get on the phone and sort it out.

If you've verified that all connections are open but your browser still won't find any addresses, the problem must lie with your **browser setup**. Check its settings and re-install it if necessary.

When a page won't display

You'll sometimes find that a page or frame inside a page instantly comes up blank. You can tell if your browser hasn't tried to fetch the page because it happens too quickly. In this case hit the **Refresh** button. If that doesn't work, reboot your browser and re-enter the address. Failing that, open **Internet Options** and clear your Temporary Internet Files or browser cache. Finally, if you're still having problems and it appears to be related to Internet Explorer security, such as the acceptance of an ActiveX control at an online banking site, check your security settings within Internet Options, disable **Content Advisor**, and consider adding the site to your Trusted sites.

When one address won't work

If only **one address fails**, you know its address is wrong or it has server problems. Now that you're familiar with error messages you can deduce the source and fix that address.

Web addresses disappear and change all the time, often because the address has been simplified, for example from: http://www.netflux.com/~test/New_Book/htm/ to http://www. newbook.com. Sometimes they'll leave a **link to the new page** from the old address, but that too might be out-of-date. Since the Web is in a constant state of construction, just about everything is a test site in transit to something bigger and more glorious. Consequently, when a site gets serious, it might change hosts and discard the old address.

If you're convinced the address is fine then try it later, perhaps even days later. It might be down for maintenance or experiencing local problems. If you can reach it on another machine but not yours, the problem might lie with your **Windows Hosts** file – especially if you've ever installed any browser acceleration software. If so, first get rid of the offending program properly through the **Add/Remove** applet in Windows Control Panel. Then locate the file called **Hosts** in your Windows folder. It will have no file extension. Open it with Notepad and remove any lines not starting with # except for the **localhost** entry. Then save the file and exit.

Finding that elusive address

The error messages will provide the most helpful clues for **tracking elusive addresses**. If the problem comes from the host name, try **adding** or **removing the www part**. For example, instead of typing http://roughguides.com try http://www.roughguides.com. Other than that you can only guess. It may only be that the host is busy, refusing entry or not connecting, so **try again later.**

If you **can connect to the host but the file isn't there**, there are a few further tricks to try. Check capitalization, for instance: book.htm instead of Book.htm. Or try **changing the file name extension** from .htm to .html or vice versa, if applicable. Then try **removing the file name** and then each subsequent directory up the path until finally you're left with just the host name. For example:

http://www.roughguides.com/old/Book.htm/
http://www.roughguides.com/old/book.htm/
http://www.roughguides.com/old/book.html/
http://www.roughguides.com/old/
http://www.roughguides.com

In each case, if you succeed in connecting, try to locate your page from whatever links appear.

If you haven't succeeded there's still hope. Try **submitting the main key words** from the site's address or title into **Google**. If Google knows the site but it's not available, you can still access Google's copy by clicking on "cached." Failing that, try searching on related subjects, or scanning through one of the subject guides like **Yahoo** or the **Open Directory**.

By now, even if you haven't found your original target, you've probably discovered half-a-dozen similar if not more interesting pages, and in the process figured out how to navigate the Net.

part two

Directory

Amusements

Looking for a chuckle or perhaps to extend your lunchbreak into the late afternoon? Click through the following directories to enter a whole new dimension of time-wasting:

Humour Sites

Ranks.com http//www.ranks.com/home/fun/top_humor_sites/
Open Directory http://dmoz.org/Recreation/Humor/
Yahoo http://dir.yahoo.com/Entertainment/Humor/

If you have a high bandwidth connection or are blessed with abnormal patience, you might like to investigate the world of online animation. Offerings range from clones of old school arcade games to feature-length Flash cartoons from renowned cartoonists such as the creators of Ren & Stimpy (http://www.spumco.com). Peruse the galleries and links from:

About Animation http://animation.about.com
Animation http://dmoz.org/Arts/Animation/
Flazoom http://www.flazoom.com
Flashkit http://www.flashkit.com
Shockwave http://www.shockwave.com

Ali G Translator
http://www.webdez.net/alig/
Make yourself comprehensible to the Staines massive.

Amused.com
http://www.amused.com
Online headquarters of the easily amused, featuring everything you need to waste several weeks at work. For even more time-wasting opportunities, try **9 to 5 Café** (http://www.9to5cafe.com).

Assassin
http://www.newgrounds.com/assassin/
Waste a few excess celebrities.

Bert is Evil
http://www.fractalcow.com/bert/
Sesame Street star exposed in photo shocker.

Bilbana
http://www.tv4.se/lattjo/kojan/bilbanan.asp/
Shockwaved online Scaletrix.

Brain Candy
http://www.corsinet.com/braincandy/
Riddles, jokes, insults and general wordplay.

Burn Maker
http://toy.thespark.com/burn/
Convert weak platitudes into powerful vitriol.

Cartoon Bank
http://www.cartoonbank.com

Every cartoon ever published in *The New Yorker*.

Comedy Central
http://www.comedycentral.com
Download full South Park episodes, listen to comedy radio and see what's screening across the network. More of a station promo than a source of laughs.

Comic Book Resources
http://www.comicbookresources.com
http://www.bigpanda.net
http://www.zapcartoons.com
http://www.cartoon-links.com
http://www.geocities.com/Area51/Aurora/2510/greatest_comics/
Comic and cartoon sites, shops, fanfare – and the hundred greatest?

Complaint Letter Generator
http://www-csag.cs.uiuc.edu/individual/pakin/complaint/
Punch in a name for an instant dressing-down.

Dean & Nigel Blend In
http://www.deanandnigel.co.uk
Witness the gentle art of urban camouflage.

Dobe's Punny Name Archive
http://www.eskimo.com/~dobe/
Thousands of unwise baby names.

Down the Pub
http://members.aol.com/downthepub/
Chained to your desk but jonesing for a pint of bitter and a discussion about David Beckham? Point your browser to this virtual pub.

The Elizabethan Curse Generator
http://www.tower.org/insult/insult.html/
Curse with grace and elegance, thou prating fen-sucked rudesby.

Face Generator
http://www.facegenerator.com
Create your spitting image from a palette of human parts.

Amusements

Funny Forwards
http://www.ilovebacon.com
http://humor.inept.net
http://www.collegehumor.com
http://www.mrjoker.net
http://www.millerinc.com
http://www.goofball.com

Most of the sight gags that arrive in your inbox courtesy of your caring friends will wind up in these, or similar, archives sooner or later. Usually before you see them. Don't go near the galleries if you're a bit sensitive.

The Guys vs The Girls Burping Contest
http://burpcontest.com

The ultimate battle of the sexes, with hundreds of MP3 files of catastrophic belches.

Horrorfind
http://www.horrorfind.com

A helpful hand into the darkness.

Hot or Not?
http://www.hotornot.com

One of the biggest Web stories of the past couple of years. Post a picture of yourself or someone else, and then the site's visitors rate your attractiveness on a scale of 1 to 10. So popular it has spawned a string of spoofs, such as:

http://www.amigothornot.com
http://www.amigeekornot.com
http://www.amifuglyornot.com
http://www.amipotornot.com
http://www.
amiallyourbase ornot.com

Am I Annoying or Not?
http://www.amiannoying ornot.com
To sort by rating, see:
http://log.waxy.org/hot/
To instantly create your own custom
"Am I" page: http://www.iamcal.
com/ami/

In the 70s/80s/90s
http://www.inthe70s.com
http://www.inthe80s.com
http://www.inthe90s.com
Re-enter the landscape that wallpapered your childhood memories.

Internet Conspiracy Generator
http://www.westword.com/extra/conspire.html/
Are you really that desperate for pub conversation fodder?

The Internet Squeegee Guy
http://www.website1.com/squeegee/
Your monitor's looking a bit dusty.

Joke Jukebox
http://www.jokejukebox.com
http://www.uselessjokes.com
http://www.humordatabase.com
http://www.humournet.com
http://www.humor.com
http://www.jokeindex.com
http://www.looniebin.mb.ca
http://www.jokecollection.com
http://www.twistedhumor.com
http://www.tastelessjokes.com
So many jokes it's not funny.

Japanese Engrish
http://www.engrish.com
Copywriters wanted, English not a priority.

Jester: the Online Joke Recommender
http://shadow.ieor.berkeley.edu/humor/
It knows what makes you laugh.

LASCO Fittings
http://www.lascofittings.com/BarCode-EDI/
Everything you ever wanted to know about the bar code . . . and a lot
more.

Amusements

Liebography
http://www.liebographytv.com
Guerilla media at its best. Every month this site posts a new
mockumentary of a celebrity, deliberately misusing footage from
American cable channel A&E's Biography series.

Misc Games
http://www.pastor2youth.com/miscgames.html/
An archive of "fun" Christian games.

National Lampoon
http://www.nationallampoon.com
Daily humour from the satire house that PJ built. Not what it was in the
'70s, as you'll see from the vault.

Newspaper Comic Strips
http://www.kingfeatures.com
http://www.comics.com
The entire works of the Phantom, Mandrake and friends.

The Official Rock-Paper-Scissors Strategy Guide
http://www.worldrps.com
Master such techniques as Speed Play, Rusty and Lowball, then make
like Gary Kasparov and play the computer.

The Onion
http://www.theonion.com
Unquestionably the finest news satire on or off the Net, and source of
inspiration to: http://www.satirewire.com
http://www.herdofsheep.com
http://www.chaser.com.au
http://www.strewth.org.au

Perpetual Bubblewrap
http://www.urban75.com/Mag/bubble.html/
Seconds of fun for the whole family.

Pet Fish
http://www.petfish.com
Turn your monitor into a virtual fishtank.

Random Name Generators

Generator of Random Bandnamesx
http://www.irz.com/robin/bandnameprogram/

Get a Gangsta Name
http://www.jasonschock.com/gangsta/

Louis Farrakhan African Name Generator
http://www.fadetoblack.com/namegenerator/

Metal Gear Solid Name Generator
http://www.buzzsite.com/goodies/MGSnamegen/

Random Old School Hip Hop Name Generator
http://www.fat-lace.com/articles/issue4/namegenerator/
namegenerator.html/

Upper West Side Manhattan
Chinese Restaurant Name Generator
http://www.novia.net/~matt/chinese/restaurant.html/

What's Your Pokéname?
http://pizza.sandwich.net/poke/pokemon.html/

The true champion of name generation, however, is the Wu-Tang Clan: WuName (http://www.recordstore.com/wuname/), Wu Name Generator (http://www.blazonry.com/scripting/wuname/php) and the Wu-Hick Name Generator (http://ryan.post891.org/cgi-bin/wu-hick.cgi/).

Piercing Mildred
http://www.mildred.com
Tattoo, pierce and scar Mildred to your heart's content – no fuss, no pus.

Pocket Internet
http://www.thepocket.com
Gadgets, games, greeting cards, cartoons and more, updated daily.

Amusements

The Post-Modernism Generator
http://www.elsewhere.org/cgi-bin/postmodern/
Sprinkle your next essay with "postsemanticist dialectical theory" and fool your teacher.

Pranksta's Paradise
http://www.ccil.org/~mika/
All the practical jokes from alt.shenanigans.

Rec.humor.funny
http://www.netfunny.com/rhf/
Archives of the rec.humor.funny newsgroup, updated daily.

Sissyfight
http://www.sissyfight.com
Scratch, tease and diss your way to playground supremacy.

The Spark.com
http://www.thespark.com
Most famous for its tests (purity, slut, bastard, etc) which have been taken by some eight million people, plus numerous other ways to laugh at your friends.

Star Wars Asciimation
http://www.asciimation.co.nz
The Star Wars saga rendered in vivid ASCII text – George Lucas would be spinning in his grave if he were dead.

Stick Figure Death Theater
http://www.sfdt.com
Stickcity citizens meet their sticky ends.

Superjam
http://www.super-jam.com
Upload a picture of yourself, paste it on one of the dancing figures and watch yourself do the Smurf.

The Tackiest Place in America Contest
http://www.thepoint.net/~usul/text/tacky.html/
A building shaped like a bulldozer, the Roadkill Café and Carhenge battle it out for the title of most soulless place in the universe.

Totally Useless Office Skills
http://www.jlc.net/~useless/
If you've exhausted all the Internet options, click here for hundreds of ways to defile office supplies.

The Ultimate Drinking Game Home Page
http://www.geocities.com/TelevisionCity/Set/7200/drinking.htm/
As if you needed more excuses to get drunk.

The Ultimate Suckup Machine
http://www.theschmoozer.com
Junk-mail your quarry with weekly compliments. For something more surreal, try: http://www.geek-boy.com/scg/

UnderGround Online
http://www.ugo.com
Vigilante gang of counterculture sites that's close to the antithesis of AOL.

Universal Translator Assistant Project
http://hometown.aol.com/JPKlingon/uta/
Translate the Bible into Klingon, Vulcan, Romulan – even Esperanto!

Web Economy Bullshit Generator
http://www.dack.com/web/bullshit.html/
Learn how to "leverage leading-edge mindshare" and "incubate compelling interfaces" at this brilliant site.

Xiaoxiao No. 3
http://www.stileproject.com/kungfu.html/
The Jackie Chan and Bruce Lee of the stick figure world battle to the death.

Antiques and Collectables

Action Figure Collectors
http://www.actionfigurecollectors.com
Looking for that elusive Lando Calrasian toy? Try here first.

Antique Quilts
http://www.antiquequilts.com
If you're after that Little-House-on-the-Prairie feel, try this excellent site which sells not only quilts but other bits of Americana like Quimper pottery and Shaker furniture.

Antiques Avenue
http://www.antiques-avenue.com
A lavish online catalogue of British furniture, clocks, art and decorative pieces from various dealers scattered throughout the south of England.

Antiques on the Web
http://www.bbc.co.uk/antiques/
The BBC's superb antiques site includes buying advice from Antiques Roadshow experts, feature articles, hints on scoring big at car boot sales, exhibition listings and the latest finds from the Roadshow.

Antiques Trade Gazette
http://www.atg-online.com
The Web home of the *Antiques Trade Gazette* features articles, auction calendars and a page where you can report stolen items.

Antiques UK
http://www.antiques-uk.co.uk
Similar to most antique portals in that it offers links to dealers and salvage warehouses, but it has an excellent want ads feature – allowing you to post a message if you're after a specific item and a dealer can then get in touch with you through the site.

Antiques Web
http://www.antiques-web.co.uk
A comprehensive database of directory information (including the best list of UK antiques fairs on the Net) for the British antiques community.

Bath Antiquities Centre
http://www.bathantiquities.freeserve.co.uk
A site hosting ten different dealers who specialize in artefacts from the ancient world like arrowheads, fossils and ancient Egyptian amulets.

Collecting Comics
http://www.collectingcomics.com
News, reviews, listings, price guides and creator interviews for fans of Marvel and beyond. See also About's comic book collecting page (http://comicbooks.about.com/hobbies/comicbooks/).

Collector Café
http://www.collectorcafe.com
A portal for the collecting community, with channels for just about every collectible from advertising memorabilia to writing instruments. For a UK based portal, try Antiques Bulletin (http://www.antiques bulletin.com), Antiques World (http://www.antiquesworld.co.uk) or World Collectors Net (http://www.worldcollectorsnet.com).

Comics International
http://www.comics-international.com
Perhaps the most useful comics site on the Web, this gateway features a near-definitive directory of UK stockists and dealers, an excellent links page, comics reviews and unusually informative FAQs.

Gallery of Antique Costumes and Textiles
http://www.gact.co.uk
Though not much more than sophisticated eye-candy, this sumptuously designed online home of the London gallery includes well-reproduced photos of their featured pieces.

I Collector
http://www.icollector.com
The eBay of the high-end collector's market, this auction site hosts more than 650 auction houses selling everything from Francis Bacon originals to George II armchairs.

Invaluable

http://www.invaluable.com

If you can't get to the Antiques Roadshow or you're a serious collector, the online branch of *Invaluable* magazine provides an appraisal service, and if you've had an item stolen, it has a tracer service to improve your odds of recovering it. These don't come cheap, but you can try them for free. A slightly less expensive service is offered by the American site, Eppraisals (http://www2.eppraisals.com).

Kitsch

http://www.kitsch.co.uk

Great British site for collectors of retro-chic featuring Dukes of Hazzard items, Presleyana, lava lamps, James Bond paraphernalia, etc. As an added bonus, they belong to the Which? Webtrader code of practice, so you know you can buy that Farrah pencil in confidence.

Labelcollector.com

http://www.labelcollector.com

Salute the golden era of fruit crates and jars.

LAPADA

http://www.lapada.co.uk

The homepage of the Association of Art and Antique Dealers features a directory of members, fair and auction listings and advice on buying, selling, taking care and providing security for antiques.

Lunchbox Bonanza
http://www.cas-
sidyframes.com/box/
Lunchbox collecting may
be a uniquely American
phenomenon, but the rare
British box goes for crazy
money in the States. Use
this site as your guide to
digging in the attic.

Numismatica
http://www.limunltd.com/numismatica/
With loads of articles, news, listings, FAQs, guides and links, this is the
best portal for coin collectors on the Web. For banknote collectors, try
Collect Paper Money (http://www.collectpapermoney.com).

Old Bear
http://www.oldbear.co.uk
Don't throw away that beat-up, stinky old teddy bear – it might be
worth a few sovereigns. This site will tell you if you can start a trust
fund with your Gund or if you're stuck for life with your Steiff.

Philatelic Resources on the Web
http://www.execpc.com/~joeluft/resource.html/
Joseph Luft's listing of some 3800 Websites devoted to stamp collecting.

Sandafayre
http://www.sandafayre.com
Auctions and information from the world's largest stamp dealer.

Architecture

TV Toys
http://www.tvtoys.com
One of the best sites to explore the ever-expanding world of TV memorabilia with knowledgeable articles about collecting certain shows and links to collectibles for sale.

Watchnet
http://www.watchnet.com
Online hub for the fine and vintage wristwatch collecting community.

World War II Collectibles
http://www.wwii-collectibles.com
Lame layout, but beneath the clutter and bad interface lies a treasure-trove of stamps, coins, posters, propaganda material and military ephemera.

Architecture

Online magazines

Architecture http://www.architecturemag.com
The Architectural Review http://www.arplus.com
Architecture Week http://www.ArchitectureWeek.com
Metropolis http://www.metropolismag.com

Adam
http://adam.ac.uk
Designed for university students, this is a search engine of internet resources for art, architecture and design.

Archibot
http://archibot.com
If you're interested in contemporary architecture and design, this very sexy site is the best portal on the Web. It features news and links that are updated daily (which you can have emailed to you), forums and an excellent metasearch engine to weed out all the building code sites.

Architecture.com
http://www.architecture.com

If you're more than a little interested in British architecture, the home page of the Royal Institute of British Architects should be your first port of call. It allows you full access to their database of article abstracts; has a find-an-architect function if you're redesigning your garden shed; and has links to over 1000 sites.

BIG Buildings
http://www.geocities.com/big_buildings1/

An excellent site offering high-quality images of the best buildings, bridges and urban environments in the world. The only problem is that the images are so good that if you're browsing at anything less than 56K you might be here for a long time.

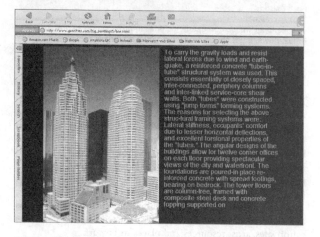

Building Conservation
http://www.buildingconservation.com
Preserve your palace.

Glass, Steel and Stone
http://glasssteelandstone.home.att.net
A fun site, with browsable galleries (including ones devoted to haunted and odd architecture), forums and news stories that are updated daily.

Great Buildings Online
http://www.greatbuildings.com
An exemplary resource. If you download free Design Lite software you can get three-dimensional models of Stonehenge, Chartres Cathedral, Falling Water and other masterpieces by Alvar Aalto, Le Corbusier and Ludwig Mies van der Rohe. Of course, there are also flat photographs and information on the architects of over 1000 great buildings. The constant pop-up ads are very irritating, though.

National Trust
http://www.nationaltrust.org.uk
The National Trust's homepage includes information on all of their properties, news, a gift shop and accommodation details.

Art

If you're an artist, photograph your work (preferably with a digital camera) and post it online: it's cheap gallery space and your disciples can visit at any time without even leaving home. But don't expect them to stumble across it randomly. You'll need to hand out its address at every opportunity, and don't forget to include news of your exhibitions and contact details. Like in the real world, finding art online is very much a click-and-miss affair (http://www.badart.com), and of course entirely a matter of taste.

If you're looking for online exhibitions, turn to the Museums and Galleries chapter. This chapter is devoted to portals, art education sites, artist resources and places to buy art.

A.A. Art
http://www.1art.com
For budding Constables, this excellent arts education site offers free online painting lessons, video workshops and forums on technique.

Aliens and UFO Art
http://www.wiolawa.com
Defy the Government by becoming as one with alien sculptures.

AllPosters.com
http://www.allposters.com
http://www.allaboutart.com
Plaster over the cracks in your bedroom walls.

Amico.org
http://www.amico.org
Thumbnails from the top North American galleries.

Anime Pitstop
http://www.animepitstop.com
http://anime.about.com
Today Japan; tomorrow a school-
yard near you.

Art.com
http://www.art.com
With an address like that, you've
got to deliver and the site does.
With its huge catalogue of repro-
ductions, limited editions, posters, photos, animation and Mona Lisa
mugs, this American site (which ships to the UK) is effectively an art
shopping mall. If you're just after posters, look no further than
Postershop (http://www.postershop.co.uk) or Barewalls
(http://www.barewalls.com), but beware of the massive shipping
charge on European orders. Of course, if you've got enough money not
to need a reproduction, you could always try Christie's
(http://www.christies.com) or Sotheby's (http://www.sothebys.com).

Artchive
http://www.artchive.com
Featuring critical biographies, links to images of art works on the Web,
excerpts from the art-theory canon and art CD-ROM reviews, this site
may be the best jumping-off point for art experts. There are also self-
portrait and landscape "tours" for those unfamiliar with art history.

Art

The Art Connection
http://www.art-connection.com
Buy British art.

Art Crimes
http://www.graffiti.org
The first and still the best graffiti site on the Web. Art Crimes features an amazing array of burners, interviews with the most well-known writers, a good FAQ page and an untouchable set of graf links.

Art Deadlines List
http://www.xensei.com/users/adl/
A bulletin board and host page of an email newsletter that alerts artists to competitions, scholarships, grants and employment opportunities.

Artists' Exchange
http://artistexchange.about.com
Artists for artists' sakes.

ArtLex
http://www.artlex.com
This visual arts dictionary is a truly superb resource for students, experts and bluffers alike. Containing extensively cross-referenced definitions of over 3000 terms and examples (reproductions appear either below the definition or are linked to another site hosting one), this is one of the most useful art sites on the Web.

Art Loop
http://www.artloop.com
An excellent resource for the collector, this site allows you to locate works of art for sale by artist or movement and then track the value of your potential investment. Its brief, keyword-heavy artist bios are also useful for budding connoisseurs. Also try Artcult (http://www.artcult.com).

Art Net
http://www.artnet.com
With its frighteningly comprehensive artists' index, excellent exhibition listings and articles both breezy and dense, the homepage of Art Net magazine probably serves as the best art portal on the Web. Other

worthwhile portals are Artstar (http://www.artstar.com) and Art Advocate (http://www.artadvocate.com).

Art-Smart
http://www.art-smart.com
If you're interested in buying original art online, this site features links to artists and galleries with lots of search options and different categories to make shopping easier. Also check out d'Art (http://dart.fine-art.com). To buy affordable work from British artists try Art Connection (http://www.art-connection.com), New British Artists (http://www.newbritishartists.co.uk) and Red Dot (http://www.reddot.co.uk).

Arts Council of England
http://www.artscouncil.org.uk
For information on everything from National Lottery funding to online exhibition spaces, this is the first place to check. Also see the Arts Council of Northern Ireland (http://www.artscouncil-ni.org), the Arts Council of Wales (http://www.ccc-acw.org.uk) and the Scottish Arts Council (http://www.sac.org.uk).

Arts Wire
http://www.artswire.org
This site from the New York Foundation for the Arts is geared to the US, but it's probably the best artist resource on the Web, with news, job openings, tutorials, workshops and a database of other arts resources.

Core 77
http://www.core77.com
Get a hand with industrial design.

Elfwood
http://www.elfwood.com
Sketches and tales from a gaggle of junior fantasy and sci-fi buffs.

Fine Art Lease
http://www.fineartlease.com
Borrow posh pictures to hang in your snooker room.

Art

Grove Dictionary of Art Online
http://www.groveart.com
Freeload for a day on the definitive work of art reference.

Interactive Collector
http://www.icollector.com
Bid for art and collectibles like celebrity cast-offs. Then, of course, there's always Ebay (http://www.ebay.com).

Internet Design & Publishing Center
http://www.graphic-design.com
Portal for the graphic design and DTP communities featuring articles, tips, reviews, forums and plenty of goodies to download. Also check out About's excellent graphic design channel (http://graphicdesign.about.com) or Graphic Design Gate (http://www.graphicdesigngate.com) for links.

Raw Vision
http://www.rawvision.com
The online presence of Raw Vision magazine is the best place to start exploring the world of Outsider Art (essentially art made by untrained artists) and Folk Art.

Roadside Art Online
http://www.interestingideas.com/roadside/artlink.htm/
Links page to such delights as the world's largest catsup bottle, Route 66 motel signs, art environments and Pancakes Across America.

Soda Connector
http://sodaplay.com/constructor/
Train ingenious spring models that obey the laws of physics and the whims of your idle mind.

Stelarc
http://www.stelarc.va.com.au
No artist has given his body to the Net like Prof. Stelarc. More hanging around at: http://www.suspension.org

3D Artists
http://www.raph.com/3dartists/
Art that looks too real to be real.

- *Hortense Fiquet in a Striped Skirt*
  1877-78 (160 Kb); Oil on canvas, 72.5 x 56 cm (28 1/2 x 22"); Museum of Fine Arts, Boston; Venturi no. 292

- *Le paysan (Peasant)*
  c. 1991 (130 Kb); Oil on canvas, 56 x 46 cm (22 x 18 1/8"); Private collection; Venturi no. 567

- *Boy in a Red Vest (Garçon au gilet rouge)*
  1888-90 (130 Kb); Oil on canvas, 65.7 x 54.7 cm (25 7/8 x 21 1/2 in); The Barnes Foundation, Merion, Pennsylvania

- *Woman in a Red-Striped Dress*
  1892-96 (120 Kb); Oil on canvas, 93.2 x 73 cm (36 3/4 x 28 3/4 in); The Barnes Foundation, Merion, Pennsylvania

Web Museum
http://www.
southern.net/wm/
Easily one of the best sites on the Web, the Web Museum hosts a fantasy collection of art – like having the Louvre, the Metropolitan Museum of Art, the Hermitage and the Prado all right around the corner. There is also an extensive glossary of terms, artist biographies and enlightening commentary on each of the works displayed.

World Wide Arts Resources
http://www.wwar.com
Its URL may lead you to believe that this is a site for military enthusiasts, but this list bank is probably the most comprehensive art search engine, with links to just about everything from art supplies and atelier services to gallery spaces and arts education courses. Also worth a gander are Artcyclopedia (http://www.artcyclopedia.com) and, for a more academic perspective, ADAM (http://adam.ac.uk).

Asian Interest

Br-Asian
http://www.brasian.co.uk
Pop culture e-zine aimed at younger British-Asians. In addition to the expected focus on Bollywood and bhangra, this site features interviews with the likes of Talvin Singh and Bally Sagoo, articles on retro chic, mainstream and Asian gig listings and a report on the issues surrounding the Satpal Ram case.

Asian Interest

Click Walla
http://www.clickwalla.com
Certainly the most comprehensive site serving Britain's Asian community, Click Walla is comprised of sections devoted to music, film, news, students, weddings, food, listings, beauty and fashion, health and Asian businesses. Other UK portals include Auntie G (http://www.auntieg.co.uk) and UK Asian (http://www.ukasian.co.uk).

800 India
http://www.800india.com
This portal includes news headlines from all of India's major newspapers (both national and regional), a song library, a collection of music videos and extensive coverage of India's technology sector.

India Abroad
http://www.indiaabroad.com
The focus here is largely on the US and Canada, but this huge site is a model portal in terms of both content and design, with extensive news coverage, a broad array of channels, immigration advice, in-depth interviews and shopping facilities.

Lankaweb
http://www.lankaweb.com
A virtual community for Sri Lankans across the world.

Sada Punjab
http://www.sadapunjab.com
Devoted to keeping Punjabi culture alive. The site's features include a literature archive of folktales, ghazals and poems; a Punjabi jukebox; an archive of Sikh religious texts; language tutorials; and a magazine. See also Punjab Online (www.punjabonline.com) and Punjabi Network (http://www.punjabi.net).

South Asia Network
http://www.southasia.net
This portal features the South Asia search engine and serves as a useful gateway to information on Bangladesh, Bhutan, India, The Maldives, Nepal, Pakistan and Sri Lanka.

Tehelka
http://www.tehelka.com
A very influential Internet newsletter from India which has had a role in exposing corruption in politics and helped to break cricket's match-fixing scandal.

Auctions

You know how auctions work: the sale goes to the highest bidder, as long as it's above the reserve price. Or, in the case of a Dutch auction, the price keeps dropping until a buyer accepts. Well, it's the same online. You simply set a starting bid and then leave an instruction to raise it in preset increments up to a ceiling. If no one outbids you, the deal is struck at your highest offer – which could be your starting bid if it's above the reserve and there weren't any other bidders.

Once the deal's been settled, it's up to the buyer and seller to arrange delivery and payment, though both can be arranged through trusted third parties. There are millions of goods for sale in thousands of categories across hundreds of online auctions. These are but a few of the best auction sites on the Web.

AuctionWatch
http://www.auctionwatch.com
The universal search feature on this site allows to search across hundreds of different auctions as well as fixed price sites, and then you can track your bid with its auction manager feature. Also try Bidder's Edge (http://www.bidddersedge.com) for similar capabilities.

eBay
http://www.ebay.co.uk
The granddaddy of all auction sites. The pages may be hectic and distracting, but underneath the clutter eBay has millions of items for sale – everything from scuzzy Def Leppard t-shirts to Scottish Masonic kilt pins to the original Robert E. Lee car from *The Dukes of Hazzard*. With features like scorecards on buyers and sellers, round-the-clock customer support, automatic insurance on items up to £120 and

chatrooms, eBay is the prototype on which all other auction sites are based. Some of the biggest sites to follow eBay's path are Amazon (http://www.amazon.co.uk), Aucland (http://www.aucland.com), eBid (http://www.ebid.co.uk), Fired Up (http://www.firedup.com), QXL (http://www.qxl.com) and Yahoo (http://uk.auctions.yahoo.com).

I Collector
http://www.icollector.com
Home to over 650 auction houses, this American site aims to be a high-end eBay with an emphasis on art and antiques. One for the serious collector.

Internet Auction List
http://www.internetauctionlist.com
This portal to the online bidding scene is the most comprehensive auction directory on the Web. Other dedicated auction directories include Auction Insider (http://www.auctioninsider.com) and Bidfind (http://www.bidfind.com).

National Fraud Information Center
http://www.fraud.com
If you're worried about getting swindled by an online auction house or dealer (in 2000, 78 percent of all Internet fraud occurred on auction sites), this excellent American site has all the information you need to protect yourself.

Priceline
http://travel.priceline.co.uk
This travel giant has added a new twist to the auction game by allowing you to state how much like you'd like to pay for airplane tickets, hotels and car hire, then waiting to see if anyone accepts. Last Minute.com (http://www.lastminute.com) offers a similar service.

Sotheby's
http://www.sothebys.com
You won't find that S Club 7 signed photo disc here, but if you've got money to burn, sites don't come any classier than this online home of the august auction house. You can bid on live auctions as well as specialist Internet bidding wars, and there are also chat rooms to make art novices feel more at home. For similar, if not quite so grand, service, try Bonham's (http://www.bonhams.com), Christie's

Specialist Auctions

Art
http://www.artconte.com

Books
Dominic Winter http://www.dominic-winter.co.uk

Cars
Birmingham Car Auctions http://www.bca-carauctions.co.uk
Blue Cycle http://www.bluecycle.com
Classic Auctions http://www.classic-auctions.co.uk
Classic Cars http://www.calssiccarsforsale.co.uk

Computers
C Net http://www.cnet.com
Computers 4 Sale http://www.computers4sale.co.uk
Morgan Auctions http://www.morgan-auctions.co.uk

Personalised Number Plates
DVLA http://www.dvla-som.co.uk

Railway Memorabillia
http://www.gwra.co.uk

Sports Memorabillia
http://www.sports-memorabillia.co.uk

Stamps
Sandafayre http://www.sandafayre.com

Toys
Vectis http://www.vectis.co.uk

The Website that Asks, "*What The Heck?*"

(http://www.christies.com) or Phillips
(http://www.phillips-auctions.com).

What the Heck
http://www.whattheheck.com/ebay/
Your guide to the bizarre stuff people try to unload on eBay. Want to see
the legendary listing of the person who auctioned their kidney for $2.5
million? It's here, as are listings for partially-used packs of cigarettes, old
toilet paper and all sorts of inappropriate ephemera. Also check out
Eday (http://eday.shutdown.com) for the day's weirdest item.

Ybag
http://www.ybag.com
At Ybag, instead of buyers bidding for the seller's wares, you type in
what you're after and then sellers approach you with their offers. You
can find similar reverse auctions at the giant American site eWanted
(http://www.ewanted.com).

Aviation and Aircraft

Aeroflight
http://www.aeroflight.co.uk
One of the best aviation resources on the Web, Aeroflight has comprehensive listings of air shows and museums, a detailed bibliography,
photos and a wealth of information on the world's air forces.

Aeroseek
http://www.aeroseek.com
If it takes off and lands, you'll find it on this aviation search engine and

portal. Other useful places to start your search are Aviation UK
(http://www.aviation.uk.com), Airliners.net (http://www.airliners.net),
About's aviation pages (http://aviation.about.com), Air Net
(http://www.AirNet.cwc.net) and Avitop (http://www.avitop.com).

Airdisaster.com
http://www.airdisaster.com
http://come.to/crashes/
http://www.aviationnewsweb.com
http://planecrashinfo.com
Way more goes wrong up in the air than you realize. Here's why you
should be frightened to fly. For firsthand tales of terror, see:
http://www.pprune.com

Airliner Photos
http://www.
airlinerphotos.com
Swiss shrine to com-
mercial air travel.

Airport City Codes
http://www.
airportcitycodes.com
A quirky site that has
details (city codes, run-
way length, etc) on
9000 airports, cheat
sheets on the world's
commercial aircraft, funny airplane stories and a crucial section on airplane etiquette.

Airport Webcams
http://www.leonardsworlds.com/airports/airframe.html/
Jumbo-jet heaven.

Airsafe
http://www.airsafe.com
Overcome your fear of plummeting.

Aviation and Aircraft

Air-Scene UK
http://www.f4aviation.co.uk
All the latest despatches from the British planespotting scene. See also
UK Airshow Review (http://www.uk-airshows.demon.co.uk).

Air Sickness Bag Virtual Museum
http://www.airsicknessbags.com
Bring up some treasured memories.

All Aviation Flightline Online
http://www.aafo.com
This American site covers the entire breadth of the aviation spectrum,
but is particularly strong on air racing and old classics like the Spruce
Goose.

All the World's Rotorcraft
http://avia.russian.ee
The copter spotter's guide to the universe.

Aviation Forum
http://www.theaviationforum.com
Complain about the awful food on your last flight or help people overcome their fear of flying.

Hot Air Ballooning
http://hotairballooning.com
More than just a load of hot air.

Live Air Traffic Control
http://www.freeweb.pdq.net/dino/liveatc.htm/
Ambulance-chasers can get a head start at this site, which has live
feeds from air traffic centres across the world.

Planes of Fame
http://www.planesoffame.org
The homepage of the Air Museum, dedicated to the preservation of
aviation history, has information on the museum's collection of aircraft,
which spans the Chanute Hang Glider from 1896 to modern spacecraft.

Sky Corner

http://www.airwar.ru

This impressive Russian site features articles, photos and drawings of over 3000 planes and 1400 weapons used on military aircraft.

Babies and Parenting

ABCs of Parenting

http://www.abcparenting.com

A large, comprehensive directory of parenting Websites organised by category, with each site given star ratings. There are also articles like "Crib Safety Tips" and Q&As with experts.

Aware Parenting Institute

http://www.awareparenting.com

A garish site, but an excellent resource for those interested in child-centred parenting.

Babycare Direct

http://www.babycare-direct.co.uk

Although ordering could be made a lot easier, this is nevertheless one of the better UK sites specialising in nursery goods. The range of their stock is very extensive and they offer some good discounts. Other specialist retailers worthy of attention are Planet Baby (http://www.planetbaby.co.uk) and the Total Baby Shop (http://www.totalbabyshop.com).

BabyCentre

http://www.babycentre.co.uk

Probably the most complete baby site on the Web, with advice on everything from conceiving to lullaby lyrics to sleep routines to coping with your kid bursting into tears on a plane.

Babies and Parenting

BabyNamer
http://www.babynamer.com
Why not give your babe a cutesy name like Adolph? It apparently means "noble hero". More suggestions to scar it for life at: (http://bnf.parentsoup.com/babyname/), Baby Names (http://www.babynames.com), Baby Names and Meanings (http://www.baby-names-meanings.com), Hawaiian Baby Names (http://www.go.to/babynames/) and Indian Baby Names (http://www.indiaexpress.com/specials/babynames/). For even more, consult the Google Baby Name Directory (http://directory.google.com/Top/Home/Family/Pregnancy/Baby_Names/).

The Baby Registry
http://www.thebaby.registry.co.uk
No, not a who's who of the baby world or a baptism gift-list but an "advice directory" of helpful organisations and Websites.

Babyworld
http://www.babyworld.co.uk
The homepage of Babyworld magazine offers all the usual chat rooms, shopping facilities and pregnancy diaries, plus one of the most detailed health sections around.

Fathers Direct
http://www.fathersdirect.com
A good site aimed at working dads, with news on the latest child development research, articles on fatherhood by Red Or Dead's Wayne Hemmingway and Laurence Llewellyn Bowen, information on the paternity leave scheme and other parental resources.

Homebirth

http://www.homebirth.org.uk

Lots of advice for parents choosing to give birth at home, including birth stories and pain relief options as well as recommended books, videos and articles.

Mother and Baby

http://www.motherandbaby.co.uk

The site of the magazine of the same title offers all the usual features with a couple of novel ones: downloadable videos of different births and a service which will email you each week of your pregnancy giving you specific advice and information.

Mothers Who Think

http://www.salon.com/mwt/

As with just about everything else on Salon, this section is funny, informative, engaging and well-written, and a perfect anecdote to all the sites and publications that treat mums as scarcely more intelligent than their babies.

National Childbirth Trust

http://www.nct-online.org

The NCT's official site is a good place to find out about antenatal classes, breastfeeding counsellors, mothers' groups and the NCT's own books on pregnancy and childbirth.

Need a Nanny?

http://www.dfee.gov.uk/nanny/

A guide for parents looking for a nanny. It's not the most exciting site in the world, but it does offer plenty of sensible advice for those seeking childcare. For more general information on childcare options, try the Day Care Trust (http://www.daycaretrust.org.uk) or the National Childminding Association (http://www.ncma.org.uk).

Net Doctor

http://www.netdoctor.co.uk/pregnancy-parenting/
http://www.netdoctor.co.uk/children/

Certainly among the best UK health sites, Net Doctor's specialist pages are filled with largely jargon-free information for mother and child. The children's health area is particularly useful as it details the symptoms and treatments of common childhood ailments and illnesses.

Babies and Parenting

Parents.com
http://www.parents.com
Unlike many sites linked to paper publications, the homepage of the American magazine *Parents* doesn't skimp on online content, and because of its ties to a respected publication, the advice and information is authoritative.

Pregnancy Calendar
http://www.pregnancycalendar.com
http://www.parentsoup.com
http://www.parenthoodweb.com
http://www.motherchild.com.au
http://www.babycenter.com
Count down the nine months from conception to pregnancy and get prepared to juggle your life around your new family member. If your baby gets sick and you can't get to a doctor, try pediatrician Dr Greene for advice (http://www.drgreene.com).

Pregnancy Today
http://www.pregnancytoday.com
Despite its name, this enormous American site coves everything from pregnancy diaries to dealing with troublesome teenagers. There's a staggering amount of useful stuff here – just avoid the celebrity section featuring Pamela Anderson's pregnancy.

SheilaKitzinger.com
http://www.sheilakitzinger.com
Sheila Kitzinger is one of the gurus of childbirth. With this background, her site may be a bit too campaigning for some, but beneath the occasionally hectoring tone and ill-advised poetry there's a wealth of information on breast-feeding, water births, home births and other childbirth issues.

UK Parents
http://www.ukparents.co.uk
A comprehensive parenting e-zine written in plain and largely unpatronising language, covering pretty much everything from pre-conception to sending the young 'uns off to school.

Betting and Gambling

It's tempting to say that online betting is for those who like that extra added element of risk, but if you stick to well-known bookmakers who've invested heavily in their security systems and avoid the casinos (which are often pretty dodgy and sometimes require you to buy a CD-ROM or download fifteen megabytes of software) you should be fine. To find a bookmaker, try Bookies Index (http://www.bookiesindex.com). Some of the UK's leading bookmakers are:

BlueSQ http://www.bluesq.com

Ladbrokes http://www.ladbrokes.com and http://www.bet.co.uk

Littlewoods http://www.bet247.com

Sporting Index http://www.sportingindex.com

Tote http://www.toe.co.uk

Victor Chandler http://www.victorchandler.com

William Hill http://www.williamhill.co.uk

Fantasy Racing
http://www.fantasy-racing.co.uk
If you're nervous or just like betting for the sport rather than the money, try this risk-free site.

National Lottery
http://www.national-lottery.co.uk
It could be you ... but it probably won't.

Oddschecker
http://www.oddschecker.co.uk
Useful site that allows you to view the odds that all the bookies are offering, linking directly to their sites so you can place a bet.

The Racing Post
http://www.racingpost.co.uk
The online home of the venerable tip sheet.

Black Interest

Settle-a-Bet
http://www.settle-a-bet.co.uk
How to beat the odds.

Sports Betting
http://www.sportsbetting.com
Glossary of betting terms and systems, particularly strong on American sports.

24 Dogs
http://www.24dogs.com
Comprehensive, Wembley-owned greyhound resource and betting service. Also see The Dogs (http://www.thedogs.co.uk).

Win 2 Win
http://www.win2win.co.uk
One of the very few free horseracing tipster services on the Web, it also has a section devoted to different betting systems.

World of Gambling
http://www.gamble.co.uk
News, reviews and advice on everything from baccarat to slot machines.

Black Interest

Africa Online
http://www.africaonline.com
This bilingual (French) portal features some of the most comprehensive African news coverage on the Web. Other African portals worth a look are Africa Guide (http://www.africaguide.com), About's African culture pages (http://africancultures.about.com), All Africa (http://allafrica.com), Channel Africa (http://www.channelafrica.com) and Africa Homepage (http://www.africahomepage.org).

Africana
http://www.africana.com
This American site is most likely the best black culture portal on the

Web. In addition to the expected channels covering lifestyle, the arts, heritage and the homefront, Africana features columns by journalists like Nelson George and Amy Alexander; radio channels playing jazz, blues, Afro-Cuban, Afro-Brazilian, gospel and R&B; and an excellent, searchable encyclopedia of the African diaspora. Also check The Black World Today (http://www.tbwt.com).

Afrisearch
http://www.afrisearch.com
Black culture search engine. Also try Black Search (http://www.blacksearch.co.uk), the Afrocentric Resource Center (http://www.jazm.com), Afro Central (http://www.afrocentral.net), Black index (http://www.blackindex.com) and Channel Africa (http://www.channelafrica.com).

Black Britain
http://www.blackbritain.co.uk
Although less authoritative than Africana (see above), this site is never-theless an extensive gateway to black British culture, with a friendly, inclusive feel. Also try Black Net (http://www.blacknet.co.uk) and Ebony City (http://www.ebonycity.net).

Black History Map
http://www.
blackhistory
map.com
In essence, this site
from Channel 4 is a
black history search
engine accessed
through a map of
Britain or a timeline.
But it also includes
features and videos
on topics like Black
Irish in the
Caribbean.

Books and Literature

Black Information Link
http://www.blink.org.uk
The 1990 Trust's bulletin board for the UK's black community serves
two functions: it provides news, events listings and links; and serves as
a forum for political advocacy.

Black Presence
http://www.blackpresence.co.uk
A forum and resource for researchers and other people interested in the
history of black culture in Britain. Also includes news, features on music
and articles on contemporary figures like Chris Ofili.

Windrush
http://www.bbc.co.uk/education/archive/windrush/
The BBC's celebration of fifty years of Afro-Caribbean culture in Britain,
with a heavy slant towards education: timelines, achievements, first-
person remembrances, poetry and a literature guide.

Books and Literature

If a squillion Web pages aren't enough to satisfy your lust for
the written word, maybe you should use one to order a book.
You'll be spoilt for choice, with hundreds of shops offering
millions of titles for delivery worldwide. That includes bumper
showings from most of the major chains alongside exclusively
online book havens such as Amazon and BOL. The superstores
typically lay on all the trimmings: user ratings, reviews, recommendations, sample chapters, author interviews, bestseller lists,
press clippings, publishing news, secure ordering and gift-
wrapping.

Major Chains

Blackwell's http://blackwell.co.uk
Borders http://www.borders.com
Hammicks http://www.hammicks.com

Books and Literature

Heffers http://www.heffers.co.uk
Ottakar's http://www.ottakars.co.uk
Tesco http://www.tesco.com/books/
Waterstone's http://www.waterstones.co.uk
WHSmith http://www.bookshop.co.uk

Only on the Web

Alphabet Street http://www.alphabetstreet.com
Amazon http://www.amazon.co.uk
BOL http://www.bol.com
Bookzone http://www.bookzone.co.uk
Buy.com http://www.buy.com
Country Books http://www.countrybookshop.co.uk
James Thin http://www.jamesthin.co.uk

Not listed here? Try browsing or subject-searching this directory of booksellers worldwide: http://www.bookweb.org/bookstores/. For a rundown on British merchants, see: http://www.books.co.uk.

While Barnes & Noble and Amazon may rightly jostle over the title of "world's most ginormous bookstore", you'll find they all offer a staggering range, usually at substantial discounts. But because books are heavy, any savings could be offset by freight charges. And naturally, the further away you are and the sooner you want it, the more it adds up. So, before you dash to the checkout, make sure you have the best deal:

AddAll http://www.addall.com
BookBrain http://www.bookbrain.co.uk
Zoomit http://www.zoomit.com

Banned Books Online
http://digital.library.upenn.edu/books/banned-books.html/
Extracts from books that riled the righteous.

Books and Literature

Bartleby
http://www.bartleby.com
Online versions of such classic reference texts
as Gray's *Anatomy*, Strunk & White's *Elements
of Style*, the King James Bible and works of
fiction and verse by HG Wells, Emily
Dickinson and many others.

Bibliofind
http://www.bibliofind.com
http://www.usedbooks.com
Millions of old, used and rare books from sell-
ers worldwide. If you can't find it here, try Advanced Book Exchange
(http://www.abebooks.com), A Book For All Reasons
(http://www.abfar.co.uk), Mr Mac (http://www.rmcd.demon.co.uk),
Alibris (http://www.alibris.com), Just Books
(http://www.justbooks.co.uk) or the Central Register of British Internet
Bookshops (http://www.clique.co.uk).

Bibliomania
http://www.bibliomania.com
Similar to Project Gutenberg (see p.72) in that it houses the digital versions of some 800 classic literary works. However, Bibliomania also features study aids as well as digital versions of reference books, plus a
shopping facility if you'd prefer the real thing.

Bodleian Library
http://www.bodley.ox.ac.uk
The homepage of Oxford's university library houses such digital library
projects as the Broadside Ballads Project, the Internet Library of Early
Journals, Allegro Catalogues of Japanese and Chinese books, the
Toyota City Imaging project plus an array of images from Medieval texts.

Book-A-Minute
http://www.rinkworks.com/bookaminute/
Knock over the classics in a lunch hour.

BookCloseouts
http://www.bookcloseouts.com
Millions of books slightly past their shelf life.

Bookwire

http://www.bookwire.com
US book trade news, bestseller lists, and author road schedules with content from *Publisher's Weekly* and *Library Journal*. For UK publishing news, see: http://www.thebookseller.com

The British Library

http://portico.bl.uk
At this stage in its development, the British Library's site is of more use to academics and researchers than to most ordinary Joes, although bookworms will delight in the ability to search the entire catalogue online as well as view select exhibits from the library's collection.

Carol Hurst's Children's Literature Site

http://www.carolhurst.com
Reviews of books for kids, as well as ideas of how to incorporate them into the curriculum.

CrimeBoss

http://www.crimeboss.com
Shock comic covers from the mid-20th century.

The Electronic Text Center

http://etext.lib.virginia.edu
The University of Virginia's digital archive project is similar to the others but it includes more foreign language texts than any of the competition, so if you're after esoterica like Mescalero Apache texts or just Voltaire's Candide in the original French, this is the place to look.

E-books

As if the Internet wasn't already the ultimate proof of the folly of democratizing publishing, along comes the electronic book. While it's tempting to dismiss e-publishing as the last refuge of desperate authors, the format does have the potential to revolutionize book writing if someone figures out how to take advantage of the possibilities the Internet has to offer. At the moment, it seems like e-books are just regular books but in .pdf format on your desktop.

E-books for You   http://www.ebooksforyou.com
Self-help and sub-Tom Clancy action thrillers for $7–10.

Electronic Books   http://www.electronicbooks.com
A good place to start, giving you all the basics with a grasp of both the potential and the shortcomings of the format, plus samples.

The Library   http://www.sealander.com/Library.html/
Check out a couple of John Sealander's e-books; they're mostly just text-based without all the multimedia hoo-ha.

Planet E-book   http://www.planetebook.com
All the latest news, plus an archive of the e-book community since 1996 and all the tools you need to become a publisher.

Riding the Bullet   http://www.simonsays.com/book/book_0743204670.html/
The only real e-book success so far has been Stephen King's thriller. Read review and an excerpt here.

Everything Romantic: Romance Novel Central
http://www.worldzone.net/arts/mrsgiggles/books.html/
Funny and opinionated news and reviews for fans of romance novels.
For more broad-chested heroes, check out All About Romance
(http://www.likesbooks.com) and The Romance Reader
(http://www.theromancereader.com).

E Server
http://www.eserver.org
Over 30,000 online works, including classic novels, academic articles,
journals, recipes and plays.

Femaledetective
http://www.femaledetective.com
She always gets her man.

Gallery of "Misused" Quotation Marks
http://www.juvalamu.com/qmarks/
A proofreader's revenge on the world.

The Internet Public Library
http://www.ipl.org
Browse online books, magazines, journals and newspapers.

January Magazine
http://www.januarymagazine.com
Dissecting books and authors.

JournalismNet
http://www.journalismnet.com
Tips and tools for tapping into the big cheat sheet. More facts for
hacks: http://www.facsnet.org and http://www.usus.org.

Literary Criticism on the Web
http://start.at/literarycriticism/
Links to literary criticism organised both by author and subject, as well
as a list of general sites.

Books and Literature

London Review of Books
http://www.lrb.co.uk
Everything you'd expect from the paper version of this literary institution, including a good – if not complete – archive of articles from writers like Christopher Hitchens, Iain Sinclair, Edward Said and Marjorie Garber. See also The New York Review of Books (http://www.nybooks.com/nyrev/).

MysteryNet
http://www.mysterynet.com
Hmm, now what could this be?

Open Letters
http://www.openletters.net
The Internet may be all about the future, but this site is all about the largely lost, age-old art of letter writing. Epistles from writers both famous and unknown recount little details from everyday life in a strangely intimate, and very readable, style.

Poetry.com
http://www.poetry.com
Your complete poetry resource: advice on rhyming and technique, online poetry slams, the 100 greatest poems and love poems, and, if you're good enough, they'll even publish your own.

Poetry Society
http://www.poetrysoc.com (UK)
http://www.poets.org (US)
Halfway-houses for budding poets and their victims. You have to start somewhere: http://crappypoetry.com

Project Gutenberg
http://www.gutenberg.net
Copyrights don't live forever; they eventually expire. In the US, that's seventy-five years after first publication. In Europe, it's some seventy years after the author's death. With this in mind, Project Gutenberg is gradually bringing thousands of old texts online, along with some more recent donations. Sounds great but you might prefer the convenience of hard copy. See also: http://digital.library.upenn.edu/books/

Pure Fiction (US, UK)
http://www.purefiction.com
For pulp worms and writers alike. Not a word of it is true.

Random Access Memory
http://randomaccessmemory.org
A truly wonder-
ful concept: this
vast repository
of memories (of
anything at all)
is the embodi-
ment of what
the Web is
meant to be all
about. Simple,
compelling,
about real peo-

ple and real lives, with no corporate intrusion.

Religious and Sacred Texts
http://davidwiley.com/religion.html/
Links to online versions of the holy books of many of the world's major
religions – everything from the Bhagavad Ghita to the Zand-i Vohuman
Yasht.

Shakespeare
http://the-tech.mit.edu/Shakespeare/
The Bard unbarred online.

The Slot: A Spot For Copy Editors
http://www.theslot.com
Soothing words of outrage for grammatical pedants.

Tech Classics Archive
http://classics.mit.edu
Hundreds of translated Greek and Roman classics. For more ancient
and Medieval literature, see: http://argos.evansville.edu and Online
Medieval and Classical Library http://sunsite.berkeley.edu/OMACL/

Books and Literature

Text files
http://www.textfiles.com
Chunks of the junk that orbited the pre-Web Internet. For a slightly more modern slant, see: http://www.etext.org

Urban Legends
http://www.urbanlegends.com
http://www.snopes.com
Separate the amazing-but-true from the popular myths.

Vatican Library
http://www.ibiblio.org/expo/vatican.exhibit.html/
The Library of Congress's online exhibit of artefacts from the Pope's library.

Village Voice Literary Supplement
http://www.villagevoice.com/vls/
The online version of *The Village Voice*'s literary supplement is the complete printed version for non-New York residents and includes writing from major new voices and insightful reviews.

Web Del Sol
http://webdelsol.com
A portal for small literary reviews and journals, hosting such prestigious American names as Kenyon Review, Mudlark, Sulfur and Prairie Schooner.

The Western Canon
http://www.geocities.com/Athens/Acropolis/6681/
Links to digital versions of the "great books" that shaped European civilization.

The Word Detective
http://www.word-detective.com
http://www.quinion.com/words/
Words never escape him.

The Yarn
http://www.theyarn.com
A story that offers you the choice of two paths at the end of each chapter. If one leads you to a dead end, you're asked to contribute.

Business

These homepages of prominent business magazines offer much of the same content as their paper versions, but often at a cost:

Advertising Age http://www.adage.com

Adweek http://www.adweek.com

Barrons http://www.barrons.com

Campaign http://www.campaignlive.com

Fast Company http://www.fastcompany.com

Financial Times http://www.ft.com

Forbes http://www.forbes.com

Upside http://www.upside.com

Wall Street Journal http://www.wsj.com

See also News, Newspapers and Magazines (p.222) and Finance (p.124)

AccountingWeb
http://www.accountingweb.co.uk
Safe playpen for British beancounters.

Adbusters
http://www.adbusters.org
Headquarters of the world's culture jammers, dedicated to declaring independence from the ever-encroaching corporate state. More culture jamming to be found at ®TMArk (http://www.rtmark.com) and Blow the Dot Out Your Ass (http://www.blowthedotoutyourass.com).

Setting Up Shop Online

Freemerchant.com

http://www.freemerchant.com
http://www.bigstep.com
http://www.bizfinity.com
http://www.jumbostore.com
http://www.clickandbuild.com
http://store.yahoo.com
http://www.zshops.com

Set up an online shop for next to nothing.

UBrandit

http://www.ubrandit.com
http://www.cafepress.com

Refab a kit commerce site in your own name.

WorldPay

http://www.worldpay.com
http://www.bidpay.com
http://www.paypal.com

Organize credit card payment.

Ad Critic

http://www.adcritic.com
http://www.superbowl-ads.com

Make a cuppa while you wait for this year's best US TV ads. For the best of the last twenty, see http://www.commercial-archive.com. For UK and Australian ads going back to the 50s:
http://www.televisioncommercials.com
http://www.tvc.com.au

Ad Forum

http://www.adforum.com
http://www.sourcetv.com
http://www.portfolios.com

Gateway to thousands of agencies, their ads and the humble creatives behind them.

Alodis
http://www.alodis.com
Specialist advice for UK freelancers.

Annual Report Gallery
http://www.reportgallery.com
View the annual reports of over 2000 publicly traded companies for free.

The Biz
http://www.thebiz.co.uk
A business-to-business portal for British companies.

Bizymoms
http://www.bizymoms.com
Crafty ways to cash up without missing the afternoon soaps.

Business.com
http://www.business.com
Attempting to become the Yahoo of business sites. For more European sites and trade data, see: http://www.dis.strath.ac.uk/business/

Business Advice Online
http://www.businessadviceonline.org.uk
Information and advice on taxes, regulations, e-commerce and consultations from the Small Business Service.

BVCA
http://www.bvca.co.uk
Homepage of the British Venture Capital Association, offering basic advice for businesses seeking funding.

City Wire
http://www.citywire.co.uk
Probably the best place to come for UK financial news. City Wire also contains research reports on what the directors are up to.

Clickz
http://www.clickz.com
The Web as seen by the marketing biz.

Business

Cluetrain Manifesto
http://www.cluetrain.org
Modern-day translation of the "customer is always right". Read it or perish. Alternatively, if you'd prefer an update on "never give a sucker an even break" consult the Ferengi Rules of Acquisition:
http://www.psiphi.org/DS9/rules.html/

CommerceNet
http://www.commerce.net
It may be US-heavy, but this is the main source for e-commerce news and an essential bookmark for any company doing business online.

Companies Online
http://www.companiesonline.com
Get the score on almost a million US companies.

Customers Suck!
http://www.customerssuck.com
Grumbling dispatches from the retail front.

Delphion Intellectual Property Network
http://www.delphion.com
Sift through a few decades of international patents plus a gallery of obscurities. Ask the right questions and you might stumble across tomorrow's technology long before the media. For UK patents see:
http://www.patent.gov.uk

DTI
http://www.dti.gov.uk
The homepage of the Department for Trade and Industry offers policy news and resources that effect every UK business.

Entrepreneur.com
http://www.entrepreneur.com
Get rich now, ask us how.

Flame Broiled
http://www.geocities.com/capitolhill/lobby/2645/
The disgruntled ex-Burger King employee homepage. If only every company had one. For more minimum wage vitriol, try Wal-Mart Sucks (http://www.walmartsucks.com).

Flounder's Mission Statement Generator
http://www.bright.net/~flounder/mission.html/
It is this site's "business to holistically re-engineer economically sound resources to exceed customer expectations".

The Foundation Center
http://fdncenter.org
Companies who might happily spare you a fiver.

Fucked Company
http://fuckedcompany.com
Join the rush to gloat over startup shutdowns.

Garage.com
http://www.garage.com
Matchmaking agency for entrepreneurs and investors founded by Apple's Guy Kawasaki. For more help milking funds to feed your online white elephant, see: http://www.moneyhunter.com

Guerilla Marketing
http://www.gmarketing.com
Get ahead by metaphorically butchering your competitors' families and poisoning your customers' water supply.

Inc
http://www.inc.com
Online presence of American magazine for entrepreneurs and small businesses; includes advice and services like assistance with creating business and marketing plans, health insurance quotes and financing.

InfoUSA
http://www.infousa.com
Find likely Americans to bug with your presentation.

International Trademark Association
http://inta.org
Protect your brand identity.

Killer Internet Tactics
http://www.killertactics.com
How to murder brain-dead Web surfers with HTML.

Mondaq
http://www.mondaq.com
Regulatory information and financial commentary on over 80 world economies.

Patent Café
http://www.patentcafe.com
Protect your crackpot schemes and see them through to fruition.

Planet Feedback
http://www.planetfeedback.com
Let US companies know what you think of their service.

Statistical Data Locators
http://www.ntu.edu.sg/library/stat/statdata.htm/
Links to economic and demographic data of just about every world economy.

Super Marketing: Ads from the Comic Books
http://www.steveconley.com/supermarketing.htm/
The ads that kept you lying awake at night wishing you had more money.

The Wonderful Wankometer
http://www.cynicalbastards.com/wankometer/
Measure corporate hyperbole. Couple with: http://www.dack.com/web/bullshit.html/

Cars and Bikes

Buying a Car

Before you're sharked into signing for a new or used vehicle, go online and check out a few road tests and price guides. You can complete the entire exercise while you're there, but it mightn't hurt to drive one first. Start here:

Autobytel http://www.autobytel.com

Autohit http://www.autohit.co.uk

Autolocate http://www.autolocate.co.uk

Autotrader http://www.autotrader.co.uk

BBC Top Gear http://www.topgear.beeb.com

Car Busters http://www.carbusters.com

Car Importing http://www.carimporting.co.uk

Car Shop http://www.carshop.co.uk

Carseekers http://www.carseekers.co.uk

DealerNet http://www.dealernet.com

Exchange & Mart http://www.ixm.co.uk

Kelly Blue Book http://www.kbb.com

Oneswoop http://www.oneswoop.com

What Car? http://www.whatcar.co.uk

Breath Testing
http://copsonline.com/online_breath_test.htm/
Slurring your swearwords, wobbling all over the road, mounting gutters and knocking kids off bikes? Pull over and blow into this site.

Car Net
http://www.carnet.co.uk
Massive automotive portal, including advice and information on collecting, research facilities, trivia, forums, links, classifieds, want ads, rallying news and more.

Cars and Bikes

Ultimate Thunder — Ultima's latest offering is the evocatively titled Can Am. With a massive 559bhp it's as fast as it looks reports Brett Fraser... more

One Hell of a Rush — With a power-to-weight ratio of 620bhp per ton the awesome Rush Hayabusa Turbo lays claim to being the fastest accelerating road car ever. Steve Bennett dons his special Kevlar reinforced overalls... more

Little big Mini — It may not be an obvious track day choice but how can we ignore BMW's interpretation of a British icon. Brett Fraser drives the new Mini... more

Circuit Driver
http://www.circuitdriver.com
This e-zine for speed junkies includes racing information (with online booking facilities), car and gear reviews, rallying and drag racing advice, car databases, photos and driving technique guides.

Classic Car Directory
http://www.classic-car-directory.com
Good resource for classic car enthusiasts, with price guides, dealer directories, events listings, classifieds and links.

Jou Jou
http://www.joujou.co.uk
"The coolest small car in the world" is for those who think the Smart Car too extravagant: this golf-cart-meets-VW-Bug is only available online, for the princely sum of £10,500 – or £11,200 for the turbo.

Layover
http://www.layover.com
Long, wide loads of truckin' stuff for prime movers and shakers.

License Plates of the World
http://danshiki.oit.gatech.edu/~iadt3mk/
Ring in sick, cancel your date, unplug the phone and don't even think about sleep until you've seen EVERY LICENSE PLATE IN THE WORLD.

Lowrider.com
http://www.lowrider.com
Online community for vatos locos and other connoisseurs of barely-street-legal motor vehicles with the lowest clearance known to man.

Mudpuppy's CB Radio Page
http://www.angelfire.com/wi/citizensband/
That's a 10-4 good, buddy, this here's the Rubber Duck and I'm about to put the hammer down.

Parkers Online
http://www.parkers.co.uk
Car price and specs database going back twenty years. For new models and insurance quotes, try New Car Net (http://www.new-car-net.co.uk).

The Speedtrap Bible
http://www.speedtrap.co.uk
Ironically this site is rather slow, but still a great resource for drivers who want to know, umm, where traffic flashpoints might occur. See also Speedtrap.com (http://www.speedtrap.com) and UK Speed Traps (http://www.ukspeedtraps.co.uk).

Street Trucks Magaazine
http://www.streettrucksmag.com
Custom trucking bible for fans of bags, grilles, rims, souped-up air intake manifolds and other things they could only dream up in the States.

Woman Motorist
http://www.womanmotorist.com
The demographic group that motor vehicle insurers prefer.

World Parts
http://www.world-parts.com
If you're seeking a hubcap or an entire engine, tell this site the car's make and model and the country in which you live, and it will tell you who stocks your part. Also try Find a Part (http://www.find-a-part.com).

Bikes

Bicyclenet
http://www.bicyclenet.co.uk
They claim to be the UK's number-one online cycle shop and it's hard to disagree. Their stock ranges from bikes for kids to high performance road bikes for pros, and they also have a wide range of accessories. Most of their merchandise is available within four working days. Other good shopping sites: Bicycle Apparel (http://www.bicycleapparel.com), Bromley Bike (http://www.bromley-bike.com) and Cycle Centre (http://www.cyclestore.co.uk).

Cars and Bikes

Bike Park
http://www.bikepark.co.uk
Not only a pretty good shop, but advice for beginners and weather reports for two-wheeled enthusiasts.

Bike Trader
http://www.biketrader.co.uk
Part of the Autotrader group, this site offers the same services as its parent site: good search tool, advice on buying and selling motor bikes and links to insurance and finance companies.

Colnago
http://www.trialtir-usa.com/colnagoproducts/cf1/cf1.htm/
The Ferrari of racing bikes is now, officially, a Ferrari. This limited edition bike (only 500 were made) uses the same materials that Ferrari use for their Formula One cars and is yours for a mere $9,500.

Cycling UK
http://www.cycling.uk.com
Portal for British cycling enthusiasts. For even more links, try Cyclesource (http://www.cyclesource.co.uk).

Mad for Mountain Biking
http://www.madformountainbiking.com
Pretty much everything a mountain biker of any skill level could want from a site: shopping area, classifieds, forums, movies, news, training tips, articles and product reviews.

Classifieds

Online classifieds need no explanation. They're like the paper version, but easier to search and possibly more up-to-date. In fact, most papers are moving their classifieds to the Net, though you might have to pay to see the latest listings. Here's a small selection:

Ad-Mart http://www.ad-mart.co.uk

Ad Trader http://www.adtrader.co.uk

Economist Classifieds Market Place http://www.classified.economist.com

eDeluxe http://www.edeluxe.com

Eureka Net http://www.eureka-net.co.uk

Exchange And Mart http://www.exchangeandmart.co.uk

Excite Classifieds http://www.excite.co.uk/classifieds/

Free Classified http://www.freeclassified.co.uk

Its Bazaar http://www.itsbazaar.com

JJ Electronic Plaza http://www.jjplaza.com/onlinead/

Local Ads http://www.localads.net

London Classifieds http://www.mercurie.co.uk/londonclassified/

Loot http://www.loot.com

Net Trader http://www.nettrader.co.uk

Photo Ads http://www.photoads.co.uk

Preloved http://www.preloved.co.uk

Reel Exchange http://www.reelexchange.co.uk

Sell It Net http://www.sellitnet.com

Computing and Tech News

Every decent PC brand has a site where you can download the latest drivers, get support and find out what's new. It won't be hard to find. Usually it's the company name or initials between a www and a com.

So you'll find Dell at: http://www.dell.com, Compaq at: http://www.compaq.com, Gateway at: http://www.gateway.com, and so forth. Most of the big names also have international branches, which will be linked from the main site. Consult Yahoo if that fails. If you're in the market for new computer bits, check out the best price across online vendors:

AnandTech http://www.anandtech.com/guides.html/

FindComp http://www.findcomp.com/uk/

Price Watch http://www.pricewatch.com

StreetPrices.com http://Europe.StreetPrices.com

Popular package software vendors include:

Buy.com http://www.buy.com

Chumbo.com http://www.chumbo.com

Jungle.com http://www.jungle.com

Bear in mind that if you buy from US sites, imports might be taxed upon arrival.

Apple
http://www.apple.com

Essential drop-in to update your Mac, pick up QuickTime and be hard-sold the latest hardware. To top up with news, software, and brand affirmations, see: http://www.macaddict.com
http://www.appleinsider.com
http://www.tidbits.com
http://www.macintouch.com
http://www.macnn.com
http://www.macslash.com
For the latest applications, hints and news on the Macintosh's new operating system, seek out Mac OS X Apps (http://www.macosxapps.com), Mac OS X Hints (http://www.macosxhints.com) and Mac Os Rumor (http://www.macosrumor.com). If you're still desperately clinging on to your old Quadra or Performa, Low End Mac (http://www.lowendmac.com) will help you from reaching absolute zero on the depreciation curve. Diagnose your ailing Mac at

MacFix-it (http://www.macfixit.com). Don't even think of looking at http://www.ihateapple.com: it will only upset you.

Bastard Operator from Hell
http://bofh.ntk.net
http://www.theregister.co.uk
If you work in a big office, you know this man.

Chankstore FreeFont Archive
http://www.chank.com/freefonts.htm/
Download a wacky Chank Diesel display font free each week. If there's still space in your font sack, arrive hat in hand at:
http://www.printerideas.com/fontfairy/
http://zapo.virtualave.net
http://www.fontface.com

Clip Art
http://webclipart.about.com
Bottomless cesspit of the soulless dross used to inject life into documents.

CNET
http://www.cnet.com
Daily technology news and features plus reviews, shopping, games, and downloads, along with schedules, transcripts and related stories from CNET's broadcasting network.

Desktop Publishing
http://desktoppub.about.com
http://desktoppublishing.com
Get off the ground in print.

Dingbats
http://dingbats.i-us.com
For when you just can't get enough symbol fonts.

Easter egg archive
http://www.eeggs.com
A racing game in Excel 2000, a basketball game in Windows 95 and a raygun-wielding alien in Quark Xpress? They're in there all right, but you'll never find them on your own. Here's how to unlock secrets in scores of programs.

Computing and Tech News

Electronic Privacy Information Center
http://www.epic.org
Since 1994, EPIC has been at the vanguard of the campaign to protect privacy over the Internet. For a withering attack on the UK's Regulation of Invesigatory Powers Act, go to the Regulation of Investigatory Powers Information Centre (http://www.fipr.org/rip/). For coverage of free speech issues on the Net, go to the Electronic Frontier Foundation (http://www.eff.org).

Forward Garden
http://www.forwardgarden.com
The resting place of every piece of junk email you've ever received.

FreeDrive
http://www.freedrive.com
http://www.myspace.com
http://www.xdrive.com
http://www.idrive.com
Free storage space on the Net that's perfect for backups and file transfers.

Gibson Research Corporation
http://www.grc.com
If you're at all interested in computer security or are a raving paranoiac, you owe it to yourself to check out this site.

The GNU Project
http://www.gnu.org
The homepage of Richard Stallman's efforts to create a free operating system. You might know it better as Linux, named after Linus Torvald's kernel. For more on GNU/Linux, try Linux Online (http://www.linux.org).

Computing and Tech News

Guide to Flaming
http://www.heenan.net/flame/
Learn how to win friends and influence people on newsgroups, forums and chat rooms.

Hackers' Homepage
http://www.hackershomepage.com
Everything you shouldn't do to your computer or someone else's. More at Attrition (http://www.attrition.org), Cult of the Dead Cow (http://www.cultdeadcow.com) and 2600.com (http://www.2600.com) – just make sure you run every antivirus utility you've got after stopping by.

InfoAnarchy
http://www.infoanarchy.org
All the latest news and views from the battle to keep information free.

Internet Speed Test
http://computingcentral.msn.com/internet/speedtest.asp/
Wallow in the grim truth that you don't have broadband access.

ISP Review
http://www.ispreview.co.uk
Compare your Internet Service Provider with the rest and get the latest broadband news. Also try Net4Nowt (http://www.net4nowt.com).

IT Reviews
http://www.itreviews.co.uk
Independent, jargon-free reviews of hardware, software, games, etc. For more reviews, try About's Computer Reviews (http://compreviews.about.com/compute/compreview/), Product Review (http://www.productreview.com) and Review Finder (http://www.reviewfinder.com).

Microsoft
http://www.microsoft.com
If you're running any Microsoft product (and the chance of that seems to be approaching 100 percent), drop by this disorganized scrapheap regularly for upgrades, news, support and patches. That includes the latest free tweaks to Windows, Office and all that falls under the Internet Explorer regime.

Computing and Tech News

Modem Help
http://www.modemhelp.com
http://www.56k.com
http://www.modemhelp.org
Solve your dial-up dramas for modems of all persuasions including cable, ISDN and DSL. And be sure to check your modem maker's page for driver and firmware upgrades, especially if it's X2 or K56flex.

The Museum of Counter Art
http://www.counterart.com
"THE showcase for over 500 sets of counter digit artwork".

Need to Know
http://www.ntk.net
Weekly high-tech wrap-up with a sarcastic bite.

Newslinx
http://www.newslinx.com
Have the top Net technology stories, aggregated from around 50 sources, delivered to your mailbox daily. Or for the highlights in a digest: http://classifieds.news.com.au/ni/netnews/

Old Computers
http://www.old-computers.com
Relive the days when your Sinclair ZX81 or Commodore Vic 20 could barely play solitaire.

Old English Computer Glossary
http://www.u.arizona.edu/~ctb/wordhord.html/
All your favourite computer terms translated into Arthurian dialect.

Palmgear
http://www.palmgear.com
Know your palm like the back of your hand. For the PocketPC, see:
http://www.pocketmatrix.com

PC Mechanic
http://www.pcmech.com/byopc/
http://www.tweak3d.net
http://arstechnica.com/tweak/hardware.html/
How to build or upgrade your own computer.

PC Tweaking
http://www.anandtech.com
http://www.arstechnica.com
http://www.pcextremist.com
http://www.pureperformance.com
http://www.sharkyextreme.com
http://www.shacknews.com
http://www.tweaktown.com
http://www.ugeek.com
http://www.mvps.org/serenitymacros/
How to overclock your processor into the next millennium, tweak your
bios and upgrade your storage capacity to attract members of the
opposite sex.

PC Tyrant
http://www.pctyrant.com
A useful corrective to the relentless optimism and gung-ho futurism of
most online computer zines.

PCWebopaedia
http://www.pcwebopedia.com
Superb illustrated encyclopedia of computer technology.

PC Help

The best place to find an answer to your computer problems is usually on Usenet. Chances are it's already been answered, so before you rush in and post, search the archives through Google Groups.

Google Groups   http://groups.google.com

That's not to say you won't find answer on the Web. You probably will, so follow up with a Web search. You'll find a choice of engines at the very bottom of the results page. If you click on Google, for example, it will perform the same search in the Web database. Apart from Usenet, there are several very active computing forums on the Web, such as:

Computing.net   http://www.computing.net
Tek Tips   http://www.tektips.com

And there are hundreds of troubleshooting and Windows news sites, such as:

ActiveWin   http://www.activewin.com
Annoyances   http://www.annoyances.org
Common Problems   http://www.users.qwest.net/
           ~careyh/fixes.htm/
Help.com   http://www.help.com
Virtual Dr   http://virtualdr.com
WinOScentral   http://www.winoscentral.com

Don't forget to keep your hardware installation drivers up-to-date. You'll find the latest files for download direct from the manufacturer's Website, or at driver guides such as these:

Driver Forum   http://www.driverforum.com
Driver Guide   http://www.driverguide.com
Drivers HQ   http://www.drivershq.com
Windrivers   http://www.windrivers.com

P2PTracker
http://www.p2ptracker.com
News on peer-to-peer systems like Napster and Gnutella.

The Register
http://www.theregister.co.uk
Punchy tech news that spins to its own tune.

SafeWeb
http://www.safeweb.com
Originally designed for surfers in countries with repressive regimes, SafeWeb is a service that encrypts all data sent from and received by your computer while surfing the Net so that all of your downloads are safe from prying eyes. For more anonymous surfing, try The Anonymizer (http://www.anonymizer.com).

Scantips
http://www.scantips.com
Become a scan-do type of dude.

Slashdot.org
http://slashdot.org
News for those who've entirely given up on the human race.

Techtales
http://www.techtales.com
http://www.helpdesktech.com
Customers – they might always be right but they sure do ask the darndest things.

Tom's Hardware Guide
http://www.tomshardware.com
One of the most important sites on the Net, at least for the hardware industry. Tom and his reporters are credited with the delayed release of Pentium's 1GHz Pentium III processor because the site gave it a thumbs down. This is the best source for bug reports and benchmark tests.

Computing and Tech News

WebReference
http://www.webreference.com
If you don't know your HTML from your XML or DHTML, try this reference and tutorials site. For more tips and tricks, try Webmonkey (http://hotwired.lycos.com/webmonkey/), and for streaming video tutorials, try Virtual Dr (http://www.virtualdr.com).

Windrivers
http://www.windrivers.com
http://www.driverforum.com
http://www.drivershq.com
http://www.driverguide.com
Driver file updates and hardware reviews compiled by a Windows fanatic of such maniacal proportions he even named his son "Gates".

Wired News
http://www.wired.com
The Net's best source of breaking technology news plus archives of Wired magazine. For more, try Geek.com (http://www.geek.com).

Woody's Office Portal
http://www.wopr.com
Beat some sense out of Microsoft Office. For Outlook, see:
http://www.slipstick.com/outlook/faq.htm/

Yahoo Computing
http://www.yahoo.com/Computers/
The grandpappy of all computing directories.

ZDNet
http://www.zdnet.com
Computing info powerhouse from Ziff Davis, publisher of *PC Magazine*, *MacUser*, *Computer Gaming World* and scores of other IT titles. Each magazine donates content such as news, product reviews and lab test results; plus there's a ton of prime Net-exclusive technochow. The best place to start researching anything even vaguely computer-related.

Play it safe

Unless you're 100 percent certain that a download or attachment is safe, even if it's been sent by your best friend, DON'T OPEN IT! Instead, save it to your Desktop or a quarantine folder and examine it carefully before proceeding. That should include running it past an up-to-date antivirus scanner such as AVG (http://www.grisoft.com). You'll find everything you need to know about viruses at:

About.com	http://antivirus.about.com
Alt.comp.virus FAQs	http://www.faqs.org/faqs/computer-virus/
AVG Ant-Virus	http://www.grisoft.com
Computer Associates	http://www.cai.com/virusinfo/
Symantec	http://www.symantec.com/avcenter/

Crafts

About Hobbies
http://www.about.com/hobbies/
Your first portal of call for any crafts search should be About's impressive hobbies page which contains links to their basketry, beadwork, candle-making and woodworking sites as well as twenty other crafts sites that they host.

Allan's Wood Miser's Workshop
http://members.aol.com/woodmiser1/
Great site full of tips and advice for the thrifty woodworker. For more carpentry tips, try About's woodworking site (http://woodworking.about.com) and Woodweb (http://www.woodweb.com) if you're a pro.

Classic Stitches
http://www.classicstitches.com
The home page of *Classic Stitches* magazine includes some 150 downloadable charts to set your needles working.

Crafts

Crafts Council
http://www.craftscouncil.org.uk
News on and listings of craft shows, events, exhibitions, seminars and workshops. The Crafts Council also provides a regional list of shops selling contemporary crafts as well as buying guides.

Crafts Unlimited
http://www.crafts-unlimited.co.uk
Over 1100 cross-stitch patterns to buy, plus downloadable beginner's and advanced guides to cross-stitch technique. Also check out Cross-Stitch Design (http://www.maurer-stroh.com).

Home Sewing Association
http://www.sewing.org
An essential bookmark for budding Gallianos and hopeless bachelors alike. The site is packed with sewing lessons for absolute beginners and tips and trends and advanced techniques for more experienced seam-stresses.

Planet Patchwork
http://www.planetpatchwork.com
Blocks and vectors of information devoted to the mystique of quilting.

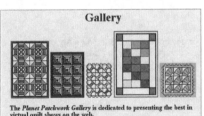

Gallery

The *Planet Patchwork Gallery* is dedicated to presenting the best in virtual quilt shows on the web.

Popular Crafts
http://www.popularcrafts.com
The digital home of *Popular Crafts* magazine includes event listings, book reviews, forums, news and online crafts projects with step-by-step instructions on decorating flower pots and making birthday party cards.

Wool Works
http://www.woolworks.org
Containing an archive of more than 250 patterns, an extensive hints and tips section on making socks and knitting for dolls and a comprehensive links page – this is a darn good knitting site.

Education

This chapter is perhaps a bit of a misnomer as the entire Internet is potentially the greatest single educational resource that's ever been invented: the latter-day equivalent of the library at Alexandria. Here you'll find educational resources (for students, teachers and parents), general homework sites, information on distance learning and admissions guides. For other study tools, try the Reference chapter or other subject headings (Art, Politics, History, etc).

About Education
http://education.about.com
They may be geared towards the US, but, as usual, About's education pages are an excellent source of information and news. Having trouble with times tables or conjugating Latin verbs? Try About Homework (http://homework.about.com).

Academic Info
http://www.academicinfo.net
Research directory for students and teachers.

A-levels
http://www.a-levels.co.uk
Links to sites that will help in A-level revision. For GCSE help, try GCSE Answers (http://www.gcse.com); Scottish Highers students should log on to Higher Still (http://www.higher-still.org.uk).

Ask an Expert
http://www.cln.org/int_expert.html/
Links to hundreds of experts who will happily answer your homework question or offer you careers advice. There are also teaching experts awaiting questions from harried pedagogues. For a more British perspective, try Questico (http://www.questico.co.uk).

Babelfish Translator
http://uk.altavista.com/trns/
If you're reading T.S. Eliot and you come across a passage that's all

Greek to you, type the text in here and it will translate it into English or virtually any language you want.

Channel 4: Homework High
http://www.homeworkhigh.co.uk
Channel 4's homework site allows you to ask experts questions and browse the archive of responses. Much better than the BBC's similar site because it's not linked to the station's programmes.

Click Teaching
http://www.clickteaching.com
A site for primary school teachers largely written by primary school teachers. For more pedagogical advice and resources, try Educare (http://www.educare.co.uk).

EduWeb
http://www.eduweb.co.uk
It claims to be the largest educational resource on the Net, but to access its Living Library (where most of these resources are stored), you have to subscribe – at £49 a year.

Evil House of Cheat
http://www.cheathouse.com
Thousands of college essays, termpapers and reports.

Good Schools Guide
http://www.goodschoolsguide.co.uk
Unfortunately, in order to gain full access to this very useful site, you need to buy the paper version of the popular book, which then lets you get to the weekly updates and the school reviews written by parents for parents.

Guide to Grammar and Style
http://andromeda.rutgers.edu/~jlynch/Writing/
Handy online guide to English language usage. It won't replace Strunk & White or the *Chicago Manual of Style*, but if you're in a pinch, could be worth a try. For more basic grammar instruction, try Pop-Up Grammar (http://www.brownlee.org/durk/grammar/) – but just make sure JavaScript is enabled on your browser.

International Centre for Distance Learning
http://www-icdl.open.ac.uk
The Open University's distance learning resource centre contains a huge database on courses and organizations as well as abstracts of journal articles and research papers pertaining to distance education. Also check out its related site, The Learning Network

(http://www.netlearn.co.uk) and the International Distance Learning Course Finder (http://www.dlcoursefinder.com).

Internet Public Library
http://www.ipl.org
Browse the catalogue of some 16,000 online texts, utilize the original resources and ask homework questions – all without a horn-rimmed librarian telling you to down your Discman.

ISIS
http://www.isis.org.uk
The homepage of the Independent Schools Information Service allows parents and teachers to search their database for information on prospective schools and employers.

Learn.co.uk
http://www.learn.co.uk
A huge resource for both students and teachers, with dowloadable sample SATs, lesson plans, an online community for teachers, revision advice and information on the national curriculum.

Maths Help
http://www.maths-help.co.uk
Send this site's boffins a question and they'll email back an answer. For more help with numbers, try Maths Net (http://www.anglia.co.uk/education/mathsnet/).

National Curriculum Online
http://www.nc.uk.net
The government's definitive national curriculum site for teachers, with outlines, goals and FAQs. For the Scottish curriculum, go to the Scottish CCC Homepage (http://www.sccc.ac.uk/).

National Grid for Learning
http://www.ngfl.gov.uk
This site is the centrepiece of the Government's plans to harness the Net as the future of education. As you might guess, it's a bit of a sprawling mess, but there are sections devoted to just about every educational issue you can think of, as well as tons of links, a virtual teacher centre and so on.

SearchEdu
http://www.searchedu.com
Search millions of university and education pages.

Study Abroad
http://www.studyabroad.com
Hop grass that's greener.

StudyWeb
http://www.studyweb.com
An absolutely enormous education portal, with links to some 160,000 resources, all organised by grade level (some translation from American required).

Topmarks Education
http://www.topmarks.co.uk
This excellent and very easy-to-use site searches the Web for educational sites pertaining to your subject and appropriate age-level, so if you're searching for sites to help you with GCSE revision it will weed out all the sites aimed at Key Stage 1 students. See also Schoolzone (http://www.schoolzone.co.uk).

UCAS
http://www.ucas.co.uk
Information on university courses, including admissions requirements and general facts and figures, from the University and Colleges Admissions Service.

Unofficial Guides
http://www.unofficial-guides.com
Get the real dope on the unis from the students themselves, not the marketing boards.

Up My Street
http://www.upmystreet.com
Type in your postcode and get quick access to the performance tables of local schools.

Employment

Web66: International School Web Site Directory
http://web66.coled.umn.edu/schools.html/
Add your school's Web page if it's not already listed.

Word Central
http://www.word
central.com
A site designed to broad-
en kids' vocabulary by
introducing to the joys of
wordplay. There's also a
section for teachers with
lesson plans and a history
of the English language.

Enter the hallway

Employment

If you're looking to move on up, beware that if you post your
CV online your boss could find it – embarrassing at the very
least. The same situation could also arise if you leave it online
once you're hired. Most job agencies have sites these days, and
the better ones update at least daily, so there are far too many to
attempt to list here. What's best for you will depend on what
field you're in and where you want to work. Bigger isn't always
better, as you'll find yourself competing with more applicants.
On the other hand, your prospective employer isn't likely to
restrict their job search to a site that isn't well known. Whether
you're looking for a job or fill a vacancy, try:

Easy Jobs http://www.easy-jobs.co.uk

Fish4Jobs http://www.fish4jobs.co.uk

Go Job Site http://www.jobsite.co.uk

Gradunet http://www.gradunet.co.uk

Guardian Jobs Unlimited http://www.jobsunlimited.co.uk

Job Search http://www.jobsearch.co.uk

Jobsin http://www.jobsin.co.uk

Monster http://www.monster.co.uk

Overseas Jobs http://www.overseasjobs.com

People Bank http://www.peoplebank.com

Personnel Net http://www.personnelnet.com

Reed http://www.reed.co.uk

Stepstone http://www.stepstone.co.uk

Total Jobs http://totaljobs.com

Work Thing http://www.workthing.com

All Jobs UK
http://alljobsuk.com
This recruitment portal claims to give access to every job vacancy on
the Internet – all two million of 'em.

The Best Resumes on the Net
http://tbrnet.com
Helpful advice on building the perfect CV, featuring a software program
– the Resume Creator 3.1 – for the lazy.

Brilliant Careers
http://brilliantcareers.channel4.com
Channel 4's employment site is a no-nonsense guide to the job market,
with advice, support, vacancies and personality tests.

Buzzword Bingo
http://www.progress.demon.co.uk/Fun/Buzzword-Bingo.html/
When your boss says something like, "proactive" or "quality management
system", check it off on your card – you're a winner if you complete a row.

Cool Works
http://www.coolworks.com
Seasonal jobs in US resorts, national parks, camps, ranches and cruise
lines.

Expat Network
http://www.expatnetwork.co.uk
Subscription placement and settling service for working globetrotters.

Employment

Hungry and Homeless
http://www.hungryandhomeless.co.uk
No, not another site mocking yesterday's dotcom millionaires, but one that houses pictures and histories of homeless people looking for work.

Integrity Based Interviewing
http://www.interviewing.net
Ex-federal agents show you how to get to the truth without drawing any blood.

Internet Career Guide
http://www.careerguide.net
This directory functions as a portal for both job seekers and employers, included are links to headhunters, CV writing services, recruitment and outplacement services.

i-resign.com
http://www.i-resign.com
Quit now while you're ahead.

Mindless Jobs of America
http://www.geocities.com/Area51/Vault/9932/mja.html/
Think your job sucks?

The Riley Guide
http://www.rileyguide.com
Messy but massive directory of job-hunting resources.

Salary Info
http://www.salary.com
http://jobsmart.org/tools/salary/
See what you're worth, and then how much you'd need in another town: http://www2.homefair.com/calc/salcalc.html/

Temp 24-7
http://www.temp24-7.com
Share the pain of temporary work at this online community for temps.

UK Jobs Sites
http://www.transdata-inter.co.uk/jobs-agencies/
An excellent resource for the jobseeker, this directory lists and ranks all
the major British online headhunters and ranks them by number of
vacancies, services, regions and industries they serve.

Washington Alliance of Technology Workers
http://www.washtech.org
This American homepage of the first dotcom union is an excellent
source of news, rumors and advice for the largely unorganised technology sector.

Working Wounded
http://www. work-
ing
wounded.com
Get back at your
boss and your co-
workers without
getting fired.

Yahoo Careers
http://careers.yahoo.com
As ever, Yahoo is in on the act, and as ever, does it superbly. This arm,
however, handles only US placements. But key "employment" as a
search term or click on "international" and you'll be awash with options
spanning the globe.

Environment

Better Planet
http://www.betterplanet.co.uk
Launched by Care4free.net, Better Planet is a simple, easy-to-use site
that extends ecological awareness even to its user interface. It contains
clear information on recycling, organic foods, energy efficiency, pollution and other green matters, all accessible with a minimum number of
mouse clicks.

Environment

eNature.com
http://www.enature.com
Vibrant field guides to North American flora and fauna.

Envirolink Network
http://envirolink.netforchange.com
Online community for the enviromentally aware, containing links to articles on sustainable energy sources and pesticides, daily news updates,
a green marketplace and forums on topics like genetic engineering. See
also EcoNet (http://www.igc.org/igc/gateway/enindex.html/).

Environmental Organization Directory
http://www.eco-portal.com
Find primary pro-
duction and
green-minded
sites.

ForestWorld
http://www.forestworld.com
http://forests.org
Timber tales from both sides of the bulldozer.

Friends of the Earth
http://www.foe.co.uk
The homepage of the environmental pressure group features information on local, national and international campaigns, and information on
the issues involved.

Greenpeace
http://www.greenpeace.org
In addition to the charity's campaigns, the Greenpeace homepage covers genetic engineering, ocean preservation, toxic waste and the transport of nuclear materials.

Rainforest Explorer
http://www.rainforestexplorer.com
A nice, general guide to rainforests and their importance which isn't
preachy. For more Amazonia try Rainforest.net
(http://www.rainforest.net) and the Tropical Rainforest Coalition
(http://www.rainforest.org).

Subsea Explorer

http://www.subseaexplorer.com

This site for scuba divers may force you to subscribe, but if you do you could win a diving expedition to the Titanic – plus there are excellent educational resources for kids, articles on the subaquatic environment, underwater Webcams and cheap diving equipment from the shop. To explore the sky as well as the sea try the equally excellent Sky and Sea (http://www.seasky.org).

UK National Air Quality Information Archive

http://www.aeat.co.uk/netcen/airqual/

Worried about foot-and-mouth pyres or diesel emissions? Check the air quality for your area here. To feel guilty about the amount of carbon dioxide you are responsible for, check out the Carbon Calculator (http://www.carboncalculator.org).

Events and Entertainment

Aloud

http://www.aloud.com

Book music, festival and event tickets online from this member of the Which? Code of Practice. See also Ticketmaster (http://www.ticketmaster.co.uk).

Ananova - Going Out

http://www.ananova.com/whatson/

Comprehensive and nationwide general entertainment listings which you can have sent to your WAP phone.

British Arts Festivals

http://www.artsfestivals.co.uk

Keep tabs on the UK's highbrow festivals from Brighton to Edinburgh on this comprehensive site.

eFestivals

http://www.efestivals.co.uk

If you can't get enough of playing your bongos in the mud, point your virtual caravan to this site which contains ticket information, line-ups, rumours and reviews of festivals like Homelands, T in the Park, Glastonbury, Creamfields and the Essential Festival.

London Theatre Guide
http://www.londontheatre.co.uk
This venerable site boasts not only excellent theatre listings but regularly updated cast news and seating plans. See also What's On Stage (http://www.whatsonstage.com) for regional as well as London listings.

Nightclubbin UK
http://www.nightclubbinuk.com
Listings and links for a large majority of Britain's clubs.

Planit4Kids
http://www.planit4kids.co.uk
Listings and events information organized by region for the most demanding audience of them all.

Scene One
http://www.sceneone.co.uk
UK-wide entertainment guide covering music, film, theatre and comedy with an excellent search facility.

This Is London
http://www.thisislondon.co.uk:80/dynamic/
The *Evening Standard*'s Website includes, film, theatre, comedy and clubbing listings for the capital as well as a visitor's guide and reviews of pubs and restaurants.

Time Out
http://www.timeout.com
Definitive London listings from the venerable magazine, as well as global city guides if you're planning to venture abroad.

Yack
http://www.yack.co.uk
Perhaps the best guide to online events, Yack lists the Webcasts, chats, film, animation and other events occurring on the Internet every day.

Regional Listings

Most UK events sites can seem like a Big Smoke screen with all the emphasis on London. Here are a few that attempt to redress the balance:

Bournemouth	http://www.bournemouth.co.uk
Cardiff	http://www.metroplex.co.uk/WhatsOn/cardiff/
Chester	http://www.chestercc.gov.uk/asp/events/
Coventry	http://www.cwn.org.uk/whatson/
Glasgow	http://www.area41.com
Hampshire	http://www.hants.gov.uk/whatson/

Fashion and Beauty

Unless it entirely erodes your reading time, the Net isn't likely to cut your guilty expenditure on glossy mags. While there's a spree of fledgling style zines and something from nearly all the big rack names, nothing compares to getting it in print. Nonetheless it will certainly supplement your vice. What you will find the Net better for is researching products, checking out brands and saving money on consumables like cosmetics at stores such as:

http://www.drugstore.com
http://www.gloss.com

http://www.ibeauty.com
http://www.perfumania.com
http://www.reflect.com
http://www.sephora.com
http://www.theperfumeshop.com
http://www.hqhair.com
http://www.beu.co.uk
http://www.thinknatural.com

Buying clothes online is tough but popular nonetheless. They're out there, if you know what you're doing, but you'll soon see why Boo.com failed. Label sites are sometimes interesting for new season looks, stockists and direct ordering.

Afro Hair and Beauty
http://www.afrohairandbeauty.co.uk
Links to, and resource pages for, black haircare and beauty products.

Bad Fads Museum
http://www.badfads.com/
Revisit your past fashion mistakes.

BK Enterprises
http://www.b-k-enterprises.com
The only place to get that authentic '70s Elvis jump suit. Prices range from $900 to $5000. Also has links to boot dealers, glasses shops and the place to get show scarves to complete the look.

Changes Live
http://www.changeslive.com
Health and beauty magazine and shop that allows you to upload a photo of yourself and then experiment with different hairstyles and make-up.

Cosmetic.org
http://www.cosmetic.org
http://www.ienhance.com
Adjust your imperfection without pills or creams.

Debenhams
http://www.debenhams.com
Do some etail therapy at the site of everyone's favourite department store.

FashionBot
http://www.fashionbot.com
Search several UK high-street retailers' catalogues.

Fashion Information
http://www.fashioninformation.com
Pay for trend forecasting reports.

Fashion Net
http://www.fashion.net
Handy shortcut to the highest-profile shopping, designer, magazine, modelling and fashion industry sites, with enough editorial to warrant an extended stopover.

Fashion Live
http://www.fashionlive.com
Splashy, sexy Parisian e-zine covering both *haute couture* and more achievable fashion trends. They've taken over the Place de Mode shopping site, allowing you quick access to the looks you see on its pages.

Fashionmall.com
http://www.fashionmall.com
http://www.brandsforless.com
http://www.bluefly.com
http://www.designersdirect.com
Mail-order familiar, and mostly American, labels.

Fashion and Beauty

Fashion UK
http://www.fuk.co.uk
Minimal but fresh vanity monthly from London.

Figleaves.com
http://www.figleaves.com
Online underwear superstore for both men and women.

Firstview
http://www.firstview.com
See what's trotting the catwalks – sometimes at a price.

Fragrance Direct
http://www.fragrancedirect.co.uk
It may look like a site for kids, but this etailer offers tremendous bargains on a good range of perfumes, cosmetics and skincare products.

The Lipstick Page
http://www.thelipstickpage.com
Cosmetic appliances for fun and profit.

Moda Italia
http://www.modaitalia.net
Patch through to the Italian rag traders.

Net-à-Porter
http://www.net-a-porter.com
Can't get to Harvey Nick's? Try here for posh frocks and accessories: Bottega Veneta, Clements Ribeiro, Missoni, Fake London and Paul & Joe are some of the cult labels this site stocks. Plus there's no snooty attitude. For Vivienne Westwood, Versace and others, try Lux Look (http://www.luxlook.com).

Organization for the Advancement of Facial Hair
http://www.ragadio.com/oafh/
Includes an archive of classic beard styles and a library of grooming tips. For more advice on beard trimmers and how to keep your hulihee at its best (or just to see pics of guys who like '70s country singers), try these other hirsute sites: Bad Burns (http://www.badburns.com), Beard Guy (http://members.aol.com/beardguy/), Men Who Look Like Kenny

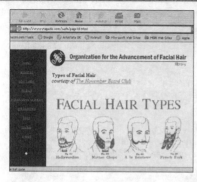

Rogers (http://www.menwholooklikekennyrogers.com) and the November Beard Club (http://my.treeway.com/beardsworld/).

osMoz
http://www.osmoz.com
They haven't invented scratch 'n' sniff technology for the Web yet, but this French site (in English) is the next best thing. A fragrance test will tell you which whether floral or hesperide scents suit you best, and if you register they will send you free samples.

Ready 2 Shop
http://www.ready2shop.com
If you're not sick to death of the *Telegraph*'s fashion writers Trinny and Susannah, this site which rates the best of the high street collections and gives you advice, according to your body shape, provides an invaluable service.

Salonweb
http://www.salonweb.com
Frizzy, fly-away, mousy, permed hair? Try this haircare portal for all the tips and advice you'll ever need.

Solemates: The Century in Shoes
http://www.centuryinshoes.com
Stepping out in the 20th century.

Style.com
http://www.style.com
With an impressive archive of images from all the major catwalk shows of the past two years, the online home of American *Vogue* is one of the

Mullets

The Kentucky Waterfall, the Soccer Rocker, the Missouri Compromise, Business Up Front/Party In The Back, Neck Blanket, Ape Drape, the Tennessee Top Hat – whatever you want to call it, no hairstyle in the history of the civilized world has generated so much scorn, derision or passion as the mullet. Here are a few sites where you can mull over "the hairstyle of the gods":

Dan's Mullet Haven
http://www.fortunecity.co.uk/southbank/pottery/3/
Wrestlers, musicians and footballers.

Football Mullets
http://www.mullets.co.uk
Site of the Mullet World Cup.

Match the Mullets
http://douno1.douno.com/matchthemullets/
Reunite the faces with the hair and win £5000.

Mullet Gods
http://www.mulletgods.com
Your complete mullet resource.

Mullet Junky
http://www.mulletjunky.com
Homepage of the mullet hunters.

Mullet Lovers
http://www.mulletlovers.com
Galleries, galleries, galleries.

Mullets Galore
http://www.mulletsgalore.com
The most comprehensive mullet site.

best resources for fashionistas. If you're after a more standard maga-zine approach, try the British equivalent (http://www.vogue.co.uk).

Victoria's Secret

http://www.victoriassecret.com
Order online or request the catalogue preferred by nine out of ten teenage boys.

Wellbeing.com

http://www.wellbeing.com
Boots' revamped site has everything you'd expect from the high street pharmacy.

Zoom

http://www.zoom.co.uk
Portal for the Arcadia group shops (Dorothy Perkins, Top Shop, Principles, Burton Menswear, etc), allowing to recreate your high street experience on the information superhighway.

Film

When it comes to movies, one site clearly rules:
The Internet Movie Database http://www.imdb.com

To say that it's impressive is an understatement. You'll be hard-pressed to find any work on or off the Net as comprehensive as this exceptional relational database of screen trivia from over 100,000 movies and a million actors. It's all tied together remarkably well – for example, within two clicks of finding your favorite movie you can get full filmographies of anyone from the cast or crew and then see what's in the cooker. Still, it's not per-fect, or without competition. You'll find a similar service with superior biographies and synopses at the colossal:
All Movie Guide http://www.allmovie.com

Or for more Chan, Li and Fat:
Hong Kong Movie Database http://www.hkmdb.com

Film

For cinema listings:

ABC Cinemas http://www.abccinemas.co.uk

Cineworld http://www.cineworld.co.uk

Popcorn http://www.popcorn.co.uk

Teletext-Cinema http://www.teletext.co.uk/bigscreen/

UCI Cinemas http://www.uci-cinemas.co.uk

Virgin Net http://www.virign.net/movies/

Warner Village http://www.warnervillage.co.uk

Ain't It Cool News
http://www.aintitcool.com

The movie news and gossip site that has Hollywood execs quaking in their boots. Founder Harry Knowles has been blamed several times when movies have tanked at the box office, and *Premiere* magazine has ranked him as one of Hollywood's most powerful people. Receive the wisdom of Harry here, along with whispers of what's in production and interviews. More production gossip can be overheard at CHUD (http://www.chud.com), Coming Attractions (http://www.corona.bc.ca/films/), Dark Horizons (http://www.darkhorizons.com) and IMDB (http://www.imdb.com/Sections/Inproduction/).

asSeenonScreen
http://www.asseenonscreen.com

Buy stuff you've seen on TV or in movies. For more, try MovieProp (http://www.movieprop.com) and The Prop Store (http://www.propstore.co.uk).

The Astounding B Monster
http://www.bmonster.com

Excellent resource for fans of Mamie Van Doren, Rondo Hatton and other cult '50s and '60s drive-in/late-show fodder. For fans of more modern fare like *Cannibal Women in the Avocado Jungle of Death*, there's Bad Movie Planet (http://www.badmovieplanet.com), The Bad Movie Report (http://www.stomptokyo.com/badmoviereport/), The Bad Movie Review (http://www.badmovies.org), Oh The Humanity (http://www.ohthehumanity.com), Shock Cinema (http://members.aol.com/shockcin/) and Trash City (http://www.trshcity.demon.co.uk). If your critical faculties are so deadened that you might actually like to own one of these celluloid atrocities, try Science

Fiction Continuum (http://www.sfcontinuum.com) – just make sure you've got a NTSC-compatible VCR.

Atom Films
http://www.atomfilms.com
Watch entertaining short films. For sixteen-colour silliness see: http://www.pixelfest.com

Bad Movie Night
http://www.hit-n-run.com
Invite a couple of mates over to your house, get in a few beers, rent an aggressively mediocre movie and hurl invective at the screen. More snide remarks available at Filthy Critic (http://bigempire.com/filthy/), Mr Cranky (http://www.mrcranky.com), The Stinkers (http://www.thestinkers.com). But to really unveil box office evil, try: Childcare Action Project (http://www.capalert.com), Movie Rat (http://www.saunalahti.fi/~mitt/movierat.htm/) and Screen It! (http://www.screenit.com).

Black Star
http://www.blackstar.co.uk
Based in Northern Ireland, this is perhaps the best British DVD and video shop on the Net: good selection, excellent search facility and great prices. Other video and DVD etailers worth checking out are DVD World (http://www.dvdworld.co.uk), Film World (http://www.film-world.co.uk), Mr Benson's World of Home Entertainment (http://www.bensonsworld.co.uk), Red Hot Monkey (http://www.red-hotmonkey.com) and The Video Shop (http://www.videoshop.co.uk). To compare prices: DVD Price Search (http://www.dvdpricesearch.com) or For Movies (http://www.formovies.com).

Blaxploitation.com
http://www.blaxploitation.com
Superfly guys and gals stickin' it to the man. More Afros and diashikis at BadAzz Mofo (http://www.badazzmofo.com).

Blooper Files
http://www.blooperfiles.com
Archive of screw-ups and inconsistencies from Hollywood's finest. More pratfalls at Film Goofs (http://www.filmgoofs.com) and more con-

tinuity errors at Movie Mistakes (http://www.movie-mistakes.co.uk)
and The Nitpickers Site (http://www.nitpickers.com).

Brutesquad Movies
http://www.brutesquad.com/MOS/movie_body.htm/
Preview movies like *Schindler's List II* (starring Arnold Schwarzenegger)
and *Titanic: Horror of the Deep* (Jeff Goldblum saving the world against
a pack of marauding blue whales).

Carfax-Abbey Horror Film Database
http://www.carfax-abbey.com
Splatter-flick Central, with loads of info on gore masters like Dario
Argento and Wes Craven. More zombies and fake blood at Arrow in the
Head (http://www.joblo.com/arrow/), while fans of Christopher Lee and
Peter Cushing should grab some garlic and head to Ghoul Britannia
(http://www.edhouse.clara.net/ghoul.html/).

Dogme95
http://www.dogme95.dk
Homepage of the Danish film movement led by Lars Von Trier, including

the manifesto, a how-to page and the latest news from the film vanguard.

Drew's Script-O-Rama
http://www.script-o-rama.com
http://www.scriptshack.com
Hundreds of entire film and TV scripts. Need help writing or selling your own? Try: http://www.celluloidmonkeys.com

DVD Debate
http://www.dvddebate.com
All the latest UK DVD release news and reviews, plus a mighty useful section on the codes that enable you to change the regional setting on your DVD player. For more on DVD hardware and software:
http://www.7thzone.com
http://www.dvdfile.com

E! Online
http://www.eonline.com
Daily film and TV gossip, news and reviews.

Empire Magazine
http://www.empireonline.co.uk
Reviews of every film showing in the UK.

555-LIST
http://home.earthlink.net/~mthyen/
Catalogue of fake telephone numbers used in TV and film.

Gil*galad's Martian Theaethyr
http://www.televar.com/~gnostran/
Applying AstroTarotry to old movies makes them so much clearer.

Golden Raspberry Award Foundation
http://www.razzies.com
The Oscars in an alternate universe.

Hollywood Reporter
http://www.hollywoodreporter.com
Tinseltown tattle, previews and reviews daily, plus a flick biz directory.

Film

In-Movies
http://www.in-movies.com
If you've got broadband access you can watch classic scenes from classic movies, trailers and short films. For shorts from closer to home, try Brit Shorts (http://www.britshorts.com). For more trailers, pull up to The Trailer Park (http://www.movie-trailers.com). For specially commissioned full-length features, point your ADSL hookup to SightSound (http://www.sightsound.com).

Melon Farmer's Video Hits
http://www.dtaylor.demon.co.uk
Challenges British screen censorship.

Movie Cliches
http://www.moviecliches.com
Nothing unfamiliar.

MovieLens
http://movielens.umn.edu
Become a member of this site and it will give you movie recommendations based on your tastes. It may be a bit of a behavioural research exercise, but it's still a pretty neat way of avoiding video shop malaise. Another site plays it safe: Greatest Films (http://www.filmsite.org).

Moviemags.com
http://www.moviemags.com
Directory of film print and ezines.

Movie Review Query Engine
http://www.mrqe.com
This specialist search engine dedicated to finding film reviews on the Web has a database of more than 25,000 titles and does an excellent job of finding info on obscure titles. But perhaps you'd prefer a summary: Rotten Tomatoes (http://www.rottentomatoes.com). For British reviews, try Filmreview (http://www.filmreview.co.uk) and Film Unlimited (http://www.filmunlimited.co.uk).

Movies.com

http://www.movies.com
http://www.mca.com
http://www.film.com

Preview box office features and trailers direct from the major studios.

The Movie Shelf of Apartment 304

http://www.compusmart.ab.ca/kroyea/movie.htm/

Cool martial arts and Yakuza flick site, with good features on Sonny Chiba and cover art.

Mr Kiss Kiss Bang Bang

http://www.ianfleming.org

An outrageously complete and obsessive guide to the shaken, not stirred universe of James Bond, with daily news and rumour updates.

A Bond-type girl poses in the same style outfit as was seen on the famous poster from *Casino Royale*.

My Movies

http://www.my movies.net

Huge film site with production news, gossip, reviews, competitions, shopping, trailers and, if you've got broadband, movies on demand.

SciFi.com

http://www.scifi.com
http://scifi.ign.com
http://www.fandom.com

Science fiction news, reviews and short films.

Showbizwire
http://www.showbizwire.com
Entertainment newsbreaks from about 50 major sources.

The Silents Majority
http://www.silentsmajority.com
This great online journal devoted to silent film is certainly one of the best film sites on the Web, even if you don't know Fatty Arbuckle from ZaSu Pitts.

Smoking List Movie Reviews
http://SmokingSides.com/asfs/m/
A history of smoking on the silver screen. Non-smokers might want to try Soup at the Movies (http://www.soupsong.com/imovies.html).

Variety
http://www.variety.com
Screen news fresh off the PR gattling gun.

VCR Repair Instructions
http://www.fixer.com
How to take a VCR apart and then get all the little bits back in so it fits easier into the bin.

Lo-tech Film Recreations

Who needs a £20 million special effects and pyrotechnics budget when you've got a couple of Lego sets?

The Fountainhead – A Parody
http://www.jeffcomp.com/ faq/parody/
Ayn Rand's capitalist parable starring Skull Force.

Lego Star Wars Trilogy
http://www.tanukikoji.or.jp/yes/lsw/
Thankfully, there's no Jar Jar Binks.

Sandou's Rising Sun Minifig Headquarters
http://www.geocities.co.jp/Hollywood/9060/english.html/
Charlie's Angels and *Akira* in ninja Lego style.

Shark Attack
http://www.exposure.co.uk/eejit/3act/sharkattack.html/
Jaws in Lego vision.

Star Wars ASCIImation
http://www.asciimation.co.nz
The ultimate Hi-tech flick rendered in glorious letter art.

Warning6
http://www.cinepad.com/warning6.htm/
If you don't want to know the twists at the end of *The Usual Suspects* or *The Crying Game*, don't you dare visit this site.

Westerns.com
http://www.westerns.com
A great site for fans of classic oaters. They've got streaming videos of some obscure low budget shoot-'em-ups like *Fury* and *Can Be Done ... Amigo*, plus MP3s of Roy Rogers and Gabby Hayes, bios and filmographies of your favourite cowboys and cowgirls, and, of course, a tradin' post.

Finance

If your bank's on the ball it should offer an online facility to check your balances, pay your bills, transfer funds and export your transaction records into a bean-counting program such as Quicken or Money. If that sounds appealing and your bank isn't already on the case, start looking for a replacement. Go for one you can access via the Internet rather than by dialling direct. That way you can manage your cash through a Web browser whether you're at home, work or in the cybercafé on top of Pik Kommunisma. For help finding a true online bank:

MyBank http://www.mybank.com
Online Banking Report http://www.netbanker.com
Qualisteam http://www.qualisteam.com

If you can resist the urge to daytrade away your inheritance, the Net should give you greater control over your financial future. You can research firms, plot trends, check live quotes, join tip lists and stock forums, track your portfolio live, trade shares and access news. By all means investigate a subscription service or two – at least for the free trial period – but unless you need split-second data feeds or "expert" timing advice you should be able to get by without paying. Start here:

Yahoo UK http://quote.yahoo.co.uk

Apart from housing the Net's most exhaustive finance directory, Yahoo pillages data from a bunch of the top finance sources and presents it all in a seamless, friendly format. Enter a stock code, for example, and you'll get all the beef from the latest ticker price to a summary of insider trades. In some markets stocks have their own forums, which, let's face it, are only there to spread rumours. In other words, be very sceptical of anything you read or that's sent to you in unsolicited email.

Yahoo is by no means complete nor necessarily the best in every area, so try a few of these as well:

Asia Gateway http://www.asiagateway.com

Bloomberg http://www.bloomberg.co.uk

CBS MarketWatch http://cbs.marketwatch.com

Digital Look http://www.digitallook.com

FinancialWeb http://www.financialweb.com

Free Real Time Quotes http://www.freerealtime.com

Gay Financial Network http://www.gfn.com

Hemscott http://www.hemscott.net

Interactive Investor http://www.iii.co.uk

Investorama http://www.investorama.com

Market Eye http://www.market-eye.co.uk

MetaMarkets http://www.metamarkets.com

Microsoft MoneyCentral http://moneycentral.msn.com

Money Extra http://www.moneyextra.com

Raging Bull http://www.ragingbull.com

Sharepages http://www.sharepages.com

Wall Street City http://www.wallstreetcity.com

Wall Street Research Net http://www.wsrn.com

You'll no doubt be after a broker next. As with banking, any broker or fund manager who's not setting up online probably doesn't deserve your business. In fact, many traders are dumping traditional brokers in favour of the exclusively online houses. E★Trade (http://www.etrade.co.uk), for example, offers discount brokerage in at least nine countries (click on "International" to find your local branch). But traditional brokers are catching on. Many have cut their commissions, and offer online services in line with the Internet competition, so it pays to shop around. You might find you prefer to research online and trade by phone. To compare brokers:

Gomez.com http://uk.gomez.com

For a British e-trading portal, try E-Trader UK (http://www.e-traderuk.com).

A word of warning, though: some online brokers have experienced outages where they were unable to trade. So if the market crashes in a big way, it mightn't hurt to play safe and use the phone instead.

BigCharts

http://www.big
charts.com
http://stock
charts.com

Whip up family-sized graphs of US stocks, mutual funds and market indices. Or if you'd prefer them streaming at you live, proceed to:
http://www.live
charts.com

BillPay

http://www.billpayment.co.uk

Pay your electricity, gas and water bills over the Net with this new service from Girobank.

Blay's Guides

http://www.blays.co.uk

Tracks and ranks finance rates across every UK market. Also links to hundreds of banking sites and investment products. For more rates, try Buy.co.uk (http://www.buy.co.uk), Moneygator (http://www.moneygator.com) and Money Supermarket (http://www.moneysupermarket.com).

Bonehead Finance

http://ourworld.compuserve.com/homepages/Bonehead_Finance/
No-nonsense financial basics for dummies.

British Bankers' Association
http://www.bankfacts.org.uk
Review the Banking Code, find a cash machine, convert currency and consult a glossary of banking terms.

Clearstation
http://www.clearstation.com
Run your stock picks through a succession of gruelling obstacle courses to weed out the weaklings or simply copy someone else's portfolio.

The Desktop Accountant
http://www.thedesktopaccountant.com
Advice and tips to help small businesses and freelancers navigate their way around the tax code.

Earnings Whispers
http://www.earningswhispers.com
When a stock price falls upon the release of higher-than-expected earnings, chances are that the expectations being "whispered" amongst traders prior to opening were higher than those circulated publicly. Here's where to find out what's being said behind your back. For the biggest surprises, see: http://biz.yahoo.com/z/extreme.html/

Financial Planning Horizons
http://www.financial-planning.uk.com
Good, unbiased information on the full range of financial products available in the UK.

Find
http://www.find.co.uk
The Financial Information Net Directory houses some 6000 links to UK financial Websites, organised into categories like investment, insurance, information services, advice and dealing, bankings and savings, mortgages and loans, business services and life and pensions.

Financial Times
http://www.ft.com
Business news, commentary, delayed quotes and closing prices from London. It's free until you hit the archives.

Finance

Foreign Exchange Rates
http://quote.yahoo.com
http://www.xe.net/ucc/
Round-the-clock rates, conversion calculators and intraday charts on
pretty close to the full set of currencies. To chart further back, see:
http://pacific.commerce.ubc.ca/xr/plot.html/

Frugal Corner
http://www.frugalcorner.com
Learn how to be thrifty from the experts.

Glossary of Financial Terms
http://centrex.com/terms.html/
At least look like you know what you're talking about.

HedgeWorld
http://www.hedgeworld.com
Allowing the average Joe a peek inside the secretive world of hedge
funds.

Hoovers
http://www.hoovers.com
Research US, UK and European companies.

iCreditReport
http://www.icreditreport.com
Dig up any US citizen's credit ratings.

iExchange.com
http://www.iexchange.com
Tracks and ranks market prophets.

Inland Revenue
http://www.inlandrevenue.gov.uk
Tax information straight from the horse's mouth. To find a qualified advisor, try the Chartered Institute of Taxation (http://www.tax.org.uk). For a
rough estimate of how much you'll have to pay, try the UK Wage/Tax
Calculator (http://listen.to/taxman/).

Insider Scores
http://www.insiderscores.com
Get the inside on US and Asian directors' trades.

Investment FAQ
http://www.invest-faq.com
Learn the ropes from old hands.

InvestorWords
http://www.investorwords.com
Can't tell your hedge rate from your asking price? Brush up on your finance-speak here.

Island
http://www.island.com
See US equity orders queued up on dealers' screens.

MAXfunds
http://www.maxfunds.com
Great site that allows you track the performance of mutual funds. You have to register, but it's free. For more on managed funds and unit trusts, try Micropal (http://www.micropal.com) and TrustNet (http://www.trustnet.co.uk).

Missing Money
http://www.missingmoney.com
http://www.findcash.com
Reclaim those US dollars you're owed.

MoneyChimp
http://www.moneychimp.com
Plain English primer in the mechanics of financial maths.

Money Origami
http://www.umva.com/~clay/money/
It's much more fun when you can make something out of it.

The Motley Fool.
Fool.co.uk

Motley Fool
http://www.fool.co.uk
Forums, tips, quotes and sound advice. More people telling you what to
do with your money at City Pigeon (http://www.citypigeon.co.uk),
Citywire (http://www.citywire.co.uk), Mrs Cohen (http://www.
mrscohen.com) and This Is Money (http://www.thisismoney.com).

Office of Fair Trade Personal Finance Guide
http://www.oft.gov.uk/html/finance/
Tips and advice from the Government.

Paypal
http://www.paypal.com
Arrange online payments through a third party.

Pension Sorter
http://www.pensionsorter.com
Protect yourself against the scandals of the '80s with this site's impartial
advice. For the Government's angle, try Pension Guide
(http://www.pensionguide.gov.uk).

Screentrade
http://www.screentrade.co.uk
General insurance site, offering quotes from a range of insurers. Try also
1st Quote (http://www.1stquote.co.uk) and InsuranceWide
(http://www.insurancewide.co.uk).

Tax & Accounting Sites Directory
http://www.taxsites.com
Links to everything you need to know about doling out your annual
pound of flesh.

Technical Analysis Tutorials
http://www.e-analytics.com/techdir.htm/
Beginner's guide to fortune-telling the markets using charts and indicators.

UK-iNvest
http://www.uk-invest.com
Very good general money site, with channels covering everything from banking to tax planning. The best feature is a section called "Around the Tipsheets" which rounds up all the day's share picks from the papers, financial rags and tipsheets.

Wall Street Journal Interactive
http://www.wsj.com
Not only is this online edition equal to the print one, its charts and data archives give it an edge. That's why you shouldn't complain that it's not free. After all, if it's your type of paper, you should be able to afford it, bigshot.

Where's George?
http://www.wheresgeorge.com
Put a tail on your greenback.

Flowers

About Flowers
http://www.aboutflowers.com
The meanings of flowers and the right ones for various occasions. See also All Occasion Flowers (http://www.all-occasion-flowers.com).

Daisys2Roses
http://www.daisys2roses.com
Despite a slight design flaw, this site allows you to create your own bouquet, a service which almost no other online florist offers. On top of that, this site has a special offer of half-a-dozen roses for £10 plus delivery.

First Flowers Direct
http://www.firstflowers.com
The flowers from this site come straight from the Covent Garden Flower Market and because of that they offer a better, less old-fashioned, range of bouquets. They also belong to the Which? Webtrader Code of Practice.

Floritel
http://www.floritel.co.uk
This site is perhaps too expensive to use for local deliveries, but it allows you to tailor a bouquet to your price limit as well as choosing flowers and colours.

Flowers Say
http://www.flowerssay.co.uk
As well as offering the real thing, Flowers Say sells artificial arrangements if you're after something a bit more permanent. Whether you want natural flowers, flowering bulbs or synthetic flora, prices are cheap, but the site is short on details.

Interflora
http://www.interflora.co.uk
Interflora may be the biggest name in flowers, but their site is pretty run-of-the-mill. Aside from reliability and name recognition, its main feature is a personal organiser that will remind you of anniversaries and birthdays.

Teleflorist
http://www.teleflorist.co.uk
Like most of the big players, Teleflorist's site seems to offer a fairly limited range of bouquets and arrangements. It does, however, feature Internet exclusives and a percentage of certain orders are donated to charity.

Food and Drink

BBC Food
http://www.bbc.co.uk/food/
A very branded site (there are lots of familiar faces) but with a good database of solid recipes that you can be sure will have been tested properly.

Beershots
http://micro.
magnet.fsu.edu/
beershots/
Beers of the world put under a microscope.

BEERSHOTS
microscopic views of beers from around the world

Berry Brothers & Rudd
http://www.bbr.co.uk
Although the site looks a little intimidating, don't be put off: this is one of the country's best wine ordering services and you can pick up wines for around £6, although at the other end the sky's the limit. Try also Oddbins (http://www.oddbins.co.uk) and Virgin Wines (http://www.virginwines.com).

Bevnet
http://www.bevnet.com
Know your new-age beverages. Here's how to brew the "real thing": http://www.sodafountain.com

Food and Drink

Breworld.com

http://www.breworld.com

None of the usual beer yarns like waking up in a strange room stark-naked with a throbbing head and a hazy recollection of pranging your car. Here beer is treated with the same dewy-eyed respect usually reserved for wine and trains. Like to send your chum a virtual beer? Stumble over to: http://www.pubworld.co.uk

Cheese

http://www.cheese.com

Excellent cheese information site with an exhaustive list of cheeses and detailed info on composition.

Chile-Heads

http://chileheads.netimages.com
http://www.ringoffire.net

Get 'em while they're hot.

Chocolate Lover's Page

http://chocolate.scream.org

The good gear: where to find recipes and dealers.

Chopstix

http://www.chopstix.co.uk

Good site for Chinese recipes (from the likes of Ken Hom) and information on ingredients too.

Cigar Aficionado

http://www.cigaraficionado.com

Archives, shopping guides, and tasting forums from the US glossy that sets the benchmark in cigar ratings. Modelled on: http://www.thethirdrail.com/crack/

Cocktail Time

http://www.cocktailtime.com
http://cocktails.about.com
http://www.webtender.com
http://www.barmeister.com
http://www.drinkboy.com

Guzzle your way to a happier home. Yes, do buy the book.

Specialist Shopping Sites

Cyber Candy http://www.cybercandy.com
Brilliant site for exploring candy from all over the world – great for US and Japanese ex-pats looking for a sugary flavour of home.

Fifth Sense http://www.fifthsense.co.uk
An excellent site if you want to adventure a bit with spices or sauces from around the globe – mostly dry or bottled goods, though.

Fortnum & Mason http://www.fortnumandmason.co.uk
Excellent luxury food shopping site sensibly separated into goods that can be sent in the UK only and those worldwide.

Marchents http://www.marchents.com
A good site that offers food delivery on everything from meat to veg, plus there's kitchen kit to buy too.

Morel http://www.morel.co.uk
Exemplary luxury online shopping – makes you salivate while you click.

Real Meat http://www.realmeat.co.uk
A decent site that sells very good products - the firm behind the site is well known in foodie circles for producing top-notch flesh.

Thornton's http://www.thorntons.co.uk
Yuumy chocolates and the site ain't bad either: easy to shop, with lots of gift ideas.

Cook's Thesaurus
http://www.foodsubs.com
Find substitutes for fatty, expensive or hard-to-find ethnic ingredients.

Cucina Direct
http://www.cucinadirect
Excellent online kitchen equipment site with a solid bricks-and-mortar business behind it.

Food and Drink

Curryhouse

http://www.curryhouse.co.uk
Make the perfect vindaloo or look up your nearest balti house if you're
too lazy. For more masala matters, try Death By Curry
(http://www.geocities.com/NapaValley/6654/).

Delia Online

http://www.deliaonline.com
A double-header of a site: lots of good recipes and useful tips plus the
alarming Delia diary for true fans who really want to know about her life.
Go to MarthaStewart.com (http://www.marthastewart.com) to see
where all the site's ideas came from or to JamieOliver.net
(http://www.jamieoliver.net) for more of the most overexposed man in
European media.

Epicurious

http://www.epicurious.com
The best food Website there is. Online marriage of Condé Nast's
Gourmet, *Bon Appetit*, and *Traveler* magazines, crammed with recipes,
culinary forums and advice on dining out worldwide.

The Espresso Index

http://www.espresso.com
http://www.espressotop50.com
Kickstart your morning with the FAQs on coffee.

Famers' Markets

http://www.farmersmarkets.net
Excellent site that helps you track down your nearest farmers' market.

Final Meal Requests
http://www.tdcj.state.tx.us/stat/finalmeals.htm/
The prospect's enough to spoil your appetite.

FoodnDrink
www.foodndrink.co.uk
A useful site with an online version of Harden's restaurant guide (created by people rather than food critics) and a restaurant booking facility (through http://www.5pm.co.uk) plus links to shopping sites, gourmet bookshop and a good cookery school directory.

Good Pub Guide
http://www.goodguides.com
Offers a good pub locator for the UK, as if you needed help.

Internet Chef
http://www.ichef.com
Over 30,000 recipes, cooking hints ("Ground Beef Meals"), kitchen talk and more links than you can jab a fork in.

Kitchen Link
http://www.kitchenlink.com
Points to more than 10,000 galleries of gluttony.

Lakeland
http://www.lakelandlimited.co.uk
Everything you could and couldn't possibly need in the kitchen.

Leaping Salmon
http://www.leapingsalmon.com
Quality prepared food that you simply assemble according to instructions – barely a chopping board required, and excellent food to boot. If you get the munchies in the middle of the night and need food cooked to order delivered to your door, try Room Service (http://www.roomservice.co.uk).

Meals For You
http://www.mealsforyou.com
A decent American recipe search engine – each recipe listing includes the details of the fat and cholesterol present in each recipe.

Food and Drink

Eating Out

The AA   http://www.theaa.co.uk
Decent search engine for nationwide restaurants and pubs.

Book2Eat   http://www.book2eat.com
A pretty decent London restaurant booking site with annoying reviews from toffs such as William Sitwell and Nick Foulkes.

This Is London   http://www.thisislondon.co.uk
The *Evening Standard* site is the best site for searching for bars and pubs and restaurants in London: comprehensive and with good-length reviews so you get an idea of exactly what you'll be getting.

Time Out   http://www.timeout.com/london/eat/
Frequently updated rundown of London eateries, searchable by area or cuisine.

Toptable   http://www.toptable.co.uk
No-nonsense site that covers London and some surrounding areas.

Zagats   http://www.zagats.com
Excellent search engine for restaurant reviews the world over plus restaurant news.

Moonshine
http://moonshine.co.nz
Get blind (possibly literally) on homemade spirits.

New York Seafood
http://www.nyseafood.org
Great site for loads of piscine information. For cod and haddock delivered to your door, try The Fish Society (http://www.thefishsociety.co.uk).

An Ode to Olives
http://www.emeraldworld.net/olive.html/
You'll never look at an olive ambivalently again.

Recipe Search
http://www.birdseye.com/search.html/
Cast your line into the Fish Finger king's own recipe database or trawl through hundreds of other Net collections. See also:
http://www.lycos.com/search/recipedia.html/
http://recipes.alastra.com
http://www.mealsforyou.com

Restaurant Row
http://www.restaurantrow.com
Key in your dining preferences and find the perfect match from hundreds of thousands of food barns worldwide.

ScotchWhisky.com
http://www.scotchwhisky.com
Excellent site with loads of info on whisky plus a shopping facility.

Spice Advice
http://www.spiceadvice.com
Encyclopedia of spices covering their origins, purposes, recipes and tips on what goes best with what.

Switcheroo
http://www.switcheroo.com
Seriously clever and useful site that offers you both an encyclopedia of ingredients and help if you're missing an ingredient when cooking. For example, if you're making a cake but there's no fat in the house, substitute mashed banana. Yes, really.

Taste
http://www.taste.co.uk
The UK's most comprehensive food site with recipe search engine plus nationwide restaurant reviews.

Tasty Insect Recipes
http://www.ent.iastate.edu/misc/insectsasfood.html/
http://www.eatbug.com
Dig in to such delights as Bug Blox, Banana Worm Bread, Rootworm Beetle Dip and Chocolate Chirpie Chip Cookies (with crickets).

Food and Drink

Tea & Sympathy
http://www.enteract.com/~robchr/tea/
Home of the Rec.Food.Tea FAQ. For more, try the Tea Council
(http://www.teacouncil.co.uk). To buy tea, try Whittard's
(http://www.whittard.com).

Thai Recipes
http://www.importfood.com/recipes.html/
Just click if you don't have an ingredient.

Tokyo Food Page
http://www.bento.com
Where and what to eat in Tokyo, plus recipes. More help packing sushi
at http://www.learn-sushi.com and http://www.sushi101.com.

Top Secret Recipes
http://www.topsecretrecipes.com
http://www.copykat.com
At least one commercial recipe,
such as KFC coleslaw, revealed
each week. Many are surprisingly
basic.

Tudocs
http://www.tudocs.com
Rates cooking links across the
web. Search under "fruit", for
instance, and get linked to such
ever-useful sites as 104 Things to
Do With a Banana.

The Ultimate Cookbook
http://www.ucook.com
Pinch recipes from hundreds of popular cookbooks. More food porn
unplugged at: http://www.cook-books.com

Vegetarian Society of the UK
http://www.vegsoc.org
Support for veggies.

Buying Groceries Online

Your chances of being able to order home-delivered groceries online will be much higher if you live in a big city, but expect to pay a premium for the convenience. Although most of the following have physical stores, they mightn't offer their full range online.

Simply Organic   http://www.simplyorganic.net
Excellent organic shopping site with a full range of 1900 products to choose from, easy to use and well-organised deliveries too. For more of Mother Nature's bounty, try Organics Direct (**http://www. organicsdirect.co.uk**).

Tesco   http://www.tesco.co.uk
Perhaps the best of the Internet shopping sites. The system takes a while for you to set up, but once it's up and running fans say it's a real doddle even if they sometimes get five kilos of tomatoes instead of five tomatoes.

Waitrose   http://www.waitrose.co.uk
One of the best supermarket shopping sites. It's not currently offering regular grocery delivery nationwide (although testing it in certain areas of the UK as this book goes to press), but this site offers organic box delivery plus wine, flowers and chocs. The site also has a link to Waitrose *Food Illustrated* magazine with access to articles and restaurant reviews.

Other sites include:
Asda	http://www.asda.co.uk
Iceland	http://www.iceland.co.uk
Sainsbury's	http://www.sainsburys.co.uk
Somerfield	http://www.somerfield.co.uk

Wine Spectator
http://www.winespectator.com
Research your hangover.

Furniture and Interiors

BBC Good Homes

http://www.goodhomes.beeb.com

The BBC's interior magazine has all the features you've come to expect, offering advice on everything from Moroccan living rooms to the good flooring guide.

Bright Beige

http://www.brightbeige.co.uk

Hip but friendly and very informative design e-zine.

Chippendale Furniture

http://ukantiques.about.com/aboutuk/ukantiques/cs/chippendale/

About's page devoted to the work of Thomas Chippendale.

Deco Deli

http://www.decodeli.com

Stylish, contemporary furniture and accessories from this Glaswegian member of the Which? Webtrader Code of Practice. More sleek, post-industrial furnishings can be found at Ocean (http://www.ocean catalogue.co.uk) and Unit 26 (http://www.unit26.com).

Design Gap

http://www.design-gap.co.uk

Directory of work by 300 contemporary British designers and furniture makers that includes everything from tchotchkes to chests-of-drawers.

Design-Online
http://www.design-online.co.uk
A database of British interior designers, feng shui consultants, building services, soft furnishing companies and other providers of interiors essentials.

Furniture Wizard
http://www.furniturewizard.com
Loads of tips on how to restore your Louis XIV chair after your cat pees on it.

Geomancy.Net – The Centre for Applied Feng Shui Research
http://www.geomancy.net
Harmonise Qi and recreate the ambience of a Chinese restuarant. For more wizard assistance, try Qi Whiz (http://www.qi-whiz.com) and Feng Shui Fanzine (http://www.fengshui-fanzine.co.uk).

Interstyle
http://www.interstyle.net
Homepage of a Florida shop that sells classics of 20th-century design by Alvar Aalto, Ludwig Mies Van Der Rohe, Le Corbusier and Charles Eames.

Let's Go Retro
http://www.letsgoretro.com
Relive your youth and get a Space Invaders machine for your living room.

Nubold.com
http://www.nubold.com
Home of lighting, glass, ceramics and tableware from contemporary designers like Bodo Sperlein and Nic Wood. They even offer a wedding list service for couples with impeccable taste.

StyleSource Design
http://www.stylesource.co.uk/design/
The peach colour-scheme and the face of Laurence Llewelyn-Bowen might suggest otherwise, but this site is a good source of information and advice on everything from frosted mirrors to colour trends and period design.

Tribu-Design
http://www.tribu-design.com/en/
A fascinating database of 20th-century furniture and design.

20th Century Design Collection
http://www.deanclough.com/arts/20thcentury1.html/
Some beautiful, well-researched pages devoted to postwar British
design, including examples of furniture by Robin Day, Basil Spence and
Terence Conran.

Wallpaper Online
http://www.wallpaperonline.co.uk
Apparently wallpaper hasn't been this trendy since the '70s, so stock
up at this easy to use site, featuring a database of 20,000 papers, borders and fabrics.

The Work of Charles and Ray Eames
http://lcweb.loc.gov/exhibits/eames/
The Library of Congress's online exhibition of the work of the most
influential designers of the 20th century.

Games

Most multiplayer games can be played across the Net. There are
also thousands of simple table, word, arcade and music games as

diverse as Chess, Blackjack, Connect 4, and Frogger that can be played on the Web courtesy of Java and Shockwave. In some cases you can even contest online opponents for prizes. Peruse the selection on offer at:

Flash Kit http://www.flashkit.com

Flazoom http://www.flazoom.com

Flipside http://www.flipside.com

FreeArcade.com http://www.freearcade.com

Gamesville http://www.gamesville.com

Playsite http://www.playsite.com

Pogo.com http://www.pogo.com

Shockwave.com http://www.shockwave.com

The Riddler http://www.riddler.com

The Station http://www.station.sony.com

Yahoo Games http://games.yahoo.com

Web Games http://www.happypuppy.com/web/

Al Menconi Ministries
http://www.gospelcom.net/menconi/topics/games/
Videogame reviews from a Christian perspective.

Games

The Atari Time Machine
http://homepage.eircom.net/~morrikar/
Museum and homage to the videogame console that just about started it all.

Autolotto
http://memelog.com/autolotto/
Arrange to enter and compete in online lotteries automatically.

The Best Games Music in the World Ever
http://gamemusic.siliconcircus.co.uk
Put someone special in the mood.

Blues News
http://www.bluesnews.com
Keep up with what's Quakin'.

Cheat Station
http://www.cheatstation.com
Get Sonic to do what you want him to do. For more devious tricks, try The Codebook (http://www.codebook.pp.se/).

ContestGuide
http://www.contestguide.com
http://www.contestworld.com
http://www.iwon.com
http://www.loquax.co.uk
http://www.uggs-n-rugs.com.au/contests/
Get junk-mailed for life by entering loads of competitions.

Croft Times
http://www.cubeit.com/ctimes/
More news about the Tomb Raider bombshell than you could ever want. For the truly smitten, you can download a customized version of Internet Explorer featuring Lara's likeness everywhere.

Electric Games
http://www.electricgames.com
Just about every free and shareware game ever.

Freeloader
http://www.freeloader.com
Download free games (like Grand Theft Auto and Hidden & Dangerous)
for your PC. The catch: you have to look at ads ... lots of ads.

Game Downloads
http://www.fileplanet.com
Stock up on even more gaming software.

GameFAQs
http://www.gamefaqs.com
Stuck on a level or just want to know more?

Gameplay
http://www.gameplay.com
Fifteen years old and still going strong, this is certainly the best British
gaming portal, with an excellent magazine, shop and loads of online
gaming options. Check out UK Games (http://www.ukgames.com) for
cheats, lotsa links and lower prices.

Gaming Age
http://www.gaming-age.com
All the latest news from the gaming frontline, plus interviews with
designers and previews of big games before they hit the shops.

Grrl Gamer
http://www.grrl gamer.com
Team up with other game grrls and prepare to kick dweeb-boy butt
right across their own turf. More reinforcement at http://www.game-
girlz.com and http://www.womengamers.com.

Games

Games

For reviews, news, demos, hints, patches, cheats, downloads, and other PC game necessities try:

Adrenaline Vault	http://www.avault.com
Daily Radar	http://www.dailyradar.com
Gamecenter	http://www.gamecenter.com
Gamers.com	http://www.gamers.com
Games Domain	http://www.gamesdomain.com
Gamespot	http://www.gamespot.com
Happy Puppy	http://www.happypuppy.com
Macintosh Gamer's Ledge	http://www.macledge.com
Old Man Murray	http://www.oldmanmurray.com

Console Games

Console Domain	http://www.consoledomain.com
Daily Radar	http://www.dailyradar.com
Hotgames.com	http://www.hotgames.com
Psx Extreme	http://www.psxextreme.com
Videogame Strategies	http://vgstrategies.about.com

Kasporov Chess
http://www.kasparovchess.com
http://chess.about.com
Take tips from the Russian master and then find an opponent.

Multi-Player Online Gaming
http://www.mpog.com
Everything you need to know to start playing Quake III and Counter-Strike online, plus patches, demos, betas, cheats and other gaming essentials.

PC Game Finder
http://www.pcgame.com
Search the leading game lairs.

RPG Vault
http://rpgvault.ign.com
Role Playing Gamers' heaven.

Vintage Gaming
http://www.vg-network.com
http://www.emux.com
http://www.download.net
Revive old school arcade games like Xevious on your home PC. More '80s fun at Smilie Games (http://www.smiliegames.com).

Gardening

About gardening
http://gardening.about.com
About's home gardening guide.

The Carnivorous Plant FAQ
http://www.sarracenia.com/faq.html/
Novel solutions for garden pests.

Crocus
http://www.crocus.co.uk
The main draw of this online garden centre is that plants are delivered by trained gardeners who will help bolster your borders. There are also sections devoted to plant finding, jargon busting and news and advice on organic gardening.

Dr Greenfingers
http://www.drgreen
fingers.com
This "advice and help clinic for the amateur and virgin gardener" may be laid out like a hospital – with a "maternity ward" for growing plants from seed and

an "operating theatre" for how-to advice – but the gimmickry ends there. If you don't find what you're looking for in the "family planning", "administration" or "health and safety" departments, you can always email your question to the site's panel of experts.

E-Garden
http://www.e-garden.co.uk
Initially this large site appears to be heavy on the hard sell, but lurking beneath the commerce are a well-organized magazine section, a Latin translator and very useful problemsolvers on subjects like diseases, climbers and herbaceous perennials.

English Country Gardening
http://www.suite101.com/welcome.cfm/
english_country_gardening/
Jane Hollis's site devoted to the grand old art of English country gardening includes discussion groups, articles, virtual tours and flower show and garden reports.

Expert Gardener
http://www.expertgardener.com
Has the usual features, with the added extra of Charlie Dimmock calendars available for purchase.

Garden Guides
http://www.gardenguides.com
Has most of the features you should expect from the better general gardening sites (plant guides, discussion forums, advice), but this site sets itself apart with its lengthy book extracts on topics like choosing bulbs and designing herb gardens.

Garden Web
http://www.gardenweb.com
One of the best horticultural resources on the Web, this site hosts a multitude of regional and specialist forums (roses, wild flowers, kitchen gardens), plus a glossary, plant database, calendar of events, plant and seed exchange, plenty of articles and shopping areas.

Gardening 365
http://www.oxalis.co.uk

The Gardening 365 homepage takes more of a magazine-style approach than many gardening sites, with short, breezy articles on weevils, wildlife and heather. However, it doesn't skimp on interactive features like a plant finder, tips of the day and virtual tours of famous gardens.

Gothic Gardening
http://www.gothic.net/~malice/

GOThiC GARDENiNG

Welcome to the Garden that mAlice built...

Grow a little greenhouse of horrors.

Growing Lifestyle
http://www.growinglifestyle.com
A dedicated home-and-garden search engine.

Internet Garden
http://www.internetgarden.co.uk
Quirky but useful links, divided by subjects like tropical, hothouse and containers.

Kitchen Gardener
http://www.taunton.com/kg/
Online presence of *Kitchen Gardener* magazine, dedicated to foodies who grow their own produce. Also check out http://www.the vegetablepatch.com for a more organic perspective.

Open Directory Gardens
http://dmoz.org/Home/Gardens/
The Open Directory Project's comprehensive set of links.

Postcode Plant Database
http://www.nhm.ac.uk/science/projects/fff/
This excellent resource from the Natural History Museum allows you to find the right native trees, shrubs and flowers for your area.

Gay and Lesbian

Royal Botanic Gardens
http://www.rbgkew.org.uk
Featuring access to its enormous academic database, the homepage of Kew Gardens is one for the real horticulturalist.

Royal Horticultural Society
http://www.rhs.org.uk
The online presence of the RHS includes plant databases, seasonal advice and a garden finder.

The Vine Weevil Advice Centre
http://www.vine.weevil.org.uk
Dedicated to combating Britain's number-one garden pest.

Gay and Lesbian

AEGIS
http://www.aegis.com
Claiming to be the largest HIV/AIDS related site on the Web, AEGIS is an amazing resource filled with the latest news from the treatment front, bulletin boards, a law library of judicial cases and an archive of publications from organizations like Gay Men's Health Crisis, Act Up and the Government. For more news, advice and despatches from the activist front, try Gay Men's Health Crisis (http://www.gmhc.org) and Act Up New York (http://www.actupny.org).

The AIDS Memorial Quilt
http://www.aidsquilt.org
View the quilt online, find out how to become involved with the project and contribute to the memory book.

Gay.com UK
http://uk.gay.com
The British version of the enormous American portal has a huge array of channels for everyone from scene queens to those not yet out of the closet. Other portals of call are Planet Out (http://www.planetout.com), Queer Theory (http://www.queertheory.com) and Queery (http://www.queery.com).

Gay Britain Network

http://www.gaybritain.co.uk
Homepage of the network that hosts sites like UK Gay Shopping, UK Gay Guide and Gay Video Shop.

Gayscape

http://www.gayscape.com/gayscape/
Probably the best gay search engine on the Web. For more Brit-specific links, try The Gay Index (http://www.gayindex.co.uk) and for less mainstream links, try Larry-bob's Queer Hotlist (http://www.io.com/~larrybob/hotlist.html/).

Gay to Z

http://www.gaytoz.com
Directory of gay-friendly hotels, bars, clubs, builders, plumbers, electricians and erotica in London, Manchester and Brighton. Give them your email address and they'll send you more complete guides on the above cities plus Paris. For more hotels in the UK and abroad, try UK Gay Hotel Guide (http://www.gayhotel.co.uk).

Gay Travel Guide

http://www.gaytravel.co.uk
This excellent site has detailed guides to destinations such as Mykonos, Benidorm, Ibiza, New York and Amsterdam, plus a good search facility for gay-friendly hotels in more exotic locales.

Holy Titclamps

http://www.holytitclamps.com
Homepage of San Francisco's fab queer zine which features fiction by the likes of Sarah Schulmann and Steve Abbot plus comics, poetry,

rants and humour from some of the best writers and artists on the scene.

Lesbian UK
http://www.lesbianuk.co.uk
A database of resources, both on- and offline, for Britain's lesbian community.

OutRage!
http://www.outrage.org.uk
Peter Tatchell's organisation fighting for equal rights and fighting against assimilation into straight society.

Pink Passport
http://www.pinkpassport.com
A site with all the usual features, but it does have one of the best gay venue selectors on the Web covering the entire world.

Rainbow Network
http://www.rainbownetwork.co.uk
As its name suggests, this site covers pretty much the entire spectrum of gay and lesbian life, from the Eurovision Song Contest to rallying the pink vote in the General Election.

Stonewall
http://www.stonewall.org.uk
The homepage of the lesbian and gay rights organisation may strike some as dull and worthy, but it's a good source of information on British activism and issues like the age of consent.

Techno Dyke
http://www.technodyke.com
Part of the Indie Gurl Network (http://www.indiegurl.com) of zines, this fun e-zine has galleries of drag kings, astrology, articles on sex and relationships and a "Biosphere" section. For an e-zine with a British perspective, try Dyke Universe (http://dykeuniverse.com).

UK Gay Guide
http://www.gayguide.co.uk
The design is slightly irritating, but this site features excellent guides to gay-friendly services throughout the UK plus advice and personals.

Genealogy

Don't expect to enter your name and produce an instant family tree, but you might be able to fill in a few gaps.

Ancient Faces
http://www.ancientfaces.com
Picture your ancestors.

Chineseroots.com
http://www.chineseroots.com
An amazing resource for people of Chinese ancestry. The site has made an agreement with the Shanghai Library allowing access to its archive of ancestral documents dating back to the 10th century.

Cyndi's List
http://www.cyndislist.com
Twenty million users can't be wrong. With just about 100,000 links, the genealogy resource you're after is undoubtedly here. For Brit-specific links, try Suzy's Genealogy Page (http://www.geocities.com/heartland/3934/britain.htm/).

Ellis Island Records
http://www.ellisislandrecords.org
If you're family had a stop over in the US in the past 150 years or so, their records will be here.

Family History
http://www.familyhistory.com
This site, a section of the massive Ancestry.com umbrella, hosts some 130,000 message boards organized by surname or location. You can also set up your own family Website here for free.

Genealogy

FamilySearch
http://www.familysearch.org
If you're going to be doing family research on the Web you'll come here at one stage or another. This site (also known as the LDS Resource) is run by the Mormons, who believe it is their duty to record the ancestry of every living soul. The religious aspect is played down in favour of sheer information, and what they have collated is nothing short of astonishing: some 450 million family names.

Freebies for Genealogists
http://www.jodenoy.clara.net/dealers/freebies.htm/
Links to free, downloadable programs of use to the genealogist.

Genuki
http://www.genuki.org.uk
This should be your first stop on your search for your family roots. They have an excellent section for beginners, offering advice on how to search and how to use the Internet's resources. More beginner's advice can be found at Starting English Research (http://www.xmission.com/~nelsonb/starte.htm/).

Historical Text Archive
http://historicaltextarchive.com
A very useful resource for people with Caribbean and African ancestry, including a Caribbean ancestry newsletter and a database of slave names. Also check Christine's Genealogy Website (http://ccharity.com).

JayKids
http://www.jaykids.com
Find out if the prodigious '50s rock 'n' roller Screamin' Jay Hawkins put a spell on your mama.

Public Record Office
http://www.pro.gov.uk
Not a great resource in itself, but if you need to approach the Public Record Office or National Archive for materials this site gives you the lowdown on how to go about it. More information can be found on the Government's new site, Family Records (http://www.familyrecords.gov.uk).

RootsWeb
http://www.rootsweb.com
The oldest, largest and probably the best free genealogy site on the Net. It features a very good search engine, links to resources and lots of humour preventing things from getting too dull. More gene gardening can be done at Ancestry.com (http://www.ancestry.com), the Family Tree Maker (http://www.familytreemaker.com), Genealogy Homepage (http://www.genhomepage.com), Genealogy Today (http://www.genealogytoday.com).

Surname Listings
http://www.surnameweb.org
Dig up dirt on your family name.

Gossip

Every celebrity has at least one obsessive fan site (http://www.ggower.com/fans/) in their honour, but finding them can sometimes be tricky. If they're not listed in Yahoo, try:
http://www.celebhoo.com
http://www.celebrityweb.com
http://www.webring.org
http://www.csotd.com

Search engines tend to find porn scuttlers who've loaded their HTML metatags with celebrity names. Easy bait, when you consider that most fans would love a glimpse of their idol in various states of undress (http://www.cndb.com). If they succeed in catching your attention, at least have the sense not to pull out your credit card. Adding **-naughty -naked -nude** to your search term, or enabling an adult filter such as Google's SafeSearch (under **Preferences**), might help weed them out.

Beat Box Betty
http://www.beatboxbetty.com/showbiznews/crowreport.htm/
Gossip and industry news "with a twist of blonde".

Bizcotti
http://bizcotti.com
Attempting to be *The Onion* of the gossip world.

Celebrity Babies

http://celebritybabies.webjump.com
What would the offspring of your favourite celebrity couple look like?

Celebrity Dreams
http://www.celebrity-dream.com
A storing-house of dreams about celebrities (some dirty), including, charmingly, "I found a floater in Seinfeld's loo".

Celebstatus
http://www.celebstatus.com
The game of 2001, this is fantasy football for celeb spotters with a cast of A, B and C list "stars" accumulating points for tabloid appearances.

Cinescape
http://www.cinescape.com
The latest insider industry news. Not as good as *The Hollywood Reporter*, but you don't have to subscribe.

Coat Hangers of the Rich and Famous
http://www.geocities.com/hangmycoat/
A revealing look inside the closet of some the world's biggest stars. For those who prefer to be walked on by their object of desire, there's always Celebrity Driveways (http://www.driveways.com) or Stars auf Krücken (http://www.fortunecity.de/spielberg/quincy/28/) – stars on crutches.

Donna's Long and Short of It
http://www.metal-sludge.com/LongShort.html/
The skinny (or the chubby) on the members of the heavy metal fraternity.

Drudge Report
http://www.drudgereport.com
Rumours from inside the Washington Beltway with a right-wing slant from the online columnist who almost brought down a president.

E! Online
http://www.eonline.com
The latest from the States courtesy of the homepage of the American cable TV channel.

Famous Birthdays
http://www.famousbirthdays.com
http://us.imdb.com/OnThisDay/
See who shares your birthday.

Famous Name Changes
http://www.famousnamechanges.com
The truth behind celebs trying to give themselves some personality.

Fanzine
http://www.fanzine.co.uk
The official addresses of stars and pop groups. For more direct access, try Chip's Celebrity Home E-mail Addresses (http://www.addresses.site2go.com). Reach out to more stars at Celebrity Addresses (http://www.writetoaceleb.com) and CelebrityEmail.com (http://www.celebrityemail.com)

Gossip

Filth2Go
http://www.filth2go.com
Outrageous, scandalous, rude gay gossip zine. Unfortunately you have to subscribe.

Find a Grave
http://www.findagrave.com
See where celebrities are buried.

Gene Simmons' Celebrity Bedroom
http://www.kissdominion.com/BEDROOM.HTM/
See how your fave celeb looks in the bedroom of the Kiss bassist who has dated Cher, Diana Ross and Shannon Tweed.

The Goldi Gossip
http://www.goldi.com
Fun, trashy tattlesheet, updated weekly.

The Gossip Lowdown
http://www.mindspring.com/%7Ealexfan/lowdown.html/
Click here to subscribe to Simone Sentral's crucial newsletter.

Groupie Central
http://www.groupiecentral.com
For adults only, this site doesn't pull any punches, but along with Popbitch it's the best gossip site on the Web.

Hello!
http://www.hello-magazine.co.uk
All the jet trash and desperate celebs you expect from the glossy, only with lower production values. For an American version of the same without the minor royalty, try People (http://people.aol.com).

ISHG?
http://www.isheshegay.com
Well, is s/he?

Mr Showbiz
http://mrshowbiz.go.com
The box office swami, the Brad Pitt worship room, the latest on Nicole

Kidman, Billy Bob Thornton's tattoos and other life-changing news and rumours, plus the Romantically Linked game.

National Enquirer
http://www.nationalenquirer.com
All the news that's not fit to print elsewhere.

New York Post
http://www.nypostonline.com/gossip/gossip.htm/
The latest dish from the columnists of the Big Apple's most notorious tabloid. For even more tittle-tattle, try their sister site, Page Six (http://www.pagesix.com).

PeopleNews
http://www.peoplenews.com
Who did what, where and when, updated twenty times a day. As recommended by Tara Palmer-Tomkinson.

Popbitch
http://www.popbitch.com
Scurrilous, rude, fun and yes, downright bitchy, this is without question the best British pop gossip site. Their weekly mailing lists have brought

down careers and halt work all over the capital every Wednesday.

RumorsRumorsRumors
http://www.rumorsrumorsrumors.com
Goss headlines, rumours, conspiracy theories and urban myths culled from around the Net.

Showbiz Wire
http://www.showbizwire.com
Entertainment newswire service, featuring stories gathered from just about every entertainment site.

Greetings Cards

The Smoking Gun
http://www.thesmokinggun.com
Tom Cruise's petition for divorce, Linda Fiorentino's nudity rider and other documents of celebrity misbehaviour. More at: http://www.apbnews.com/media/gfiles/

TeenHollywood.com
http://www.teenhollywood.com
All the latest dirt and news on Tinsletown's pretty young things.

Variety
http://www.variety.com
Screen news fresh off the PR gattling gun.

Who would you kill?
http://www.whowouldyoukill.com
So who would you toss into Dawson's Creek?

Greetings Cards

http://www.freegreetingcards.org
http://www.postcard-heaven.com
http://www.postcards.com
http://www.cardlady.com

If stretching the bounds of good taste doesn't bother you, you'll find thousands of sites that will gladly speckle your message with multimedia tutti-frutti. Rather than forward your "card" directly, your victim will generally receive an invitation to drop by and collect it from the site. And of course being masked by a third party makes it perfect for harassing valentines and sending ransom notes. The above directories list hundreds of virtual card dispensers but check out the most popular ones first:

Blue Mountain http://www.bluemountain.com
eGreetings http://www.egreetings.com
Hallmark http://www.hallmark.com
Pulp Cards http://www.pulpcards.com

Regards.com http://www.regards.com
Tackymail http:/www.tackymail.com
Virtual Insults http://www.virtualinsults.com
Yahoo Greetings http://greetings.yahoo.com

Banner Greetings
http://www.bannergreetings.com
Create your own personalized greetings by uploading your photo and
choosing from their music or art library.

Card Corp
http://www.cardcorp.co.uk
Need some business cards or invitations fast? Design them online for
snappy delivery via email or on the paper of your choice. Naturally, the
latter option costs.

Digital Voodoo
http://www.pinstruck.com
Curse thy neighbour.

Guycon
http://www.guycon.com
Have a Lambada guy or psychiatrist guy send your regards.

Hotpaper.com
http://www.hotpaper.com
Fill in the blanks to create handy everyday documents like greetings
cards, references, eviction notices and credit card disputes.

Invites
http://invites.yahoo.com
http://www.regards.com
http://www.egreetings.com
Throwing a slide night? Here's an easy way to create an instant email
invitation and manage the thousands of RSVPs. For help planning:
http://www.theplunge.com

Matoox
http://www.matoox.com
Tell your boss he's a male chauvinist pig, tell your neighbour he's got

bad breath, tell that fox in History lectures your true intentions – but all under the cover of anonymity.

Postcardland
http://postcardland.com
Confuse your parole officer by sending them a postcard from the other side of the world.

Transeden
http://www.transeden.com
If you visit one of Transeden's kiosks in numerous tourist destinations, you can send virtual postcards with your picture and a photo of your locale.

Virtual Beer Server
http://beer.trash.net
Say it with a brew.

Virtual Presents
http://www.virtualpresents.com
http://www.it3c.co.uk
Why waste money on real gifts when, after all, isn't it the thought that counts?

Web Greeting Cards
http://www.web-greeting-cars.com
If you're after something classier than the average e-card, this site offers high quality images that can be extensively customized.

Health

While the Net's certainly an unrivalled medical library, it's also an unrivalled promulgator of the 21st-century equivalent of old wives' tales. So by all means research your ailment and pick up fitness tips online, but like the pill bottles say, check with your doctor before putting them to work. And while you're with your GP, ask if they use the Net for research and if so, which sites they recommend.

Don't expect to go online for first-aid advice. If it's an emergency, you won't have time. The Net is better for in-depth research and anecdotal advice, none of which comes quickly. But once you've spent a few sessions online studying your complaint, you'll be fully prepared to state your case. To find a doctor, dentist or specialist, try: http://www.medavenue.com (US) or http://www.netdoctor.co.uk (UK).

WorldClinic (http://www.worldclinic.com) provides phone, fax or email response that could save your life on the road.

It's hard to say where to start your research. Perhaps a directory: Yahoo et al have seriously stacked medical sections, or you could try one of the specialist health portals:

Achoo http://www.achoo.com

Hospitalweb UK http://www.hospitalweb.co.uk

MedExplorer http://www.medexplorer.com

Patient UK http://www.patient.co.uk

SearchBug http://www.searchbug.com/health/

Or a government gateway:

Health on the Net http://www.hon.ch

NHS Direct (UK) http://www.nhsdirect.nhs.uk

US National Library of Medicine http://www.nlm.nih.gov

World Health Organization http://www.who.int

You'll find tons of excellent self-help megasites, though the presence of sponsors may raise ethical questions. Their features vary, but medical encyclopedias, personal health tests and Q&A services are fairly standard fare. Starting with the former US Surgeon General's site, try:

Dr Koop http://www.drkoop.com
HealthAtoZ.com http://www.healthatoz.com
HealthCentral http://www.healthcentral.com
HealthWorld http://www.healthy.net
Intellihealth http://www.intelihealth.com
Mayo Clinic http://www.mayoclinic.com
Netdoctor.co.uk http://www.netdoctor.co.uk
Surgery Door http://www.surgerydoor.co.uk
ThriveOnline http://www.thriveonline.com
24Dr.com http://www.24dr.com
WebMD http://www.webmd.com
WebMD (Lycos) http://webmd.lycos.com
Yahoo Health http://health.yahoo.com

But for serious research go straight to Medline, the US National Library of Medicine's database. It archives, references and abstracts thousands of medical journals and periodicals going back to 1966. You can get it free at PubMed, but the subscription services may have access to more material. These are aimed more at health pros and students:

BioMedNet http://www.bmn.com
Medscape http://www.medscape.com
Medline Plus Medline Plus http://www.nlm.nih.gov/medlineplus/
Ovid http://www.ovid.com
PubMed http://www.ncbi.nlm.nih.gov/PubMed/

Despite first appearances, Martindale's maintains an outstanding directory of medical science links:

Martindale's Health Science guide http://www-sci.lib.uci.edu/HSG/
HSGuide.html/

If you know what you have and you want to contact other
sufferers, use a search engine (http://www.google.com) or directory (http://dmoz.org) to find organizations and personal home
pages. They should direct you to useful mailing lists and discussion groups. If not, try Google Groups (http://groups.google.com)
to find the right newsgroups, and PAML (http://www.paml.org)
for mailing lists.

Acne Regimen
http://www.acneregimen.com
Out, out damn spot.

Acupuncture.com
http://acupuncture.com
Probably the best and certainly the most comprehensive site dealing
with Chinese medicine. As well as acupuncture, it covers Chinese
herbal remedies, Qi Gong and Tui Na (massage) for patients, students
and practitioners alike. For more information, try Oriental Medicine
(http://www.orientalmedicine.com).

Alex Chiu's Eternal Life Device
http://www.alexchiu.com
Live forever or
come back for
your money.

All Nurses
http://www.
allnurses.com
Springboard to
chat groups,
research data,
professional
bodies, jobs and
other nursing
resources.

Alternative Medicine

http://altmedicine.about.com
http://www.alternativemedicine.com
http://www.wholehealthmd.com
http://www.alternativedr.com
http://dmoz.org/Health/Alternative/

Part of the Net's ongoing research function is the ability to contact people who've road-tested alternative remedies and can report on their efficacy. Start here and work your way to an answer. See also the entry for Quackwatch.

Aromatherapy

http://www.aromaweb.com

Psuedoscience it might be (http://skepdic.com/aroma.html/), but you'll be on the way to smelling better. And surely that can't be a bad thing.

Ask Dr Weil

http://www.drweil.com

Popdoctor Andrew Weil's eagerness to prescribe from a range of bewildering and often conflicting alternative therapies has seen him called a quack in some quarters, but not by Warner. *Time* put him on the front cover and gave him a job peddling advice beside vitamin ads. Whether or not you believe in food cures, his daily Q&As are always a good read.

Biopharm Leeches

http://www.biopharm-leeches.com

Cure your ailments the old-fashioned way.

Calorie Counter

http://www.caloriecounter.co.uk

Diet sensibly. For more dieting advice, check out the Open Directory's Weight Loss pages (http://dmoz.org/Health/Weight_Loss/). To lose "weight and hair through stress and poor nutrition", try The Hackers' Diet (http://www.fourmilab.to/hackdiet/www/hackdietf.html/).

CancerHelp UK

http://www.cancerhelp.org.uk

Jargon-free guide to living with the disease, plus information on treatments, ongoing studies and trials.

Chirohelp.com

http://www.chirohelp.com
Don't get bent out of shape: this is a good introduction to chiropractic
health care.

Color Vision Test

http://www.umist.ac.uk/UMIST_OVS/UES/COLOUR0.HTM/
Do you dress in the dark or are you merely colour-blind?

ConsumerLab

http://www.consumerlab.com
An independent testing authority which publishes its studies online. It
tests herbal remedies, vitamins, supplements, sports products and
functional foods for effectiveness, purity, potency, consistency and
bioavailability (ie whether the body can deal with the product properly).

Dr Squat

http://www.drsquat.com
http://www.weightsnet.com
Avoid getting sand kicked in your face through deep full squats.

Drugs

http://www.erowid.org
http://www.lycaeum.org
http://www.trashed.co.uk
http://www.perkel.com/politics/issues/pot.htm/
http://www.neuropharmacology.com
http://www.druglibrary.org
Everything you ever wanted to know about the pleasure, pain and politics of psychoactive drugs and the cultures built around them. Even
more at Drugs, Solvents and Intoxicants
(http://area51.upsu.plym.ac.uk/~harl/).

GYN101

http://www.gyn101.com
Swot up for your next gynaecological exam. But if you're after honours
go straight to: http://www.obgyn.net

Gyro's Excellent Hernia Adventure

http://www.cryogenius.com/mesh/
Holiday snaps from under the knife.

HandHeldMed
http://www.handheldmed.com
http://medicalpocketpc.com
http://www.pdamd.com
Arm your pocket computer with medical software and references.

Health Fitness Tips
http://www.health-fitness-tips.com
Ironically, the site itself is somewhat flabby, but hopefully the exercise tips, low-fat recipes and motivational quotes will help you shed the inches. For more instruction, try Netsweat (http://www.sickbay.com/netsweat/).

Medicinal Herb Faq
http://metalab.unc.edu/herbmed/mediherb.html/
If it's in your garden and it doesn't kill you, it can only make you stronger. More leafy cures and love drugs at:
http://www.algy.com/herb/
http://www.botanical.com
http://www.herbal-ahp.org

Mental Health
http://www.mentalhealth.com
It's guaranteed that you'll come out of this site convinced there's something wrong with you. Worry your way along to http://www.anxiety network.com or http://www.onlinepsych.com

Museum of Questionable Medical Devices
http://www.mtn.org/ quack/
Gallery of health-enhancing products where even breaks weren't bundled free.

National Institute of Ayurvedic Medicine
http://niam.com/corp-web/
A good, low BS guide to balancing your life energies with the ancient Indian practice.

Nutritional Supplements
http://www.nutritionalsupplements.com
First-hand experiences with vitamins, bodybuilding supplements, and other dubious health shop fodder.

Quackwatch
http://www.quackwatch.com
http://www.ncahf.org
http://www.hcrc.org
http://nccam.nih.gov
Separating the docs from the ducks. Don't buy into any alternative remedies until you've read these pages.

Reuters Health
http://www.reutershealth.com
Medical newswires, reviews, opinion and reference.

RxList
http://www.rxlist.com
http://www.virtualdrugstore.com
http://www.pharminfo.com
Look up your medication to ensure you're not being poisoned.

Spas Directory
http://www.thespasdirectory.com
Locate a British spa or health resort.

Talk Surgery
http://www.talksurgery.com
Discuss your operation with people who appear interested.

ThinkNatural
http://www.thinknatural.com
Order homeopathic, herbal, Ayurvedic and Chinese remedies for next-day delivery, plus advice on how to use them properly.

The Virtual Hospital
http://www.vh.org
Patient care and distance learning via online multimedia tools such as illustrated surgical walkthroughs.

Virtual Periodontology
http://www.odont.lu.se/depts/par/virtual.html/
Click here if you don't want to end up in *The Simpsons*' "Big Book of British Smiles".

The Visible Human Project
http://www.nlm.nih.gov/research/visible/
Whet your appetite by skimming through scans of a thinly filleted serial killer, and then top it off with a fly-through virtual colonoscopy. For higher production values, see the Virtual Body:
http://www.medtropolis.com

What Have I Got?
http://www.whathaveigot.net
Worry yourself sick through self-diagnosis.

Wing Hop Fung
http://www.winghopfung.com
Chinese cures by mail-order.

World Sexual Records
http://www.sexualrecords.com
Go for gold in slap and tickle.

World Wide Online Meditation Center
http://www.meditationcenter.com
Connect with your essence.

The Yoga Site
http://www.yogasite.com
A good, general site on the various asanas and vinyasas so you can stretch yourself back into shape. For even better karma, try the Yoga Homepage (http://www.holisticonline.com/Yoga/hol_yoga_home.htm/), Yoga Nation (http://www.yoganation.com) and Yoga Studio (http://www.timages.com/yoga.htm/).

History

ArchNet
http://archnet.asu.edu
Digital directory to online archaeology sites with a leaning towards the academic. See also the Archaeological Resource Guide to Europe (http://odur.let.rug.nl/arge/), or for general history links, try History Links on the Internet (http://www.nyu.edu/gsas/dept/history/internet/).

BBC Online – History
http://www.bbc.co.uk/history/
As you'd expect, the Beeb's history pages are well-designed and informative – if a bit too traditional and not as complete as you'd like.

Britannia
http://britannia.com/history/
Easily the best British history site on the Web, with biographies of the "bravest knights of the fourteenth Century", virtual tours of Sussex churches, a history of Welsh royalty and an electronic version of the *Anglo-Saxon Chronicle*.

Dead Media Project
http://www.deadmedia.org
Documenting the roadkill on the information superhighway.

History Channel
http://www.historychannel.com
This Web home of the American cable TV channel has perhaps too much of an American slant for most British users, but it does have some great features like an amazing archive of great speeches, both as text and as RealAudio documents.

Hobbies

History House
http://www.historyhouse.com
Dedicated to rescuing history from the historians, this excellent American site tells the stories of real people with very real human foibles who have impacted on the world's major and not so major events. A necessary corrective to the "great man of history" myths.

History Ring
http://members.tripod.com/~PHILKON/ring.html/
Homepage of the history ring, linking you to hundreds and hundreds of non-commercial history sites.

Internet History Sourcebooks Project
http://www.fordham.edu/halsall/
Professor Paul Halsall's site is a fantastic resource for students of history, especially the marginalized varietry. His directory of Internet articles has links to thousands of articles on women's history, Jewish history, Islamic history, African history, lesbian and gay history, medieval studies and the more standard ancient and modern cultures.

1940s Sound Library
http://freespace.virgin.net/ian.bayley/sounds/sounds.htm/
Ian Bayley's amazing sound archive of the 1940s, including Lord Haw Haw's broadcasts.

All Magic Guide
http://www.allmagicguide.com
Your passport to the world of illusion.

Antler Art
http://www.wic.net/antler/
Only in America number 2,346: "Enjoy antler art in a variety of settings" including a table and chairs, bed stand, chandelier, hall table and mirror.

The Art & Science of Dumpster Diving

http://www.geocities.com/CollegePark/Union/7807/

Reconnect with your ancestral roots as a hunter-gatherer.

The Contortion Home Page

http://www.contortionhomepage.com

Hey, Stretch, how
do you do that?

Experimental Aircraft

http://exp-
aircraft.com

Online resource for
lunatics interested in
building their own
planes.

Firewalking.com

http://www.fire
walking.com

The official Website of Tolly Burkan, the father of the firewalking movement.

International String Figure Association

http://www.isfa.org

Perfect your cat's cradle technique.

Joseph Wu's Origami Page

http://www.origami.vancouver.bc.ca

Gateway to the wide world of paper folding, including diagrams, galleries and links.

Juggling Information Service

http://www.juggling.org

If you can't keep your balls up, this site has just about everything any
sane human could ever want to know about juggling. There's a collection of juggling software so you can see how the pros do it, a history of
juggling and other arcane stuff. For the "best beanbag kit on the market" try Juggling Store (http://www.jugglingstore.com).

Kitez
http://www.kitez.com
Go fly a kite at this dedicated search engine for kitesurfers.

Knots on the Web
http://www.earlham.edu/~peters/knotlink.htm/
Why knot?

Model Crafts
http://www.modelcrafts.net
Model online community for modelers. There's more putty filler at Scale Models Central (http://www.geocities.com/Athens/Crete/1111/) and Modelmasters Online (http://www.modelmasters-online.com).

NMRA Directory of World Wide Rail Sites
http://www.ribbonrail.com/nmra/
The National Model Railroad Association's vast site of model railway links across the world.

Potato Cannon Fun Page
http://www.geocities.com/Yosemite/Rapids/1489/
Charm and delight your parents for years to come.

The Puppetry Homepage
http://www.sagecraft.com/puppetry/
The ups and downs of puppetry, from Animatronics to ventriloquism.

Reenactors World
http://www.reenactorsworldplus.com
A Web directory of sites devoted to historical re-enactment and living history.

Rocketry.org
http://www.rocketry.org
Send your worst enemy to the Moon. To buy a "really big, potentially dangerous aircraft loaded with large amounts of propellant", try Suborbital (http://www.suborbital.com).

TreasureNet
http://www.treasurenet.com
Exchange tall tales and learn about metal detection.

Home Improvement

Ask the Builder

http://www.askthebuilder.com

An excellent site from American DIY columnist Tim Carter offering tons of advice from his archived columns and e-zines with a very good search engine.

Ask the Master Plumber

http://www.clickit.com/bizwiz/homepage/plumber.htm/

Save a small fortune by unblocking your own toilet.

B&Q

http://www.diy.com

They may dominate the British DIY market, but B&Q's Website is ugly (it looks like a circular inserted in a Sunday paper), clumsy and too expensive. Homebase (http://www.homebase.co.uk) is only slightly better.

BarPlans

http://www.barplans.com

Move the Queen Vic into your basement.

Buy.co.uk

http://www.buy.co.uk/Personal/

Clinch the best deal on UK utilities and loans.

Cooksons

http://www.cooksons.com

The best place for power tools on the Net, with loads of special offers and free delivery if you spend more than £45.

Coping With Winter

http://www.ag.ndsu.nodak.edu/coping/

Building a ski house in the Alps or moving to Irkutsk? Follow these building and DIY tips from North Dakota State University.

Home Improvement

DIY Fix It
http://www.diyfixit.co.uk
Since most of the best DIY sites are American, this decent UK home improvement encyclopedia is very useful for information regarding Brit-specific problems.

Fine Homebuilding
http://www.taunton.com/fh/
American magazine for real DIY enthusiasts, with loads of information on frame construction, garage doors, tools and safety.

HomeCentral
http://homecentral.sierrahome.com
Standard DIY site, but with a range of calculators and estimators that will tell you the exact amount of paint and wallpaper you need for your job or how much leaving the outside light on all night will cost.

Home Improvement Encyclopedia
http://www.bhglive.com/homeimp/
Lots of step-by-step guides and illustrated how-tos from the American *Better Homes and Gardens* magazine. Again the information is designed for Yanks, but the language is simple, the illustrations clear and the animated guides are a very clever idea.

Home Repair Stuff
http://www.factsfacts.com/MyHomeRepair/
Design-free site answering questions like "Which caulk?" and "Squirrel in your belfry?", plus beginner's guides and basic tool kits.

Home Sewing Association
http://www.sewing.org
Pick up hints from a bunch of sew and sews.

Home Tips
http://www.hometips.com
http://www.homestore.com
http://www.doityourself.com
http://www.naturalhandyman.com
Load your toolbox, roll up your sleeves and prepare to go in.

How to Clean Anything
http://www.how
tocleananything.com
Just add elbow grease.

Improveline
http://www.
improveline.com
http://www.
homepro.com
Peruse the latest design
ideas and find someone
to do the job. You can even screen your local builders against public
records and find the one least likely to quaff all your home brew and
sell your nude holiday snaps to the *National Enquirer*.

ImproveNet
http://improvenet.com
Yankee DIY giant with more advice, calculators, shopping facilities and
so on than any sane person can handle. It even includes archives from
Popular Mechanics and *Today's Homeowner* as well as energy conservation articles, project guides and personal project managers. For even
more, see HouseNet (http://www.housenet.com).

MFI
http://www.mfi.co.uk
Redo your kitchen with some modular cabinets. For more chi-chi
options, try Kensington Kitchens (http://www.kensington-
kitchens.co.uk), Magnet (http://www.magnet.co.uk) and PS4 Kitchens
(http://www.ps4kitchens.co.uk).

The Old House Web
http://www.oldhouseweb.net
An excellent resource for those restoring the old money-pit. Again, the
site is American so the product info may not be entirely appropriate,
but there are good articles on choosing the right primer, selecting synthetic slates and quick fixes for wallpaper repair problems.

ThePlumber.com
http://www.theplumber.com
Includes tips and online repair handbooks plus the history of plumbing

from Babylonia through the inventions of Thomas Crapper to water-works in the White House. For more plumbing sites, try The PlumbingWeb (http://www.PlumbingWeb.com).

Skills Register
http://www.skills-register.com
Thinking of hiring a plumber or handyman? Try this great service: a directory of British tradespeople who have passed site owner Will Stevens' stringent quality assurance tests. For a bigger database, try Improveline (http://www.improveline.com).

This to That
http://www.thistothat.com
So what would you like to glue today?

Wacky Uses
http://www.wackyuses.com
Using Coca-Cola to clean corrosion from batteries, pantyhose to polish furniture and other wacky household hints from Joey Green.

Horoscopes and Fortune-telling

American Federation of Astrologers
http://www.astrologers.com
Impress your hairdresser by becoming a fully accredited seer by corre-spondence course.

Astro Advice
http://www.astroadvice.com
Aside from its treasure-trove of arcane astrological systems (like Nine Star Ki) and slightly dodgy advice pages (astrological financial fore-casts, for example), this site's best feature is its free, in-depth astrologi-cal charts.

Astrology.com
http://www.astrology.com
This sprawling site contains advice and predictions from just about every soothsaying system under the sun. There are horoscopes both

Ask the Eight Ball

There must be a hundred sites on the Web based on the old Magic Eight Ball toy. Here are some of the most novel twists on the theme.

Archie McPhee's Ask the Sarcastic Ball
http://www.archiemcphee.com/goodies/sarcastic.html/
Yeah, right.

Ask Bubba
http://www.arkansas-web.com/rednecksonly/askbubba/
Redneck agony uncle.

Ask Frank's Magic Hi-Ball
http://www.snarkbite.com/askfrank.htm/
Pearls of wisdom from Ol' Blue Eyes.

Ask a Klingon
http://www.ai.mit.edu/people/paulfitz/plank/advice.html/
Highly illogical advice.

The Magic Mr T Head
http://www.uidaho.edu/~bokm9606/magic/magict.htm/
Pity the fool who doesn't listen to him.

Mystical Smoking Head of Bob
http://www.resort.com/~banshee/Misc/8ball/
Articles of faith from the head of the Church of the Subgenius.

free and charged, past-life reports, celebrity horoscopes, self-empowerment guides, karmic profiles, crystal balls, Chinese astrological readings and plenty more.

Astrology – Atlas and Time Zone Database
http://www.astro.com/atlas/

Horoscopes and Fortune-telling

Know exactly what was happening upstairs the second of your birth. Or if you prefer your cold readings (http://www.skepdic.com/coldread.html) with a touch less pseudoscientific mumbo-jumbo, try http://astrology.about.com or http://www.astrocenter.com. Then see what old sensible shoes has to say:
http://www.skepdic.com/astrolgy.html/

Biorhythm Generator
http://www.facade.com/attraction/biorhythm/
Generate a cyclical report that can double as a sick note.

Dreamstop
http://www.dream-stop.com
Analyse your night visions and jot them into a journal to share with your friends.

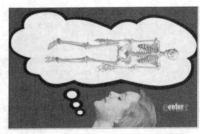

800 Predict
http://www.800predict.com
Put your hands on your mouse for free psychic readings, love compatibility charts, daily lottery numbers, love casts and star gossip.

Free Will Astrology
http://www.freewillastrology.com
The home page of guerrilla oracle and the funniest astrologer around, Rob Brezsny.

Metalog
http://www.astrologer.com
The home of the Astrological Association of Great Britain and the Centre for Psychological Astrology, this site " is devoted to promoting serious quality astrology; hopefully a place where many people will discover the richness of their own unique chart and learn that they are more than 'just' their sun-sign."

Mood Ring
http://www.ajcockrell.com/ajcockrell/moodring.htm/
Put your hands on your mouse and this site will tell you how you're really feeling.

Oracle of Changes
http://www.iching.com
This excellent site enables you to virtually consult the I Ching, the ancient Chinese book of divination and soothsaying. The user casts coins into a pool six times which creates a hexagram that the oracle interprets according to the laws of ancient wisdom. See also: http://www.facade.com/Occult/iching/

Panchang
http://www.panchang.com
Get a personalised time-planner based on this ancient Indian astrological system.

Past Life Regression
http://www.pastlives.cc
All the information you need to send your worst enemy back to the Stone Age.

Psyche Tests
http://www.psychtests.com
http://www.keirsey.com
http://www.queendom.com/tests.html/
http://www.emode.com
ttp://buster.cs.yale.edu/implicit/
So, what breed of dog are you? Smug sceptics (http://www.skepdic.com/myersb.html/) say you'll get closer to the truth here: http://www.learner.org/exhibits/personality/

RealAge
http://www.realage.com
Compare your biological and chronological ages. Here's how long you can expect to live: http://www.msnbc.com/modules/quizzes/lifex.asp/

Horoscopes and Fortune-telling

Russell Grant Astrology
http://www.russellgrant.com
Chirpy, cheerful advice from the chubby prognosticator, thankfully without having to look at his collection of garish sweaters.

Sarena's Tarot Page
http://www.talisman.net/tarot/
Look no further if you need help with your chandelier, fan or 7 triplet spreads. Also, for the expert only, a section on tarot spells. Also consult Tarot Magic (http://www.tarot.com).

Spirit Network
http://spiritnetwork.com
Portal for horoscopes, psychic readings, biorhythms, I Ching readings, paranormal activity and other New Age pursuits.

Stichomancy
http://www.facade.com/stichomancy/
Type in your question and the computer will choose a book and a passage at random that miraculously will apply to your query. See also Bibliomancy (http://www.facade.com/bibliomancy/), which chooses Bible passages at random to aid you on your quest for the answers.

The Voice of the Woods
http://www.pixelations.com/ogham
Seek guidance from the Ogham, an ancient Celtic divination method.

What's in your name?
http://www.kabalarians.com/gkh/your.htm?
The Kabalarians claim names can be boiled down to a numerical stew and served back up as a character analysis. Look yourself up in here and see what a duff choice your parents made. Then blame them for everything that's gone wrong since.

Kids and Teens

It's your choice whether to let them at it headlong or bridle their experience through rose-coloured filters. But if you need guidance or pointers towards the most kidtastic chowder, set sail into these realms:

About.com (Kids) http://kids.about.com

American Libraries Assoc http://www.ala.org/parentspage/greatsites/

Australian Families Guide http://www.aba.gov.au/family/

Kids Click http://www.worldsofsearching.org

Kids Domain http://www.kidsdomain.com

Kids Identifying and Discovering Sites http://kids.library.wisc.edu

Lightspan http://www.lightspan.com

NetMom http://www.netmom.com

Open Directory: Kids http://dmoz.org/Home/Kids/

Scholastic International http://www.scholastic.com

Surfing the Net with Kids http://www.surfnetkids.com

Yahooligans (Yahoo for kids) http://www.yahooligans.com

The search engines Google and Altavista can also be set to filter out adult content. For encyclopedias and dictionaries, see p.255.

Adolescent Adulthood
http://www.adolescentadulthood.com
How to flirt, date, kiss and ultimately dump, so you won't spend the rest of the year being teased at the bus stop.

Barbie
http://www.barbie.com
It's a huge, Flash-intensive, slow-loading site, but there's a massive amount of stuff here to keep any girl entertained for hours – so just give in to the inevitable.

Kids and Teens

Beakman & Jax
http://www.beakman.com
Answers to typical kid questions from the likes of "why poo is brown" and "why farts smell" to "why your voice sounds different on a tape recorder" and "why the TV goes crazy while the mixer is on".

The Belch Page
http://www.goobo.com/belch/
Gross out your parents and your little sister.

Bigchalk
http://www.bigchalk.com
Study collections for all grades through to college.

Bizarre Things You Can Make In Your Kitchen
http://freeweb.pdq.net/headstrong/
Rainy-day science projects and general mischief such as volcanoes, stink bombs, cosmic ray detectors, fake blood and hurricane machines.

Bob the Builder
http://www.bobthebuilder.org
Yes, he can.

Bullying Online
http://www.bullying.co.uk
Advice and support channels for bullied children and their parents. Perhaps a few sessions of self-defence might be a good place to start: http://www.blackbeltmag.com/bbkids/

The Bug Club
http://www.ex.ac.uk/bugclub/
Creepy-crawly fan club with e-pal page, newsletters and pet care sheets on how to keep your newly bottled tarantulas, cockroaches and stick insects alive.

Children's Literature Web Guide
http://www.ucalgary.ca/~dkbrown/
Critical roundup of recent kids' books and links to texts.

Club Girl Tech
http://www.girltech.com
Encourages smart girls to get interested in technology without coming across all geeky.

Cyberteens
http://www.cyberteens.com
Submit your music, art or writing to a public gallery. You might even win a prize.

Decoding Nazi Secrets
http://www.pbs.org/wgbh/nova/decoding/
http://www.thunk.com
Use World War II weaponry to exchange secret messages with your clued-in pals.

Disney.com
http://www.disney.com
Guided catalogue of Disney's real-world movies, books, theme parks, records, interactive CD-ROMs and such, plus a squeaky-clean Net directory. For an unofficial Disney chaperone, see:
http://laughingplace.com

Kids and Teens

eHobbies
http://www.ehobbies.com
Separating junior hobbyists from their pocket money.

Funbrain
http://www.funbrain.com
Tons of mind-building quizzes, games and puzzles for all ages.

Funschool
http://www.funschool.com
Educational games for preschoolers.

Goosebumps
http://www.tcfhe.com:80/goosebumps/thrillold.html/
Scary stories for your next sleepover.

The History Net
http://www.thehistorynet.com
http://www.historybuff.com
Bites of world history with an emphasis on the tough guys going in with guns.

Horse-Country.com
http://www.horse-country.com
A great site for horse-crazy kids, with a seemingly endless array of games and quizzes designed to teach children about horses and how to care for them.

The Idea Box
http://www.theideabox.com
If your preschoolers are bored of *Teletubbies* already, try this site for activities to keep them entertained.

Kid's Domain
http://www.kidsdomain.com
Huge array of stuff here for kids and their parents: brain-builders, games (both online and downloadable), tips on safe surfing, Pokémon, crafts, desktop icons, etc. A similar service is provided by atkidz (http://www.atkidz.com).

Kids' Games

http://kidsnetgames.about.com
http://dmoz.org/Home/Kids/Games/
http://www.wicked4kids.com
http://www.kidsdomain.com/games/
http://www.randomhouse.com/seussville/games/
http://games.yahoo.com/games/yahooligans.html/
Give the babysitter a break.

Kids' Jokes

http://www.kidsjokes.co.uk
http://www.users.bigpond.com/lander/
Reams of clean jokes, riddles and knock-knocks.

Kids-Party

http://www.kids-party.com
Ideas to prevent your child from crying at their own birthday party.

Kids' Space

http://www.kids-space.org
Hideout for kids to swap art, music and stories with new friends across
the world.

Learn2

http://learn2.com
Figure out how to do all sorts of things from fixing a zipper to spinning
a basketball. While the interests aren't strictly for kids, there's nothing
here that's too hard for a whippersnapper.

Liana's Paper Doll Boutique

http://www-personal.umich.edu/~lsharer/paperdolls/
If you've got a printer you've now got a rather large paper doll collection, with costumes ranging from ballerina outfits to Scarlett O'Hara.

The Little Animals Activity Centre

http://www.bbc.co.uk/education/laac/
The second the music starts and the critters start jiggling you know
you're in for a treat. Let your youngest heir loose here after breakfast
and expect no mercy until afternoon tea. As cute as it gets.

Magic Tricks
http://www.magictricks.com
http://www.trickshop.com
http://www.magicweek.co.uk
Never believe it's not so.

Neopets
http://www.neopets.com
Nurture a "virtual pet" until it dies.

Poketech
http://www.poketech.com
Study at the academy of Pokémon trainers.

Roper's Knots
http://www.realknots.com
It's not what you know; it's what knots you know.

Seussville
http://www.randomhouse.com/seussville/
The online home of the Cat in the Hat, Sam-I-Am, Horton, The Grinch and The Whos.

Sing Along Midis and Lyrics
http://www.niehs.nih.gov/kids/musicchild.htm/
Gather round for a spot of keyboard karaoke.

StarChild
http://starchild.gsfc.nasa.gov
Nasa's educational funhouse for junior astronomers. See also
http://www.earthsky.com and http://www.starport.com.

Starwars Origami
http://ftmax.com/ArtLife/Origami/SW/sw.htm/
Graduate from flapping birds onto Destroyer Droids and Tie Fighters.
Prefer something that will actually fly? See: http://www.aricraft.com
For more paperfolding, try: http://www.origami.com

Teen Advice
http://www.teenadvice.net
Part of the enormous Student Center Network, this site has loads of
forums and experts for advice on anything from acne to (surprise, surprise) sex. For more advice on tricky subjects, try Embarrassing
Problems (http://www.embarrassingproblems.co.uk).

Toy Stores
http://www.faoschwartz.com
http://www.imaginarium.com
http://www.toysrus.co.uk
It's just like Christmas all year round.

Tukids Art Barn
http://greenapple.tukids.tucows.com/crafts/
Endless rainy-day fun with this treasure-trove of crafts ideas.

The Unnatural Museum
http://www.unmuseum.org
Lost worlds, dinosaurs, UFOs, pyramids and other mysterious exhibits
from the outer bounds of space and time.

The Yuckiest Site on the Internet
http://www.yucky.com
Fun science with a leaning towards the icky-sticky and the creepy-

crawly. But if you want to get thoroughly engrossed in the gross, slither
right along to: http://www.grossology.org

Law and Crime

For legal primers, lawyer directories, legislation and self-help:

Delia Venables http://www.venables.co.uk
FindLaw http://www.findlaw.com
InfoLaw http://www.infolaw.co.uk
Lawrights http://www.lawrights.co.uk
UKLegal http://www.uklegal.com

For more on criminal activities, trends, arrests and law
enforcement, rustle through the following guides:

About Crime http://crime.about.com
Crime.com http://www.crime.com
Crime Spider http://www.crimespider.com
Open Directory http://dmoz.org/Society/Crime/

A–Z Guide to British Employment Law
http://www.emplaw.co.uk
Get the upper hand on your boss.

The Absolute Worst Things to Say to a Police Officer
http://www.geocities.com/Heartland/Prairie/7559/copjokes.html/
"Aren't you the guy from The Village People?"

APBnews.com
http://www.apbonline.com
Highly acclaimed network news service focusing on crime, justice and
safety.

Brutal.com
http://www.brutal.com
Bad news from around the world, as it breaks.

Burglar.com

http://www.theburglar.com

Profit from stolen goods that some- how happened to be in your possession.

Copyright Myths

http://whatis-copyright.org

http://www.templetons.com/brad/copyright.html/

Just because it's online doesn't make it yours.

The Court Service

http://www.courtservice.gov.uk

In amongst all the dull information and legalese is a collection of recent judgements handed down by the country's Justices.

Crime Magazine

http://www.crimemagazine.com

Encyclopedic collection of outlaw tales.

Cybercrime

http://www.cybercrime.gov

How to report online crooks.

Desktop Lawyer

http://www.desktoplawyer.net

Cut legal costs by doing it online.

Divorce Online

http://www.divorce-online.co.uk

DIY D.I.V.O.R.C.E. for residents of England and Wales.

Dumb Crooks

http://www.dumbcrooks.com

Let the masters teach you how not to do it.

Law and Crime

Dumb Laws
http://www.dumblaws.com
Foreign legislation with limited appeal.

ECLS
http://www.e-commercelawsource.com
Global monitor and directory of online business law.

The Evidence Store
http://www.evidencestore.com
"Need a hand for your day in court? How about a foot or a skull? ...
Accident reconstructions? The Evidence Store's experts will create all
the visual exhibits you'll need to educate even the toughest jury."

Famous Mugshots
http://www.mugshots.org
Lifestyles of the rich and famous.

FBI Files
http://foia.fbi.gov/alpha.htm/
Download the FBI's reports released by the Freedom of Information Act
on the Black Panthers, Al Capone, Pablo Picasso, Elvis and Winston
Churchill.

Freelawyer
http://www.freelawyer.co.uk
Ask a legal question and get a jargon-free response from a qualified
solicitor with a list of local specialists as well as no-obligation estimates.

Gang Land
http://www.ganglandnews.com
This amazing site from former New York *Daily News* reporter Jerry
Capeci has just about everything you could want to know about
Salvatore "Sammy Bull" Gravano, John Gotti, Wing Yeung Chan and
their ilk.

Guide to Lock Picking
http://www.lysator.liu.se/mit-guide/mit-guide.html/
Never climb in through the window again.

Legal Services Commission
http://www.legal-aid.gov.uk
Information on Community Legal Service and Criminal Defence Service from the public body that oversees their administration.

Police Officer's Directory
http://www.officer.com
http://www.cops.aust.com (AUS)
http://www.crimespider.com
Top of the pops cop directory with more than 1500 baddy-nabbing bureaux snuggled in with law libraries, wanted listings, investigative tools, hate groups, special ops branches and off-duty home pages. To see who's in Scotland Yard's bad books: http://www.met.police.uk

Police Scanner
http://www.policescanner.com
Listen in on busts in progress by the NY, LA, Dallas and San Diego police departments.

PursuitWatch
http://www.
pursuitwatch.com
Get paged when there's a
live police chase on TV.

Rate your risk
http://www.nashville.
net/~police/risk/
See if you're likely to be
robbed, stabbed, shot or beaten to death in the near future.

Society of Will Writers
http://freespace.virgin.net/society.willwriters/
Information on wills and bequests from the will writers' professional body.

The Speedtrap Bible
http://www.speedtrap.co.uk
Ironically, this site is rather slow, but still a great resource for drivers who want to know, umm, where traffic flashpoints might occur. See

also Speedtrap.com (http://www.speedtrap.com) and UK Speed Traps (http://www.ukspeedtraps.co.uk).

Museums and Galleries

Home pages of bricks-and-mortar museums

British Museum http://www.british-museum.ac.uk
Guggenheim http://www.guggenheim.org
The Hermitage http://www.hermitagemuseum.org
Louvre http://www.louvre.fr
Metropolitan Museum of Art http://www.metmuseum.org
Museo Del Prado http://museoprado.mcu.es
Museum of Modern Art http://www.moma.org
National Gallery http://www.nationalgallery.co.uk
National Portrait Gallery http://www.npg.org.uk
Natural History Museum http://www.nhm.ac.uk
Tate Gallery http://www.tate.org.uk
Uffizi Gallery http://www.uffizi.firenze.it
Victoria & Albert Museum http://www.vam.ac.uk

Artists

Leonardo da Vinci http://www.webgood.net/leonardo/
Monet http://www.claudemonet.com
Picasso http://www.tamu.edu/mocl/picasso/
Van Gogh http://www.vangoghgallery.com

The Art Canvas
http://www.theartcanvas.com
Superb and very high quality images of some of the masterpieces from the Modernist canon (Picasso, Pollock, de Kooning, Degas, Cézanne, Manet, etc).

ArtMuseum
http://www.artmuseum.net
Infrequent exhibitions of modern US classics.

Bad Art
http://www.badart.com

Di With Sty, Orange Maiden and *Still Life With Agony Faces* are just some of the masterpieces enshrined here – you won't see them anywhere else but your local charity shop. Meanwhile, http://www.glyphs.com/moba/ is the Web presence of Boston, Massachusetts' bricks-and-mortar shrine to good artists gone bad.

Bitstreams
http://www.whitney.org/bitstreams/
A fine exhibit of minimal digital art from New York's Whitney Museum, with downloadable art.

British Lawnmower Museum
http://www.lawnmowerworld.co.uk
SEE: the world's fastest lawnmower. SEE: Prince Charles's lawnmower. SEE: the water-cooled egg boiler lawnmower. SEE: Vanessa Feltz's lawnmower.

Dia Center for the Arts
http://www.diacenter.org
Web exclusives from "extraordinary" artists, plus the lowdown on the NY Dia Center's upcoming escapades.

The Exploratorium
http://www.exploratorium.edu
No substitute for visiting this great San Francisco museum in the flesh, but The Exploratorium's Website is filled with fun and educational sections on sports medicine, the solar system, the Hubble Telescope and the Panama Pacific Exposition.

Museums and Galleries

Isometric Screenshots
http://whitelead.com/jrh/screenshots/
An online exhibition by artist Jon Haddock in which he has rendered
some of the 20th century's defining moments (the protests at Tianamen
Square, the beating of Rodney King, the assassination of Martin Luther
King) in the visual style of video games.

Museum of Menstruation and Women's Health
http://www.mum.org
Its curator may be a man, but this is a rather weird and wonderful site
that takes its subject pretty seriously.

24 Hour Museum
http://www.24hourmuseum.org.uk
Portal for British museums, with an excellent search feature which
allows you to look for museums with food, baby changing facilities or
that tie in with national curriculum requirements. Also try
MuseumNetwork (http://www.museumnetwork.com) or Museums
Around the World (http://www.icom.org/vlmp/world.html/). For galleries
as well as museums see The Art Guide (http://www.artguide.org) or
The Gallery Channel (http://www.thegallerychannel.com).

Unusual Museums of the Internet
http://www.unusualmuseums.org
Homepage of the Unusual Museums Webring, your gateway to such
exotic destinations as the Toilet Paper Museum, World of Crabs, Cigar
Box Art and the Toilet Seat Art Museum.

Washington Banana Museum
http://www.geocities.com/NapaValley/1799/
The world's greatest collection of banana ephemera. No plantains, please.

Web Gallery of Art
http://gallery.euroweb.hu
For fans of everything from Giotto frescoes to Rembrandt's *The
Nightwatch*, this fantastic site houses digital reproductions of some
8000 works from between 1150 and 1750.

Web Museum
http://www.southern.net/wm/

Easily one of the best sites on the Web, the Web Museum hosts a fantasy collection of art – like having the Louvre, the Metropolitan Museum of Art, the Hermitage and the Prado all right around the corner. There is also an extensive glossary of terms, artist biographies and enlightening comment on each of the works displayed.

Music

If you're at all into music you've certainly come to the right place. Whether you want to hear it, read about it or watch it being performed you'll be swamped with options. If you're after a specific band, label or music genre, the Ultimate Band List on Artists Direct should be your first port of call:

Ultimate Band List http://www.ubl.com

Then try these directories:

About.com http://home.about.com/musicperform/
Open Directory http://dmoz.org/Arts/Music/
SonicNet http://www.sonicnet.com/allmusic/
Yahoo http://music.yahoo.com

As ever, if these fail to satisfy, try:

Google http://www.google.com

For an astoundingly complete music database spanning most popular genres, with bios, reviews, ratings, and keyword crosslinks to related sounds, sites, and online ordering, see:

All Music Guide http://www.allmusic.com

And don't overlook our own printed guides to Rock, Reggae, Drum & Bass, Jazz, Classical, House, Techno, Soul, World and Opera:

Rough Guides to Music http://www.roughguides.com

Much of the mainstream music press is already well established online. For the latest music news:

Artists Direct http://artistsdirect.com

Music

Buying records online

Shopping for music is another area where the Net not only equals but outshines its terrestrial counterparts. Apart from the convenience of not having to tramp across town, you can find almost anything on current issue, whether or not it's released locally, and in many cases preview album tracks in RealAudio. You might save money, too, depending on where you buy, whether you're hit with tax and how the freight costs stack up. Consider splitting your order if duty becomes an issue.

The biggest hitch you'll find is when stock is put on back order. Web operators can boast a huge catalogue simply because they order everything on the fly, putting you at the mercy of their distributors. The trouble is your entire order might be held up by one item. The better shops check their stock levels before confirming your order and follow its progress until delivery.

As far as where to shop goes, that depends on your taste. In terms of sheer innovation, **Tunes.com** stands out by profiling your preferences, recommending selections, linking to reviews and serving up ample samples. Amazon is also impressive – but then you can't go too far wrong with most of the blockbusters:

Amazon http://www.amazon.co.uk
AudioStreet http://www.audiostreet.co.uk
BOL http://www.bol.com
CDNow http://www.cdnow.com
HMV http://www.hmv.com
Tower Records http://uk.towerrecords.com
Virgin Megastore http://www.virginmega.com

Or, if you're after something more obscure, you'll find no shortage of options under the appropriate Yahoo categories or at: http://www.offitsface.com/links.html/

Like these, for example:
Aquarius http://www.aquariusrecordssf.com
The online presence of one of America's best record shops is

perhaps even better than visiting its hallowed halls in person. Simple to navigate and constantly updated, the selection (everything from *Sounds of North American Frogs* to *Super Duck Breaks*) is hard to beat and the reviews are funny, engaging and informative.

CDEmusic http://www.cdemusic.org

This American site carries not only electronic music from a time when it was made only by men in white labcoats but specialist books, music software and seriously sexy musical equipment like the Moog Moogerfooger processor.

CD Wow http://www.cd-wow.com

Cheap chart CDs (£9 at press time). See also Play 247 (http://www.play247.com).

CyberCD http://www.cybercd.de
http://www.musicexpress.com

German outfits with enormous catalogues, though not so cheap.

Desscarga http://www.descarga.com

If you are a fan of Latin music, you must, must check out this site. *¡Sabroso!*

Dusty Groove http://www.dustygroove.com

The Web site of this renowned Chicago record shop created the blueprint for Internet-based record mail order services, and they're still doing it better than anyone else. If you're interested in hip-hop, funk, soul, reggae, Latin or obscure soundtracks, it's nearly impossible to leave the site empty-handed.

Forced Exposure http://www.forcedexposure.com

This Massachusetts distributor is the colossus of underground music, and its informative, easy-to-use Website is another jewel in its crown. Along with an excellent search feature (which, unlike too many mail order sites, searches the personnel lists as well as the main artist name), the reviews are opinionated and informative.

Global Electronic Music Market
http://gemm.com
One-point access to over two million new and used records from almost two thousand sources. See also: **http://www.second spin.com**

Hard to find records
http://www.htfr.com
Record-finding agency that specializes in house, hip-hop, soul and disco vinyl.

Other Music
http://www.othermusic.com
Since opening in 1996 opposite Tower Records, New York City's bastion of the weird, wacky and just plain great has made a name for itself as one of America's best record emporia. Divided into sections like "Out" (avant garde music from this world and others), "In" ('90s indie rock) and "Le Decadanse" (sophisto pop), its site embodies the virtues that made it so good in the first place: friendly, helpful and attitude-free.

Penny Black
http://www.pennyblackmusic.com
Indie pop, punk and electronica.

Record Finder
http://www.recordfinders.com
Deleted vinyl, including over 200,000 45s.

You'll find thousands of archived reviews, charts, gig guides, band bios, selected features, shopping links, news, and various sound artefacts courtesy of these familiar beacons:

Rough Trade http://www.roughtrade.com

The Web site of London's underground landmark is housed in a slick designer package. It would benefit from less time-consuming graphics, but the stock is excellent and the prices, while not the bargain level of the giants, ain't bad. Additional bonuses include an old t-shirt section, chat rooms and downloads – plus there's no tricky spiral staircase to navigate.

Sandbox Automatic http://www.sandboxautomatic.com

Without a doubt the best source for independent hip-hop on the Net. There are no bells and whistles, but what a choice.

Secondsounds http://www.secondsounds.com

Buying used CDs online may be even more risky than in an actual shop because you can't check out the merchandise, but if you're after a bargain this site is hard to beat.

Sterns African Records Centre http://www.sternsmusic.com

The UK's number-one retailer of world music does a fine job online as well.

For a listing of price comparison agents, see Shopping (p.280).

Cooking your own CD

Fancy whipping up your own custom CD? Simply run through the catalog, preview what looks good, submit your track listing, and they'll burn it to disc:

CD Now http://www.cdnow.com
Emusic http://www.emusic.com
Razorcuts http://www.razorcuts.co.uk

Billboard http://www.billboard-online.com
Blues and Soul http://www.bluesandsoul.co.uk
Dirty Linen http://kiwi.futuris.net/linen/

Music

Folk Roots http://www.froots.demon.co.uk
NME http://nme.com
Q http://www.q4music.com
Rolling Stone http://www.rollingstone.com
Spin http://www.spin.com
Vibe http://www.vibe.com

And if your concentration is up to it, MTV:
Europe http://www.mtveurope.com
UK http://www.mtv.co.uk

Don't buy a stereo component until you've consulted the world's biggest audio opinionbases:
AudioReview.com http://www.audioreview.com
AudioWeb http://www.audioweb.com
What Hi-Fi http://www.whathifi.com

Or if you wouldn't settle for less than a single-ended triode amp:
Audiophilia http://www.audiophilia.com
GlassWare http://www.glass-ware.com
Stereophile http://www.stereophile.com
Triode Guild http://www.meta-gizmo.com

Consult these directories for manufacturers, shops and other audio sites:
AudioWorld http://www.audioworld.com
Hifiheaven.com http://www.hifiheaven.com
UK Hi-Fi Dealers http://hifi.dealers.co.uk

Addicted to Noise
http://www.addict.com
Monthly news and reviews with a heavy bias towards the rowdy end of the pop rock spectrum.

African Music
http://www.africanmusic.org
World Music aficionados should make a beeline for this library, search-

able by country or artist, and with an accompanying shopping area.

All About Jazz

http://www.allaboutjazz.com

Don't let the expensive corporate layout fool you, this American site doesn't just cover Kenny G. As its name suggests, it aims to deal with the entire spectrum of jazz from Anthony Braxton to John Scofield. That it succeeds is down to an easily navigable layout, a wealth of info and contributions from the biggest names in jazz journalism.

Ari's Simple List of Record Labels

http://www.guxx.com/recordlabels/

Exactly what it says on the tin.

Art of the Mixed Tape

http://www.artofthemix.org

"If you have ever killed an afternoon making a mix, spent the evening making a cover, and then mailed a copy off to a friend after having made a copy for yourself, well, this is the site for you". Kind of says it all, really.

Canonical List of Weird Band Names

http://www.geminiweb.net/bandnames/

Just be thankful your parents weren't so creative. Here's the story behind a few: http://www.heathenworld.com/bandname/

CDDB

http://www.cddb.com

Automatically supplies track listings for the CDs playing in your PC drive.

Classical Hub

http://www.classicalhub.com

This relatively new site is designed for both the neophyte (glossary, introduction to the main composers and to reading music) and the expert (in-depth bios, a Listening Booth with background on each of the pieces). See also Classical Net (http://www.classical.net).

Classical Music on the Net

http://www.musdoc.com/classical/
http://www.gmn.com/classical/

Gateway to the timeless.

Music

The Dance Music Resource
http://www.juno.co.uk
New and forthcoming dance releases for mail order, UK radio slots and a stacked directory.

Dancetech
http://www.dancetech.com
One-stop shop for techno toys and recording tips. For more on synths, try http://www.synthzone.com and http://www.sonicstate.com.

Dial-the-Truth Ministries
http://www.av1611.org
So why does Satan get all the good music?

DJ University
http://dju.prodj.com
Become a wedding spinner.

Donna's Long and Short of it
http://www.metal-sludge.com/LongShort.htm/
The most essential music resource on the Net: Donna and her gaggle of groupies give you the lowdown on the vitals of 150+ heavy metal gods.

dotmusic
http://www.dotmusic.com
Top source of UK and global music news, weekly charts, and new releases in RealAudio. See also:
http://www.music3w.com

The Droplift Project
http://www.droplift.org
Join in some plunderphonic fun by smuggling some avant-garde sampladelic CDs onto the shelves of major chain retailers.

Electronic Musical Instruments

http://www.obsolete.com/120_years/
From the ondes martenot to the sampler, this online museum is the liveliest, least techie source of information on the rapidly expanding world of music technology.

Evil Music
http://www.evilmusic.com
Don't know the difference between Black Metal and Doom Metal, or what constitutes Original Death Metal as opposed to Brutal Death Metal? Let Spinoza Ray Prozac be your guide to the dark world of the Metal underground.

Fat Lace
http://www.fat-lace.com
The Internet presence of the hilarious "Magazine for ageing B-boys" contains mostly copy from the print version which covers hip-hop with an irreverent slant only possible in the UK. An added bonus is the Random Old School Name Generator for all the Lord Disco Loves out there.

Freestyling

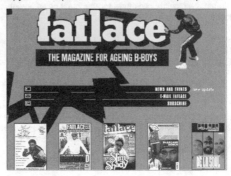

http://www.freestyling.com
Fancy yourself as the next Tupac or Jay-Z? Post your best rhyme here and wait to be discovered. For more traditional battling, try the Home Grown Hip Hop Zone (http://www.HomeGrownHipHopZone.com) and Ughh (http://www.ughh.com).

Funk45.com
http://www.funk45.com

A great entrée into the murky world of deep funk collecting. The site is chock-full of MP3s and Real Audio files of hopelessly obscure funk records. The only catch is that the files are only one minute long, with the aim being to introduce people to this arcane world rather than destroying its informal economy.

Funky Groovy Lexicon
http://www.access.ch/funkymusic/
Over 322 pages (in PDF format), the FGL catalogues nearly everything that can be construed as funky, from 100 Proof Aged in Soul to Zzebra. There's also a gallery of suave cats in daishikis and killer Afros. Believe it or not, it's from Switzerland.

Garage Music
http://www.garagemusic.co.uk
If you don't live in the East End and want to keep up with what the pirates are playing, click here for the latest news, events and downloads.

Get Out There
http://www.getoutthere.bt.com
Expose your unsung talents or listen to other unsigned acts.

Gramophone
http://www.gramophone.co.uk
There is no better site for serious classical music aficionados. The Web home of *Gramophone* magazine boasts access to its database of 25,000 CD reviews. Need more reasons to visit? How about audio clips, the option to buy from the site, links, listings, glossary, artist bios and feature articles?

Groupie Central
http://www.groupiecentral.com
More than just a repository of tales of decadence and bad sex, this often eye-popping forum is by turns sly, knowing, empowering, brutal and, of course, risqué.

Harmony Central

http://www.harmonycentral.com
Directory and headspace for musicians of all persuasions.

Hyperreal

http://www.hyperreal.org
Perhaps the godfather of all music sites, Hyperreal has been going since 1992. It's a one-stop window shop for all things rave and Ambient. Erowid's Psychoactive Vaults host the raver's version of the *Physician's Desk Reference* – a library of info on mind-altering substances.

Independent Underground Music Archive

http://www.iuma.com
Full-length tracks and bios from thousands of unsigned and indie-label underground musicians.

Jazz

http://www.jazzreview.com
http://www.allaboutjazz.com
http://www.downbeat.com
Bottomless drawer of beard-stroking delights.

Kareoke.com

http://www.kareoke.com
Sing along in the privacy of your own home.

Kompaktkiste

http://www.kompaktkiste.de
The bluffer's guide to electronic music: an extensive list of CDs of electronic music organised by artist with track listings and running times. It makes no judgements, but if you're looking for that hard to find Phthalocyanine remix, come here first.

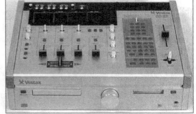

Music

Large Hot Pipe Organ
http://www.lhpo.org
Thrill to the throb of the world's first MIDI controlled, propane-powered, explosion organ.

Launch.com
http://www.launch.com
Thousands of music videos, audio channels, record reviews and chat forums.

Libretto List
http://php.indiana.edu/~lneff/libmlist.html/
A fantastic resource for opera buffs, this site has links to just about every public domain libretto available on the Net.

Live Concerts
http://www.liveconcerts.com
Major gigs live in RealAudio.

London Musicians Collective
http://www.l-m-c.org.uk
The LMC has been promoting the cause of improvised music in the Big Smoke for over a quarter of a century. Their site features content from their journal, *Resonance*, streaming audio from their radio show and information on studio facilities.

The Manual
http://www.klf.de/online/books/bytheklf/manual.htm/
Think you can do better than Hear'Say? Have a glance at the essential guide to pop superstardom, written by the ace pranksters in The KLF.

Metal Sudge
http://www.metal-sludge.com
Heavy metal portal that treats the genre with the dignity and respect it deserves.

MIDI Farm
http://www.midifarm.com
Synthesized debasements of pop tunes, TV themes, and film scores. Cheesy listening at its finest.

Minidisc.org
http://www.minidisc.org
Keep in tune with Sony's troubled Minidisc format.

Mr Lucky
http://www.mrlucky.com
Get smooth with rhythm 'n' booze.

Motion
http://motion.state51.co.uk
A great resource for fans of experimental music of all stripes. Record Shop Finder is a database of independent record shops all over the world, while the Motion Filter delivers email updates of reviews, events and release information culled from specialist mailing lists that are selected according to parameters you key in.

Niceup
http://www.niceup.com
Probably the most irie reggae site on the Net, Niceup contains discographies, articles on topics like "Studio One Riddims", a lyrics archive, histories, news and a Patois dictionary.

Online DJ
http://www.onlinedj.com
You gotta have all manner of plug-ins to visit this comprehensive resource for DJs, but if you want help on your transformers, chirps, flares and crabs this is the only place to come. Well, there's also Hitsquad (http://www.hitsquad.com) and Turntablism.com (http://www.turntablism.com).

Online Guitar Archive
http://www.olga.net
A truly awesome site for guitarists and bassists. No more scurrying through back issues of *Guitar Player* for tablature for Blue Öyster Cult's "Godzilla" – OLGA boasts some 40,000 tabs.

Opprobrium
http://www.info.net.nz/opprobrium/
No longer printed on paper, the legendary *Opprobrium* has been strictly digital ever since editor Nick Cain moved to London. Nevertheless, its

coverage of avant jazz, Japanoise, Improv and radical minimalism remains almost peerless.

Original Hip Hop Lyrics Archive
http://www.ohhla.com
Mind-blowingly complete archive of all of your favourite rhymes.

Perfect Sound Forever
http://www.furious.com/perfect/
Calling itself "the online magazine with the warped attitudes", PSF is one of the best music sites on the Net. Although most of the articles are straight interview transcripts and don't take advantage of the Web format, the writing on leftfield heroes is passionate and informative.

Rap Dictionary
http://www.rapdict.org
Can't understand your teenage son anymore? Log on here, dun, and you'll get the 411.

Rare Music
http://www.raremusic.com
One for all the crate diggers, with articles focusing on rare funk, old school hip-hop, instructional records and Muhammad Ali.

Roadie.net
http://www.roadie.net
No backstage pass necessary.

The Sample FAQ
http://members.accessus.net/~xombi/intro.html/
Ever wondered what beat The Beastie Boys ripped off for "Shadrach" or who's sampled Isaac Hayes? This whistle blowing Website tears the lid off of the record crates of hip-hop's most famous producers.

Scorchin' Soul
http://www.scorchinsoul.co.uk
http://www.soulcity.ndo.co.uk
Listen to hundreds of '60s and Northern Soul clips.

Scratch Simulator

http://www.turntables.de/scratchit8.htm/

Can't afford a pair of SL 1200s? Practise your reverse orbit scratches and beat juggling here, or at the Beat Bomb (http://www.hookt.net), Infinite Wheel (http://www.infinitewheel.com), Live Jam (http://livejam.com) or ScratchOMatic (http://www.fm-productions.com/scratch.html/).

Shareware Music Machine

http://www.hitsquad.com/smm/

Tons of shareware music players, editors and composition tools, for every platform.

Show and Tell Music

http://www.showandtellmusic.com

Albums much cooler than anything you own.

Smithsonian Institution

http://web2.si.edu

Although this site is as gigantic as the famous American museum itself, if you're interested in folk music (from both America and the rest of the world) it's an absolute paradise, with info on their Folkways record label, Webcasts, galleries and articles (augmented with RealAudio files).

Music

Bizarre Records

American Song Poem Archives   http://www.aspma.com
Archive of the bizarre mid-century phenomenon where studio hacks set music to the lyrics of ordinary Joes – resulting in some of the weirdest records ever.

Collecting Crap Records   http://www.78rpm.sonow.com/
                                                 002/Crmain.htm
The what, why, where and hows of collecting records like Rolf Harris's "Pukka Chicken" and King Uszniewicz & His Uszniewicztones' "She Won't Turn Over for Me".

Frank's Vinyl Museum   http://franklarosa.com/
                                                 $spindb.query.new.vinyl/
Exhibition of charity shop flotsam, including such timeless classics as *Ken Demko Live at the Lamplighter Inn* and an album of Beatles covers done by dogs.

The Internet Museum of Flexi/   http://www.wfmu.org/MACrec/
Cardboard/Oddities
Records made out of metal, souvenirs from the Empire State Building and other curios.

Songs in the Key of Z   http://www.keyofz.com/keyofz/
Irwin Chusid's fantastic introduction to the world of outsider music.

Songfile
http://www.songfile.com
If you've got the right software, you can search the site's database of lyrics to 130,000 songs. Also try Lyric Hound (http://www.lyrichound.com), Sing365 (http://www.sing365.com) and Top 3 (http://www.top3.net/FH/).

Songplayer
http://www.songplayer.com
Can't read music and still want to play guitar like Hendrix or keyboards like Keith Emerson? Try this music tuition site which has some 4000 songs in its files, and there are no cumbersome staves, bars or clefs to wrestle with.

Sonic Net
http://www.sonicnet.com
Big-name live cybercasts, streaming audio and video channels, chats, news and reviews.

Sony
http://www.sony.com
Think about everything that Sony flogs. Now imagine it all squeezed under one roof.

Sounds Online
http://www.soundsonline.com
Preview loops and samples, free in RealAudio. Pay to download studio quality. If it's effects you're after, try: http://www.sounddogs.com

Spaceage Bachelor Pad Music
http://www.chaoskitty.com/sabpm/
Make like Hef and slip into something more comfortable for this journey into the heart of Loungeland.

SS7x7 Sound System
http://www.ss7x7.com
Mix your own tracks in Shockwave. Or have a bit of a scratch: http://www.turntables.de

Taxi
http://www.taxi.com
Online music A&R service. And guess what? You and your plastic kazoo are just what they're looking for.

This Day in Music
http://www.thisdayinmusic.com
Find out which member of the Bay City Rollers shares your birthday and other essential music trivia.

MP3s

Unlike every music delivery system since the development of 33⅓ and 45rpm records, MP3 is the first format not forced upon consumers by the record industry. Short for "MPEG-1 audio layer 3", MP3 is a format that compresses digital music files without a significant degradation in sound quality and has become the standard way of storing music on the Internet. In order to take advantage of MP3 you need some up-to-date kit: at least 32MB of RAM, a 56K modem, lots of room on your hard drive and, if you have an older PC, a sound card. You will also need to download MP3 player software like Soundjam for Macintosh or Winamp or RealJukebox for PC which are usually available in basic, free versions or more advanced versions for $29.95.

The best place to start is MP3.com (**http://www.mp3.com**) which has links to all the downloadable MP3 player software, lots of information for beginners and a vast catalogue of files. The software allows you to download MP3 files (which you can also do using your browser) and play them through the speakers on your computer. Many of the software programs have "ripping" options which allow you to convert a track on a CD into an MP3 file. This is where the rub comes. Peer-to-peer file sharing programs like Napster (**http://www.napster.com**) and Gnutella (**http://gnutella.wego.com**) allow(ed) people to trade files with one another – without any record company mediation, of course. The Record Industry Association of America, however, stepped in and a put a stop to free Napster file exchanges and at the time of writing the state of music on the Net is now very much up in the air.

The most likely answer to the conundrum is a subscription service like:

Emusic   http://www.emusic.com
For $10 a month you can download MP3s from established artists.

For more MP3 options, try:
Audio Galaxy Satellite   http://www.audiogalaxysatellite.
                                                                      com/satellite/

CMJ   http://www.cmj.com/mp3/
Wippit   http://www.wippit.com

The industry players' sites weren't ready as this book went to press, but the names to look out for are:
Duet
HitHive   http://www.hithive.com
MusicNet   http://www.musicnet.com

For some of the copyright issues involved, go to Free Music Philosophy (http://www.ram.org/ramblings/philosophy/fmp.html/).

Advanced Audio Coding   http://www.aac-audio.com
Learn the news on the audio compression format destined to replace MP3.

Coalition for the Future of Music   http://www.
futureofmusic.org
Run by riot grrl Jenny Toomey, this organisation campaigns for the rights of the independent musician in the Napster furore and is a good place to get to grasp with what's at stake for both the musician and label.

To discover the next Hear'Say or Slipknot, try:
Clickmusic   http://www.clickmusic.co.uk
Get Signed   http://www.get-signed.co.uk
Popwire   http://www.popwire.com
Vitaminic   http://www.vitaminic.co.uk

Don't want to pay for Napster but still want free MP3s? Try some of the following sites, although we can't vouch for the legality of all of them:
Classic Outtakes   http://www.fadetoblack.com/outtakes/
Actual recordings by William Shatner and the legendary tape of Linda McCartney singing "Hey Jude".

Music

Bob Dylan
http://www.bobdylan.com
Rare live recordings released by the Great White Wonder himself.

Musicblitz
http://musicblitz.com
Headline names like Eminem, Madonna and Beck, but inevitably not the tracks you want.

Punk: Hyped to Death
http://www.hyped2death.com

RealAudio Punk Archive
http://members.nbci.com/ spiritof1977/

Smashing Pumpkins
http://spfc.org
Download their final *Machina II* album which the group decided to give away after record company indifference.

360HipHop
http://www.360hiphop.com
A victim of dotcom overexcitement, this site still houses the best hip-hop writing on the Net. The 411 on hip-hop culture can also be found at Davey D (http://www.daveyd.com) and Rapstation (http://www.rapstation.com).

Uplister
http://www.uplister.com
Playlists from your favourite musicians and regular Joes, with RealAudio samples and links to purchase the tracks.

Urban Sounds
http://www.urbansounds.com
Excellent, well-planned and designed electronica site from the US. The Minimalism issue features hot names on the underground and is sexily intercut with Rem Koolhaas sketches and Donald Judd reproductions.

WholeNote
http://www.wholenote.com
Guitar resources and chat boards. For live lessons, see:
http://www.riffinteractive.com

The Wire
http://www.thewire.co.uk
Subtitled "Adventures in Modern Music", the online home of the British avant-garde music magazine *The Wire* features in-depth articles from past issues on a pantheon of underground gods and goddesses and a comprehensive set of links to set you exploring the labyrinthine demi-monde of experimental music.

3D Insects
http://www.ento.vt.edu/~sharov/3d/3dinsect.html/
Whiz around a selection of 3D bugs. They're not real insects but at least they don't have pins through their backs. For a bigger range of bug bios, see: http://insects.org

African Wildlife Foundation
http://www.awf.org
Great site covering everything from the aardvark to the zebra.

Aquatic Network
http://www.aquanet.com
A good site promoting sustainable aquaculture, with some great photography and solid information saving it from being too earnest.

ARKive
http://www.arkive.org.uk
Electronic archive of the world's endangered species.

Birding
http://birding.about.com
http://www.camacdonald.com/birding/
http://dmoz.org/Recreation/Birdwatching/
Birds are such regional critters that one site couldn't hope to cover them all. Use these to find the chirpiest one on your block.

Nature

Birds of Britain
http://www.birdsofbritain.co.uk
Web zine devoted to our fine feathered friends, with an illustrated guide to some 100 species.

Cetacea.org
http://www.cetacea.org
Excellent encyclopedic source of information on whales, dolphins and porpoises.

Dinosaur Interplanetary Gazette
http://www.dinosaur.org
It may be as slow and cumbersome as a Brontosaurus stuck in the LaBrea tar pits, but patience does pay off with a wealth of information and features.

The Electronic Zoo
http://netvet.wustl.edu/e-zoo.htm/
Up and running since 1993, this virtual menagerie is the best collection of animal-related links on the Web.

eNature.com
http://www.enature.com
Vibrant field guides to North American flora and fauna.

Field Trips
http://www.field-guides.com
A neat idea, if not perfectly executed: visit this site and take virtual field trips involving deserts, oceans, hurricanes, sharks, fierce creatures, salt marshes, volcanoes and other natural wonders of the world.

Forces of Nature
http://library.thinkquest.org/C003603/
Thinkquest's student-designed Website devoted to avalanches, droughts, landslides, earthquakes and other natural disasters.

ForestWorld
http://www.forestworld.com
http://forests.org
Timber tales from both sides of the dozer.

Great Cats of the World

http://www.greatcatsoftheworld.com

The home page of the Bridgeport Nature Center in Texas functions as a mini-encyclopedia of lions, tigers, leopards and cougars.

Insects on the Web

http://www.insects.org

Definitely not one for your little girl, this excellent educational resource of creepy-crawlies features some rather too detailed photography of everyone's least favourite bugs.

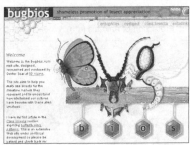

Mr Winkle

http://www. mrwinkle.com

Okay, so how cute is Mr Winkle? But is he really real?

Nature Explorer

http://NatureExplorer.com

Based on the series of CD-ROMs with the same name, this fantastic site hosts pretty much the entire series online. It may be slow, but the information and pictures are nearly unbeatable.

Nessie on the Net

http://www.lochness.co.uk

Watch the Loch Ness Webcam, spot the monster and win £1000.

Predator Urines

http://www.predatorpee.com

Bewitch neighbouring Jack Russells with a dab of bobcat balm or true blue roo poo: http://www.roopooco.com

Roadkill

http://earth.simmons.edu/roadkill/roadkill.html/

Documenting incidents of vehicular homicide throughout the US.

Sea turtle migration-tracking
http://www.cccturtle.org/satwelc.htm/
Adopt a bugged sea reptile and follow its trail.

World Wildlife Fund
http://www.worldwildlife.org.uk
Teach your kids that the WWF isn't all about pile drivers and steroid cases in skimpy shorts. More animal lovers at the World Society for the Protection of Animals (http://www.wspa.org) and the Royal Society for the Protection of Animals (http://www.rspca.org).

ZooNet
http://www.zoonet.org
Perhaps the best virtual zoo on the Web.

News, Newspapers and Magazines

Now that almost every magazine and newspaper on the globe from *Ringing World* (http://www.ringingworld.co.uk) to the *Falkland Island News* (http://www.sartma.com) is discharging daily content onto the Net, it's beyond this guide to do much more than list a few of the notables and then point you in the right direction for more. The simplest way to find your favourite read would be to look for its address in a recent issue. Failing that, try entering its name into a subject guide or search engine. If you don't have a title name and would prefer to browse by subject or region, try:

Open Directory http://dmoz.org/News/

Yahoo http://dir.yahoo.com/News_and_Media/

Newspapers rarely replicate themselves word for word online, but they often provide enough for you to live without the paper edition. Not bad considering they're generally free online before the paper even hits the stands. Apart from whatever proportion of their print they choose to put online, they also tend to delve deeper into their less newsy areas such as travel, IT, entertainment and culture. Plus they often bolster this with exclusive content such as breaking news, live sports coverage, online shopping, opinion polls and discussion groups. In most cases they'll also provide a way to search and retrieve archives, though this might incur a charge. There are also a few sites that index multiple news archives, again usually at a price. Such as:

Electric Library http://www.elibrary.com

FindArticles.com http://www.findarticles.com

NewsLibrary http://www.newslibrary.com

Northern Light http://www.nlsearch.com

A few of the more popular news bugles, to get you started:

Arab News http://www.arabnews.com

Brill's Content http://www.brillscontent.com

Christian Science Monitor http://www.csmonitor.com

Daily Mail & Guardian http://www.mg.co.za

Economist http://www.economist.com

Evening Standard http://www.thisislondon.co.uk

Express http://www.express.co.uk

Financial Times http://www.ft.com

Guardian http://www.guardian.co.uk

News, Newspapers and Magazines

The Hindu http://www.hinduonline.com
Independent http://www.independent.co.uk
International Herald Tribune http://www.iht.com
Irish News http://www.irishnews.com
LA Times http://www.latimes.com
Mirror http://www.mirror.co.uk
Le Monde http://www.lemonde.fr
National Enquirer http://www.nationalenquirer.com
National Geographic News http://www.ngnews.com
News of the World http://www.newsoftheworld.co.uk
Newsweek http://www.newsweek.com
NY Times http://www.nytimes.com
Observer http://www.observer.co.uk
El País http://www.elpais.es
Scotsman http://www.scotsman.com
South China Morning Post http://www.scmp.com
La Stampa http://www.lastampa.it
Sun http://www.the-sun.co.uk
Tehelka http://www.tehelka.com
Telegraph http://www.telegraph.co.uk
Time Daily http://www.time.com
Times http://www.thetimes.co.uk
Times of India http://www.timesofindia.com
USA Today http://www.usatoday.com
Village Voice http://www.villagevoice.com
Washington Post http://www.washingtonpost.com
Weekly World News http://www.weeklyworldnews.com

Like much you do online, reading news is addictive. You'll know you're hooked when you find yourself checking into newswires throughout the day to monitor moving stories. Try these for a fix:

Breaking News

Ananova http://www.ananova.com

Associated Press http://wire.ap.org

BBC http://news.bbc.co.uk

CNN http://www.cnn.com

ITN http://www.itn.co.uk

NBC http://www.msnbc.com

Reuters http://www.reuters.com

Satayam http://www.news.satyamonline.com

Sky http://www.sky.com

Wired News http://www.wired.com

While most magazines maintain a site, they're typically more of an adjunct to the print than a substitute. Still, they're worth checking out, especially if they archive features and reviews or break news between issues. Again, check a recent issue or one of the directories for an address. If you'd rather subscribe to the paper edition, try:
http://www.britishmagazines.com
http://www.magsuk.com

American Newspeak
http://www.scn.org/news/newspeak/
Celebrating the arts of doublethink, spin, media coaching and other ways to mangle meaning.

Clique
http://clique.org.uk
Roundup of stories that didn't get coverage from the mainstream news sources, whether because they were too controversial, too bizarre or just too stupid.

Crayon
http://www.crayon.net
Most of the major portals such as Excite, Yahoo and MSN also allow

E-zines

"E-zines" are magazines that only exist online or are delivered by email. But because almost any regularly updated Web page fits this description, the term has lost much of its currency. Although most e-zines burn out as quickly as they appear, a few of the pioneers are still kicking on.

For more, try browsing one of the directories listed at:
http://dmoz.org/News/Ezines/Directories/

Ammo City http://www.ammocity.com
Hip online lifestyle zine, peppered with music from The Avalanches and Orbital and articles like "Top Ten Luncheon Meats" and the "Ol' Dirty Bastard Watch".

The Chap http://www.artfink.demon.co.uk/chap/
"Dressing for Golf" and other essential manners guides for the modern male.

ChickClick http://www.chickclick.com
Zine network dedicated to hip young things that's pitched somewhere between the original *Sassy!* and *Jane*.

Drudge Report http://www.drudgereport.com
The shock bulletin that set off the Lewinsky avalanche. A one-hit wonder perhaps, but still a bona-fide tourist attraction on the info goat track.

Future File http://futurefile.com
Thought-provoking e-zine portal from technocrat Todd Maffin, featuring ideas and trends to look for in the next decade.

IGN http://www.ign.com/affiliates/
IGN (Internet Gaming Network) treads similar – though generally tamer – ground to UGO, partnering mostly with high quality gaming, sci-fi, wrestling and comic sites.

NTK
http://www.ntk.net

Sarcastic high tech media magazine. For geeky Popbitch (see Gossip) fans.

Salon
http://www.salon.com

The real e-zine success story. It spans the arts, business, politics, lifestyle and technology in a style that's both smart and breezy.

See Thru
http://www.seethru.co.uk

Intermittently funny and sharp e-zine for media-saturated urban smart-alecs.

Slate
http://slate.msn.com

Microsoft's long-suffering Slate marks similar territory to Salon, but succeeds more in being terribly dull.

Spiked
http://www.spiked-online.com

Caustic, political e-zine from former Living Marxism supremo Mick Hume.

Suck
http://www.suck.com

Arguably the only e-zine that mattered, Suck sits in a smug class all by itself. Worth reading daily, if not for its cocked eye on all that's wired and painfully modern then at least for Terry Colon's cartoons.

Underground Online
http://www.ugo.com

Big men's magazine-style network devoted to music, wrestling, film, TV, books, technology and so on.

you to create a custom news page that draws from several sources –
though none do it quite so thoroughly as Crayon. Infobeat
(http://www.infobeat.com) does similar things but delivers by email.

Electric Library
http://www.elibrary.com
A great resource that allows you to view full text versions of some
seven million articles, books, pictures, TV and radio transcripts.
Unfortunately you have to pay $59.95 a year for the privilege.

Inside
http://www.inside.com
Media news with a heavy US slant.

A Journalist's Guide to the Internet
http://reporter.umd.edu
No design whatsoever, but a useful set of links to resources for journalists.

Moreover
http://www.moreover.com/news/
The best free service for searching current or recent stories across hundreds of international news sources. Also try News Index
(http://www.newsindex.com) and What the Papers Say
(http://www.whatthepaperssay.co.uk). Like someone to monitor the
Web and assorted newswires for mention of your product or misdeeds?
Try Webclipping.com (http://www.webclipping.com).

NewsNow
http://www.newsnow.co.uk
News aggregators allow you to tap into several sources simultaneously.
This one might be the best: it has more UK-specific content than any of
the others and is apparently updated every five minutes. For more, try:

Arts & Letters Daily http://www.cybereditions.com/aldaily/

Asia Observer http://www.asiaobserver.com

Excite Newstracker http://nt.excite.com

FastAsia (Asia) http://www.fastasia.com

NewsHub http://www.newshub.com

Russian Story http://www.russianstory.com

TotalNews http://www.totalnews.com

Yahoo News http://dailynews.yahoo.com

The Onion
http://www.theonion.com
News the way it was meant to be.

The Paper Boy
http://www.thepaperboy.com
This site is perhaps the best specialist directory of newspapers and news organisations on the Web, with links to everything from Bulgarian National Radio to eight different papers from Zambia. Other directories to check out include AJR NewsLink (http://ajr.newslink.org/news.html/), Editor & Publisher (http://www.mediainfo.com), Metagrid (http://www.metagrid.com), NewsDirectory (http://www.newsdirectory.com), Online Newspapers (http://www.onlinenewspapers.com) and Publist (http://www.publist.com). To find magazines, try The Magazine Boy (http://www.themagazineboy.com).

Tech News
http://www.news.com
Computing and technology newswire. Of course, there's no shortage of similar sites: NewsLinx (http://www.newslinx.com), SiliconValley (http://www.siliconvalley.com), TechWeb (http://www.techweb.com) and ZD Network News (http://www.zdnet.com) are some of the best. For e-business news: InternetNews (http://www.internetnews.com).

This Is True
http://www.thisistrue.com
Randy Cassingham's weekly column of preposterous-but-true news stories and headlines collated from the major wire services.

Wireless Flash News Service
http://www.flashnews.com
News service specialising in pop culture stories, featuring some of the least newsworthy headlines in history.

News Tickers

A news ticker is like having a wire service on your desktop, complete with scrolling headlines. Click on one and you'll taken to the full story. You have to be online in order to receive the news, so they are best for those with ADSL or ISDN connections. Usually, all getting a news ticker entails is downloading the software (sometimes at a cost) and installing it on your computer. Tickers range from the very basic to customizable ones with loads of options; some can even be placed in the Windows taskbar.

BBC Newsline   http://www.bbc.co.uk/newsline/
A straightforward but very good news ticker.

Desktop News   http://www.desktopnews.com
Powerful, customizable ticker with plenty of different channels to choose from.

InfoGate   http://www.infogate.com
One of the best tickers for business news.

My Yahoo Ticker   http://my.yahoo.com/ticker.html/
One of the smallest tickers available, but it's only available to users of Yahoo's My Yahoo portal.

WorldFlash   http://www.worldflash.com
Extensive ticker with a keyword alert feature allowing you to keep track of stories of particular interest.

World Press Review
http://www.worldpress.org
Keeping tabs on the people who keep tabs on us. Also keep an eye on News Watch (http://www.newswatch.org).

Outdoor Pursuits

Birdlinks
http://www.birdlinks.co.uk
Gateway to the world of birdwatching.

The Butterfly Website
http://www.butterflywebsite.com
The Monarch of butterfly sites, with galleries, lists of gardens and butterfly gardens and loads of information on biology, conservation and behaviour.

Camp Sites
http://www.camp-sites.co.uk
Find a place to pitch your tent in the UK.

Go Fishing
http://www.go-fishing.co.uk
Your compleat angling resource. Other sites that would make Isaak Walton proud: Angler's Net (http://www.anglersnet.co.uk), Angling News (http://www.angling-news.co.uk) and Sea Angler (http://sea-angler.org).

Great Outdoor Recreation Pages
http://www.gorp.com
Ignore all the multivitamin and SUV adverts and the American bias because this is the best outdoors site on the Web. The superlative how-to pages alone make it worth navigating the pop-up ads, plus there are good articles, trail finders, destination guides, discussion groups, photo galleries and you can book holidays and buy gear from the site.

Ramblers' Association

http://www.ramblers.org.uk

All the latest news on walking and other pedestrian pursuits. For more info, take your browser on a stroll over to Walking World (http://www.walkingworld.com) or Walking Britain (http://www.walkingbritain.co.uk).

Rock Climbing in the UK

http://www.ukcrags.com

Great resource for British rock climbers, with news, articles, Webcams, events listings, routes and crag descriptions. More handholds can be found at Climb Guide (http://www.climb-guide.com).

Pets

About Veterinary Medicine

http://vetmedicine.about.com

About's vet pages are an excellent resource for pet owners worried about their moggie or pet lizard and are filled with advice, news, disease indexes and forums.

The Aviary

http://www.theaviary.com/ci.shtml/

Everything you'd ever want to know about companion birds – and then some.

Barbara's Canine Café

http://www.k9treat.com

Only In America part 346: If your mutt's got a food allergy or you just want to get your hound a "celebration gift basket" made from all-natural ingredients, look no further.

Cat Tips

http://www.cat-tips.com

"Understanding kitty psychology", "Litterbox blues" and other feline facts.

Chazhound
http://www.chazhound.com
Resources for dog lovers as well as screen savers, games and doggie greeting cards.

The Dogpatch
http://www.dogpatch.org
Advice on training your pooch, plus the best canine links on the Web.

Dogs Online
http://www.dogsonline.co.uk
Directory pages for British dog owners, including lost and found, breeders, puppies for sale and dog-friendly accommodation.

Equine World
http://www.equine-world.co.uk
Great site covering all things equestrian. See also Equiworld (http://www.equiworld.net).

FishDoc
http://www.fishdoc.co.uk
All the information you need if your goldfish is looking a bit green around the gills. For aquarium links go to Fish Link Central (http://www.fishlinkcentral.com).

Kingsnake.com
http://www.kingsnake.com
A mind-bogglingly enormous portal for reptile and amphibian enthusiasts.

Museum of Non-Primate Art
http://www.monpa.com
Online home of the people behind the "Why cats paint" caper, with special exhibitions devoted to dancing with cats and "bird art".

New Pet.com

http://www.newpet.com

Friendly and informative site for new or soon-to-be owners of a cat or dog.

Pet Cat

http://www.petcat.com

In addition to the usual information and advice, this feline resource allows you to create a virtual cat and even offers horoscopes for Tiddles. See also Moggies (http://www.moggies.co.uk).

Pet Mad

http://www.petmad.com

Despite first appearances, this Irish site is probably the best (and cheapest) online pet shop for UK surfers. For organic food and alternative remedies try Pets' Park (http://www.petspark.com).

Pet Planet

http://www.petplanet.co.uk

Not to be confused with the American site listed below, this site houses one of the UK's best online pet shops, with special features like a lost pet service and rehoming facilities.

The Pet Project

http://www.thepetproject.com

There's a whiff of New Age aromatherapy here ("the special bond between human and animal") and the focus is firmly on the US, but this is surely the most comprehensive pet resource on the Web, with all manner of advice on everything from canine nutrition to interpreting the sounds your chinchilla makes. Other good resources are Acme Pet (http://acmepet.petsmart.com), Pet Channel (http://www.thepet channel.com) and Pet Planet (http://www.petplanet.com).

The Pet Rabbit Web

http://www.petrabbit.com

Online community and resource for rabbit owners. Also try the British House

Rabbit Association (http://www.houserabbit.co.uk) and the House Rabbit Society (http://www.rabbit.org).

Rodent Fancy
http://www.rodentfancy.com
With information on everything from African rock rats to Mongolian gerbils, rodent fanciers shouldn't look anywhere else.

RSPCA Online
http://www.rspca.co.uk
The RSPCA's homepage offers advice, allows the kids to adopt a cyber-pet before getting the real thing and features news and information on campaigns for animal welfare.

Photography

American Museum of Photography
http://www.photographymuseum.com
Exhibitions from back when cameras were a novelty.

Black & White World
http://www.
photogs.com/
bwworld/
A celebration of black-and-white photography.

Digital Camera Resource Page
http://www.dcresource.com
A simple, easy-to-use site, offering reviews of loads of digital cameras and equipment as well as product news and information on issues like Mac OS X compatibility.

Digital Photography Review
http://www.dpreview.com
Considering a new digital camera? Read on.

Photography

Digital Truth: Photo Resource
http://www.digitaltruth.com
Perhaps the best photographic resource for the advanced photographer, with loads of tips, downloadable f-stop calculation software and "the world's largest" film development chart.

Exposure
http://www.88.com/exposure/
A beginner's guide to photography, whose neatest feature is the simulated camera which mimics the effects of adjustments in shutter speed and aperture on pictures.

Life
http://www.lifemag.com
View *Life* magazine's Picture of the Day then link through to some of the world's most arresting photographs. There's even more over at *Time*'s Picture Collection (http://www.thepicturecollection.com) and Australia's Newsphotos (http://www.newsphotos.com.au).

Masters of Photography
http://www.masters-of-photography.com
An excellent collection of the works of some of history's greatest snappers, from Berenice Abbott to Garry Winogrand. In addition to the images there are links to articles and other Websites with biographical and technical information.

Photodisc
http://www.photodisc.com
Plunder these photos free, or pay for the hi-res versions.

PhotoWave
http://www.photowave.com
Portal for professional photographers. Amateurs should try PhotoNet (http://www.photo.net), PhotoLinks (http://www.photolinks.net) or About's photography pages (http://photography.about.com).

PhotoZone
http://www.photozone.de
This site offers comparative analysis of cameras and lenses, and loads of technical information on all sorts of equipment.

Photography

Online Photo Albums

Got some snaps you'd like to show the world – or just your friends (through selective password access)? Upload them here:

Album Pictures http://www.albumpictures.com
Club Photo http://www.clubphoto.com
Photobox http://www.photobox.co.uk
PhotoLoft http://www.photoloft.com
Photopoint http://www.photopoint.com
Yahoo! Photos http://photos.yahoo.com

Pinhole Visions
http://www.pinhole.com
A great site devoted to the art of pinhole photography, a primitive form of picture-taking that creates a dreamlike effect unattainable with conventional photography. There are two gallery spaces, discussion groups, news and links to other resources.

Shutterbug
http://www.shutterbug.net
The online home of the American *Shutterbug* magazine includes a massive archive of past articles, product reviews, news, hints, galleries, competitions and more. Digital photographers should focus on eDigital Photo (http://www.edigitalphoto.com).

Take Better Photos
http://betterphotos.cjb.net
No-nonsense site offering tricks and tips on correcting common photographic errors, picking the best viewpoint, compensating for parallax, computer enhancement, etc, etc. For more serious (really serious) tuition at a cost, try Photo Seminars (http://www.photo-seminars.com).

Year in the Life of Photojournalism
http://www.digitalstoryteller.com/YITL/
Tag along with pros and see what they do day to day.

24 Hours in Cyberspace
http://www.cyber24.com
One thousand photographers save the day.

Politics and Government

Most governmental departments, politicians, political aspirants and causes maintain Websites to spread the word and further their various interests. To find your local rep or candidate, start at their party's home page. These typically lie dormant unless there's a campaign in progress, but can still be a good source of contacts to badger. Government departments, on the other hand, tirelessly belch out all sorts of trivia right down to transcripts of ministerial radio interviews. So if you'd like to know about impending legislation, tax rulings, budget details and so forth, skip the party pages and go straight to the department. If you can't find its address through what's listed below, try:

Yahoo http://dir.yahoo.com/Government/
Open Directory http://dmoz.org/Society/Government/

For the latest election night counts, check the breaking news sites (p.222). Below is a selection of the most useful starting points.

British Politics Links http://www.ukpol.co.uk
Government Portal http://www.open.gov.uk
Green Party http://www.greenparty.org.uk
Labour http://www.labour.org.uk
Liberal Democrats http://www.libdems.org.uk
Natural Law http://www.natural-law-party.org.uk
National Assembly for Wales http://www.wales.gov.uk
Northern Ireland Assembly http://www.ni-assembly.gov.uk
Plaid Cymru http://www.plaidcymru.org
Prime Minister http://www.pm.gov.uk
Scottish National Party http://www.snp.org
Scottish Parliament http://www.scottish-parliament.com
Sinn Féin http://www.sinnfein.ie
Social Democratic and Labour Party http://www.sdlp.ie

Socialist Party http://www.socialistparty.org.uk
Socialist Workers Party http://www.swp.org.uk
Tories http://www.conservatives.com
Ulster Unionist Party http://www.uup.org

Adopt-A-Minefield
http://www.adoptaminefield.com
Help clear war-torn communities of deadly explosives.

Amnesty International
http://www.amnesty.org
Join the battle against brutal regimes and injustice.

Animal Concerns Community
http://animalconcerns.netforchange.com
Online community for animal rights advocates.

Antiwar
http://www.antiwar.com
http://www.iacenter.org
Challenges US intervention in foreign affairs, especially the Balkans and Middle East.

The Big Breach
http://www.thebigbreach.com
Download a free copy of the British MI6 spy-and-tell book.

The British Monarchy
http://www.royal.gov.uk
Tune into the world's best-loved soap opera.

British Politics Pages
http://www.ukpolitics.org.uk
News and history for politicos, with a great links page.

The Complete Bushisms
http://slate.msn.com/Features/bushisms/bushisms.asp/
The subliminal wit and wisdom of George Dubya.

Politics and Government

Center for the Moral Defense of Capitalism
http://www.moraldefense.com
http://www.aynrand.org
Is greed still good in the Y2Ks? Maybe not good but legal, says
Microsoft's last bastion of sympathy.

Central Intelligence Agency
http://www.cia.gov
Want the inside on political assassinations, arms deals, Colombian drug
trades, spy satellites, phone tapping, covert operations, government-
sponsored alien sex cults and the X-files? Well, guess what? Never
mind, you won't go home without a prize see http://www.copvcia.com
and http://www.magnet.ch/serendipity/cia.html/.

Communist Internet List
http://www.cominternet.org
http://www.yclusa.org
Angry intellectuals and workers unite.

Conspiracies
http://www.mt.net/~watcher/
http://www.conspire.com
Certain people are up to something and, what's worse, they're probably
all in it together. If these exposés of the sixty biggest cover-ups of all
time aren't proof enough, then do your bit and create one that's more
convincing: http://www.turnleft.com/conspiracy.html/

Council for Aboriginal Reconciliation
http://www.reconciliation.org.au
Unfinished business in the Lucky (for some) Country.

Disinformation
http://www.disinfo.com
The dark side of politics, religious fervour, new science, along with
current affairs you won't find in the papers.

Doonesbury
http://www.doonesbury.com
Over thirty years of Gary Trudeau's legendary political cartoon.

Electronic Frontier Foundation
http://www.eff.org
Protecting freedom of expression on the Internet.

Fax Your MP
http://www.faxyourmp.com
Pester your local member through an Internet-to-fax gateway.

FBI FOIA Reading Room
http://foia.fbi.gov
FBI documents released as part of the Freedom of Information Act.
Includes a few files on such celebrities as John Wayne, Elvis, Marilyn
and the British Royals. Check out who's most wanted now at:
http://www.fbi.gov

Federation of American Scientists
http://www.fas.org
Heavyweight analysis of science, technology and public policy including national security, nuclear weapons, arms sales, biological hazards,
secrecy and space policy.

Foreign Report
http://www.foreignreport.com
Compact subscription newsletter with a track record of predicting international flashpoints well before the dailies.

Free Tibet
http://www.freetibet.org
Favourite Website of the Beastie Boys and Richard Gere.

Freedom Forum
http://www.freedomforum.org
Organization dedicated to free-speech issues, newsroom diversity and freedom of the press.

The Gallup Organization
http://www.gallup.com
Keep track of opinion trends and ratings.

Gates Foundation
http://www.gatesfoundation.org
See where the world's richest man is spreading it around.

Gay & Lesbian Alliance against Defamation
http://www.glaad.org
Stand up against media stereotyping and discrimination of those deviating from the heterosexual norm.

Gendercide
http://www.gendercide.org
Investigates mass killings were a single gender is singled out.

German Propaganda Archives
http://www.calvin.edu/cas/gpa/
Who did you think you were kidding, Mr Hitler?

Grassroots.com (US)
http://www.grassroots.com
Tracks political action and election policies across the board, aided by *TV Nation* champ Michael Moore: (http://www.michaelmoore.com).

Greenpeace International
http://www.greenpeace.org
Rebels with many a good cause.

Hate Monitor

http://www.hatemonitor.org
http://www.splcenter.org
http://www.publiceye.org
http://www.paragraph175.org
Shining the public flashlight on hate groups and political forces that threaten to undermine democracy and diversity.

Hindu Holocaust Museum

http://www.mantra.com/holocaust/
Contends that the massacre of Hindus during Muslim rule in India was of a scale unparalleled in history, yet an event that has largely gone undocumented.

Illuminati Links

http://www.newnetizen.com/illuminati/illuminatilinks.htm/
All the Web resources you need on the elitist One World government. For a more jovial version, play Illumiati: New World Order The Game (http://www.sjgames.com/inwo/).

InfoWar

http://www.infowar.com
Warfare issues from prank hacking to industrial espionage and military propaganda.

Jane's IntelWeb

http://intelweb.janes.com
Brief updates on political disturbances, terrorism, intelligence agencies and subterfuge worldwide. For a full directory of covert operations, see: http://www.virtualfreesites.com/covert.html/

Liberty

http://www.liberty-human-rights.org.uk
Championing human rights in England and Wales.

MediaAttack

http://www.mediaattack.com
Video clips of talking heads and their celebrity guests put on the spot with awkward questions.

Politics and Government

National Charities Information Bureau
http://www.ncib.org
http://www.charity-commission.gov.uk
Investigate before you donate.

National Forum on People's Differences
http://www.yforum.com
Toss around touchy topics such as race, religion, and sexuality with a sincerity that is normally tabooed by political politeness.

One World
http://www.oneworld.org
Collates news from over 350 global justice organizations.

Open Secrets
http://www.opensecrets.org
Track whose money is oiling the wheels of US politics.
More keeping 'em honest at: http://www.commoncause.org

Oxfam
http://www.oxfam.org
Pitch in to fight poverty and inequality.

The Political Graveyard
http://www.politicalgraveyard.com/
Find out where over 81,000 politicians, diplomats and judges are buried.

Political Wire
http://politicalwire.com
In-depth political news aggregator that is US-heavy but which does cover international politics as well.

Politics Online
http://www.PoliticsOnline.com
It may be subtitled "Fundraising and Internet tools for politics", but this is actually a good general political site, with an emphasis on how connectivity is changing the face of the game.

The Progressive Review
www.prorev.com
Washington dirt dug up from all sides of the fence. For darker soil, try:
http://www.realchange.org

Protest.net – A Calendar of Protest Worldwide
http://protest.net
Find a nearby riot you can call your own.

Revolutionary Association of the Women of Afghanistan
http://www.rawa.org
And you think you have problems with men: http://www.taleban.com

Skeleton Closet
http://www.realchange.org
Exposing the dark side of American politics. More depressing news at
House of Crooks (http://www.sit.wisc.edu/~lsfitzge/).

Spin On
http://www.spinon.co.uk
Play games such as "Stay to the Right of Jack Straw", "Egg Prescott"
and the Hague Goes Trucking Simulator.

Spunk Press
http://www.spunk.org
http://www.infoshop.org
All the anarchy you'll ever need, organized neatly and with reassuring
authority.

Politics and Government

This Modern World
http://www.thismodernworld.com
Archive of Tom Tomorrow's scathing political cartoon.

Threelinewhip.com
http://www.threelinewhip.com
British political e-zine with columns, news, rebel of the month and MPs' voting records. More backbench murmurs at ePolitix (http://www.epolitix.com).

Trinity Atomic Web Site
http://www.fas.org/nuke/trinity/
See what went on, and what went off, fifty-odd years ago, then file into the archives of high-energy weapon testing and see who else has been sharpening the tools of world peace.

UK Census
http://www.statistics.gov.uk
More statistics on the UK and its citizens than you'd care to know.

UK Online
http://www.ukonline.gov.uk
Not to be confused with the ISP, this UK Online aims to be the place where people interact with the government. Like most governmental policies, it seems pretty hazy and to get anywhere you have to dig far too hard.

US Presidential Candidates and their Evil Genes
http://www.nenavadno.com/usaelections2000.html/
Biocybernetic criminals from the 33rd dimension take America.

YouGov
http://www.yougov.com
A good attempt at using the Internet to make government more accountable. There are columns and comment from John Humphrys, Fay Weldon and Ian Hargreaves, plus constantly updated political news. The best features, though, are the People's Parliament, which allows users to vote on the same issues as parliament, a service to create e-petitions and GovDoctor, which identifies MPs, councillors and service managers.

Property

08004homes.com
http://www.08004homes.com
General property portal with sale and rental listings, mortgage advice,
area guides – even an interiors channel.

Bamboo Avenue
http://www.bambooavenue.com
If you're moving house, all the help you'll need under one roof. Also try
The Move Channel (http://www.themovechannel.com) and Really
Moving (http://www.reallymoving.com).

BBC Good Homes
http://www.goodhomes.beeb.com/features/advice/property/
Sensible advice from Auntie on legal issues, dealing with damp and
subsidence and financing.

British Association of Removers
http://www.barmovers.com
Search for a mover who meets the BAR's standards of service.

FinanCenter
http://www.financenter.com
Figure out your monthly payments or what you can't afford.

Home Check
http://www.homecheck.co.uk
An excellent service for prospective home buyers: type in your future
postcode and it will tell you if you need to worry about subsidence,
pollution, air quality, flood risk or if the Triads are likely to firebomb the
flat below.

HouseWeb
http://www.houseweb.co.uk
http://www.findaproperty.com
http://www.propertylive.co.uk
http://www.propertyfinder.co.uk

http://www.propertyfile.co.uk
http://www.property-sight.co.uk
Rent, buy or sell property within the UK. More properties at
Accommodation Directory (http://www.accommodation.com),
Assertahome (http://www.assertahome.com), Easier (http://www.
easier.co.uk), Global Resident (http://www.globalresident.co.uk),
Homefile (http://www.homefileuk.co.uk), Home Free Home
(http://www.homefreehome.co.uk), Homepages (http://www.
homepages.co.uk), Home Sale (http://www.home-sale.co.uk), Home
to Home (http://www.home-to-home.co.uk), HouseNet
(http://www.housenet.co.uk), Let's Direct (http://www.letsdirect.co.uk),
LondonHomeNet (http://www.londonhomenet.com), Mooov
(http://www.mooov.com), Move.co.uk (http://www.move.co.uk),
Pavilions of Splendour (http://www.heritage.co.uk), Property World
(http://www.propertyworld.com), Property Watch (http://www.
propwatch.com) and UK Property Gold (http://www.ukpg.co.uk). For
commercial property, try Comproperty (http://www.comproperty.com).

ihavemoved.com
http://www.ihavemoved.com
Bulk-notify UK companies of your new address.

International Real Estate Digest
http://www.ired.com
Locate real estate listings, guides, and property-related services world
wide.

Islands for Sale
http://www.islandsforsale.com
Get away from it all.
For more opportuni-
ties for isolation, try
Tropical Islands
(http://www.tropical-
islands.com) or
World of Private
Islands (http://www.
vladi-private-islands.de/).

Property Broker
http://www.propertybroker.co.uk
If you live within the M25 you can avoid the middleman and advertise your property here for a flat fee of £78.

UpMyStreet
http://www.upmystreet.com
Astounding wealth of house prices, health, crime, schools, tax and other statistics on UK neighbourhoods. Mighty useful if you're shifting base.

Web Guide to Household Packing
http://www.avatar-moving.com/support/doc_packing_guide.html/
Stock up on bubblewrap.

Radio and Webcasts

While almost all radio stations have a Website, only a fraction pipe their transmissions online. The ever-increasing percentage that do usually broadcast (Webcast) in RealAudio and/or Windows Media Format, so grab the latest copies of both before setting out. Both players come with in-built station directories along with Web-based event guides which are fine for starting out but nowhere near complete. Yahoo and Voquette also run services that keep tabs on notable audiovisual happenings:

RealGuide http://realguide.real.com
Voquette http://www.voquette.com
Windows Media Guide http://windowsmedia.com
Yahoo Events http://www.broadcast.com

Not enough? Then try one of the specialist radio directories. These list physical radio stations with Websites along with full-time stations that only exist online, normally lumped together by country or genre. If they don't provide a direct link to the live feed, visit the station's site and look for a button or link that says "live" or "listen". For a more complete listing of directories, see: http://radiodirectory.com/Stations/Web_Directories/

Internet Radio Directories

ComFM http://www.comfm.fr/live/radio/
Internet Radio List http://www.internetradiolist.com
Listen http://www.listen.com
Live Radio http://www.live-radio.net
Radio Locator http://www.radio-locator.com
RadioNow http://www.radionow.co.uk
RadioWise http://www.radiowise.com.au/stations_live.htm/
Sunset radio http://sunsetradio.com
Virtual Tuner http://www.virtualtuner.com

Apart from the traditional single-stream broadcasters, dozens of sites host multiple feeds. These might be live, on demand, on rotation, archived or one-off events. They tend to work more like inflight entertainment than radio.

Multistream Webcasters

113 Audio http://www.113audio.com
Anime Hardcore http://www.animehardcoreradio.net
Betalounge http://www.betalounge.com
CD Now http://www.cdnow.com/radio/
GoGaGa http://www.gogaga.com
House of Blues http://www.hob.com
Interface http://interface.pirate-radio.co.uk
Listen Radio http://radio.listen.com
LiveConcerts http://www.liveconcerts.com
NetRadio http://www.netradio.net
Online Classics http://www.onlineclassics.net
Radio SonicNet http://radio.sonicnet.com

Spinner http://www.spinner.com
StarCD http://www.starcd.com
The Womb http://www.thewomb.com
Yahoo! Radio http://radio.yahoo.com

There are thousands upon thousands of Webcasters sending their signals into the ether. These are some of the more familiar names and some of the oddest:

BBC Radio
http://www.bbc.co.uk/radio1/
http://www.bbc.co.uk/radio2/
http://www.bbc.co.uk/radio3/
http://www.bbc.co.uk/radio4/
Auntie online, with something for everyone.

BitBop Turner
http://www.audiomill.com
Stupid name, but a great tool: download the software and it monitors online radio stations most likely to play your favourite songs, then records them for playback at your leisure.

De Concertzender
http://www.omroep.nl/concertzender/
A real boon for lovers of "highbrow" music: jazz, classical and New Music from this Dutch terrestrial station.

Dance Portal
http://www.danceportal.co.uk
Can't get out on Friday night? Put on your dancing shoes and point your browser here for Webcasts from, as Pete Tong would probably say, "the most upfront clubs" in the UK. Also check out Clubbed.com (http://www.clubbed.com).

MTV
http://www.mtv.com
It may not be radio, but it does have hundreds of video streams available.

Radio and Webcasts

On the Wire
http://onthewire.hypermart.net
The best reggae on the Web from BBC Lancashire's Steve Barker, with an extra-special 24 hour dub loop for echo fanatics. Try also Black Ark (http://www.blackark.com).

ORANG
http://www.orang.orang.org
The Net may be on big open mic night, but the open access archives here (you can upload your own content) are of an artier, more avant-garde bent.

Solid Steel
http://www.ninjatune.net/solidsteel/
Coldcut have been airing their essential mixes since 1988 on various terrestrial stations; you can listen to almost all of them (with playlists) here.

Swank Radio
http://www.swankradio.com
Spaceage bachelor pad muzak for cocktail enthusiasts and Tiki lovers everywhere.

TM Selector
http://www.tmselector.net
Great resource for those interested in setting up their own online radio station, with tools, advice and links to other underground broadcasters.

Van Halen Radio Network
http://www.vhradio.com
Yup, all Van Halen, all the time.

WFMU
http://www.wfmu.org/radio.html/
Lucky residents of the New York metropolitan area have been able to call this treasure theirs for thirty-odd years. Now you can listen to the best freeform radio station on earth no matter where you live.

WNUR

http://www.wnur.org
Another great American station (from Chicago) covering experimental
and local music better than nearly anyone else.

World of Dance

http://www.wod1.com
Trance, House, Techno and Hard House 24/7. For more Techno, see
Gaialive (http://www.gaialive.co.uk), Inaudible
(http://www.inaudible.com).

Xfm

http://www.xfm.co.uk
Catch London's indie station live online, all the time.

If you fancy setting up your own station or listening to the
online equivalent of pirate radio, try:

GiveMeTalk (Talk only) http://www.givemetalk.com
Icecast.org http://www.icecast.org
Live365 http://www.live365.com
MyPlay http://www.myplay.com
Radio SonicNet http://radio.sonicnet.com
Shoutcast http://www.shoutcast.com
Spotlife http://www.spotlife.com

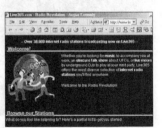

To promote your own sta-
tion or search for a song or
artist currently playing across
thousands of others:

RadioSpy http://www.radiospy.com

For everything else related to professional or amateur radio
broadcasting:

Radio Directory http://www.radiodirectory.com

Crystal Radio
http://www.midnightscience.com
Build a simple wireless that needs no battery.

Interface Pirate Radio
http://www.pirate-radio.co.uk/interface/
Attempting to bring the aural ambience of east London to the Net.

Phil's Old Radios
http://www.antiqueradio.org
If you've ever drifted to sleep bathed in the soft glow of a crackling Bakelite wireless, Phil's collection of vacuum-era portables may instantly flood you with childhood memories.

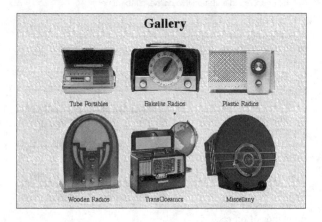

Gallery

Tube Portables | Bakelite Radios | Plastic Radios

Wooden Radios | TransOceanics | Miscellany

Pirate Radio
http://pirateradio.about.com
Stake your claim on the airwaves. More piracy info at How to Be a Radio Pirate (http://www.irational.org/sic/radio/).

Police Scanner
http://www.policescanner.com
http://www.apbnews.com/scanner/
http://www.javaradio.com
Live emergency scanner feeds piped into RealAudio. Eavesdrop on busts in progress. More on scanners at: http://www.strongsignals.net

Reference

With the Net threatening the very foundations of the encyclopedia industry, it should come as no surprise to find most of the household names well entrenched online. While they're not all entirely free, they're certainly cheaper and more up-to-date than their bulky paper equivalents.

Britannica http://www.eb.com
Columbia http://www.bartleby.com/65/
Encarta http://www.encarta.com
Funk & Wagnalls http://www.funkandwagnalls.com
Macquarie http://www.macquariedictionary.com.au

BRITANNICA ONLINE

The premier Web encyclopedia
Now just $5 a month

Subscribers enter here ▼
Individual & Family subscribers
► Forgot Log-In?
College, School, Library & Business users

► Subscription Info
► Use it FREE for 14 days
► Try a sample search
► Learn more about this site
► Purchase a gift certificate for an annual subscription

Acronym Finder
http://www.acronymfinder.com
http://www.ucc.ie/info/net/acronyms/acro.html/
Before you follow IBM, TNT and HMV into initializing your company's name, make sure it doesn't mean something blue.

All Experts

http://www.allexperts.com
http://www.askme.com
http://www.abuzz.com
Ask any question and let unpaid experts do the thinking.

alt.culture

http://www.altculture.com
Witty, digital A-Z o '90s pop culture. Fun to browse, maybe even
enlightening – but don't blow your cool by admitting it.

Alternative Dictionary

http://www.notam.uio.no/~hcholm/altlang/
Bucket your foreign chums in their mother tongue.

American ASL Dictionary

http://www.handspeak.com
http://www.bconnex.net/~randys/
Learn sign language
through simple anima-
tions.

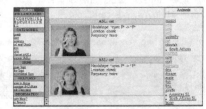

Anagram Genius

http://www.anagram
genius.com
Recycle used letters.

Aphorisms Galore

http://www.
aphorismsgalore.com
Sound clever by repeating someone else's lines.

Babelfish Translator

http://babelfish.altavista.com/translate.dyn/
Translate text, including Web pages, in seconds. Though run some text
back and forth a few times (http://www.telalink.net/~carl/multibabel/)
and you'll end up with something that wouldn't look out of place on a
Japanese T-shirt. If you can't pick the language, try:
http://www.dougb.com/ident.html/

Bartleby Reference
http://www.bartleby.com/reference/
Free access to several contemporary and classic reference works such as the American *Heritage* dictionaries, *Columbia Encyclopedia*, Fowler's *King's English*, Emily Post's *Etiquette*, the *Cambridge History of English and American Literature* and Gray's *Anatomy*.

Biography
http://www.biography.com
Recounting more than 25,000 lives.

Calculators Online
http://www-sci.lib.uci.edu/~martindale/RefCalculators.html/
Awesome directory of some 10,000 online tools to calculate everything from how much sump-oil one puts in soap to the burden of bringing up brats.

Cliché Finder
http://www.westegg.com/cliche/
Submit a word or phrase to find out how not to use it.

Earthstation1
http://www.earthstation1.com
The 20th century captured in sound and vision.

eHow
http://www.ehow.com
Make yourself useful through step-by-step tutorials.

Encyclopedia Mythica
http://pantheon.org/mythica/
Hefty album of mythology, folklore and legend.

Reference

Famous Quotations Network
http://www.famous-quotations.com
Perk up essays and letters with a witticism from Oscar Wilde or a
Senegalese proverb. For more quotes, try The Quotations Page
(http://www.quotationspage.com) or Silly Quotes (http://www.
sillyquotes.com) or Motivational Quotes (http://www.motivational-
quotes.com).

Find Articles
http://www.findarticles.com
No fuss, no muss search engine of more than 300 magazines and journals. The results are all printable and free.

How Stuff Works
http://www.howstuffworks.com
Learn the secrets behind fake tans, animal camouflage and cable
modems.

How to Speak to an Extraterrestrial
http://adrr.com/lingua/alien.htm/
Crash course in ET101.

InfoPlease
http://www.infoplease.com
Handy, all-purpose almanac for stats and trivia.

Ka-BOOM! A Dictionary of Comic Book Words
http://www.geocities.com/Athens/Marathon/5150/dictionary/
Become fluent in the language favoured by leading superheroes.

Librarian's Index
http://www.lii.org
Naturally there are oodles of reference portals brimming with helpful reference tools. These are some of the best:

LibrarySpot http://www.libraryspot.com

Open Directory http://dmoz.org/Reference/

Refdesk.com http://www.refdesk.com

Yahoo http://dir.yahoo.com/reference/

Megaconverter 2

http://www.megaconverter.com/mega2/
Calculate everything from your height in angstroms to the pellets of lead per ounce of buckshot needed to bring down an overcharging consultant.

Nonsensicon

http://www.nonsensicon.com
Non-existent words and their meanings.

Nupedia

http://www.nupedia.com
Nupedia is a new open content encyclopedia project collated by volunteers. You're invited to contribute.

Rap Dictionary

http://www.rapdict.org
Hip-hop to English. Parental guidance recommended.

RhymeZone

http://www.rhymezone.com
Get a hoof up in putting together a classy love poem.

Roget's Thesaurus

http://www.thesaurus.com
New format; useless as ever.

Skeptic's Dictionary

http://www.skepdic.com
Punch holes in mass media funk and pseudo-sciences such as homeopathy, astrology and iridology.

Spellweb

http://www.spellweb.com
http://bodin.org/altameter/
Compare two words or phrases and see which gets more hits in a search engine. If it demonstrates anything, it's that the Web is strung together with a lot of bad spelling.

Slang dictionaries

Playground Slang
http://www.odps.cyberscriber.com
Bridge the generation gap.

A Prisoner's Dictionary
http://dictionary.prisonwall.org
Shhh, a 5-0 is coming.

Silicon Valley Slang Page
http://www.sabram.com/site/slang.html/
For your next meeting with Bill Gates.

Twists, Slugs and Rocoes
http://www.miskatonic.org/slang.html/
Talk like Mike Hammer.

Wizard's Gay Slang Dictionary
http://www.hurricane.net/~wizard/19a.html/
For adults only.

The Straight Dope
http://www.straightdope.com
Cecil Adams's answers to hard questions. Find out how to renounce your US citizenship, what "Kemosabe" means and the difference between a warm smell of colitas and colitis.

Streetmap.co.uk
http://www.streetmap.co.uk
Find a location anywhere in the UK with a postcode, phone number, street name or latitude and longitude. If you're planning a US road trip, try Mapquest (http://www.mapquest.com).

Strunk's Elements of Style
http://www.bartleby.com/141/
The complete classic of English usage in a nutshell, though unfortunately not the latest edition. For more on grammar and style:

alt.usage.English FAQ http://homepages.tcp.co.uk/~laker/faq/
Education Finder http://www.edunet.org/english/grammar/
Garbl's Writing Resources http://www.garbl.com
Montreal Gazette Style Guide http://www.montrealgazette.com/styleguide/

Symbols

http://www.symbols.com

Ever woken up with a strange sign tattooed on your buttocks? Here's where to find what it means without calling in Agent Mulder.

What is?

http://www.whatis.com
http://www.webopedia.com

Unravel cumbersome computer and Internet jargon without having even more thrown at you.

Whoohoo

http://www.whoohoo.co.uk

If you come from Berwick and find yourself in the East End unable to understand a word anyone says, this site may be of help.

The Why Files

http://whyfiles.org

The science behind the headlines.

World Atlas

http://www.worldatlas.com

Maps, flags, latitude and longitude finder, population growth and so on – though you might prefer the maps on paper. For more maps, geography and GPS resources, try About Geography (http://geography.about.com), National Geographic (http://www.nationalgeographic.com/mapmachine) and the Open Directory (http://dmoz.org/Refernce/Maps/).

Learn a language

Arabic http://i-cias.com/babel/arabic/

The French Tutorial http://www.hello.org/education/french/

German For Travellers http://www.germanfortravellers.com

The Japanese Tutor http://www.japanese-online.com

Spain Is Moving http://www.spainismoving.com

World Factbook
http://www.odci.gov/cia/publications/factbook/
Information for spies from the CIA.

Xrefer
http://www.xrefer.com
Consult this site to query a broad selection of prominent reference
works from Oxford University Press, Houghton Mifflin, Penguin,
Macmillan, Bloomsbury and Market House Books.

Yellow Pages
http://www.yell.co.uk
If you're too lazy to flip through the book.

YourDictionary.com
http://www.yourdictionary.com
For one-point access to over a thousand dictionaries across almost
every language. Try also Dictionary.com (http://www.dictionary.com)
and One Look (http://www.onelook.com).

Relationships, Dating and Friendship

The Internet is the biggest singles bar humankind has ever created: with millions and millions of users from around the world,
even the most lovelorn are bound to find someone worth cyber-
flirting with. However, it's worth bearing in mind that the World

Relationships, Dating and Friendship

Wide Web is no different from the real world and there are plenty of scam artists, hustlers, leeches and other unsavoury characters lurking in unsuspected corners. By all means enjoy dropping virtual handkerchiefs to perspective suitors, but keep your wits about you. Before engaging in any social intercourse on the Net, go to Wildx Angel (http://www.wildxangel.com) for advice on the safest way to go on the pull online.

To help you on your way, here are some of the Web's biggest dating agencies:

Dateline http://www.dateline.uk.com
Elite Dating http://www.elite-dating.co.uk
Friendfinder http://www.friendfinder.com
Lovefinder http://www.lovefinder.co.uk
Match.com http://www.match.com
SocialNet http://www.relationships.com
The Switch http://www.theswitch.co.uk
UDate http://www.udate.com
UK Singles http://www.uksingles.co.uk
Web Personals http://www.webpersonals.com
Where's My Date? http://www.wheresmydate.com
WooWho http://www.woowho.co.uk

To find a chat room, try a chat portal like:
The Chat Room Directory http://www.webarrow.net/chatindex/
Chatseek http://chatseek.com
Chat Shack Network http://chatshack.net
The Ultimate Chatlist http://www.chatlist.com

For more, try the Open Directory's chat portal list:
http://dmoz. org/Computers/Internet/Chat/Link_Lists/

Ask-a-Chick
http://www.ask-a-chick.com
Boys ask girls to set them straight.

Relationships, Dating and Friendship

Breakup Girl
http://www.breakupgirl.com
How to mend a broken heart and get on with your life. Here's how not to do it: http://www.crazy-bitch.com

ClassMates.com
http://www.classmates.com
You haven't forgotten. Now track them down one by one. More people who teased you in the common room are at Friends Reunited (http://www.friendsreunited.co.uk).

Cyberspace Inmates
http://www.cyberspace-inmates.com
Strike up an email romance with a prison inmate – maybe even one on death row.

Dating
http://dating.miningco.com/people/dating/
About's dating advice page hosts a motherload of sensible information on dating both on- and offline.

Dating Directories
http://www.cupidnet.com
http://www.singlesites.com
http://www.100hot.com/directory/lifestyles/dating.html/
Come aboard, they're expecting you.

The Divorce Support Page
http://www.divorcesupport.com
Lots of friendly ears and shoulders to cry on.

Hot or Not?
http://www.hotornot.com
http://www.ratemyface.com
Submit a flattering photo and have it rated by passing chumps. So popular it has spawned a string of spoofs, such as: http://www.amigothornot.com; http://www.amigeekornot.com; http://www.amifuglyornot.com; http://www.amipotornot.com; http://www.amiallyourbaseornot.com. To sort by rating, see: http://log.waxy.org/hot/. To instantly create your own custom Am I page: http://www.iamcal.com/ami/l/

Relationships, Dating and Friendship

The Hugging Site
http://members.tripod.com/~hugging/
The history of embracing, hugging stories and tips to improve your cuddling technique.

Javina's Prostitution FAQ
http://www.javina.com/JJ3/faq.html/
Learn the truth behind the *Pretty Woman* fantasy.

Love Calculator
http://www.lovecalculator.com
Enter your respective names to see if you're compatible.

Pen Pal Directory
http://www.yahoo.com/Society_and_Culture/Relationships/Pen_Pals/
Exchange email with strangers.

PlanetOut
http://www.planetout.com
http://www.rainbownetwork.com
http://www.qrd.org
http://www.datalounge.com
http://www.queertheory.com
Directories to all that's that way inclined.

Romance 101
http://www.rom101.com
Chat-up lines, compatibility tests and advice from men to women like "Never buy a 'new' brand of beer because 'it was on sale'."

Secret Admirer
http://www.secretadmirer.com
http://www.ecrush.com
Find out whether your most secret crushed one digs you back.

So There
http://www.sothere.com
A place to post your parting shots.

Swoon
http://www.swoon.com
Dating, mating, and relating. Courtesy of Condé Nast's *Details*, *GQ*, *Glamour*, and *Mademoiselle*. For dessert, try: http://dating.about.com

Tips for Dating Emotional Cripples
http://www.grrl.com/bipolar.html/
The site all women must visit.

Vampire Exchange
http://www.vein-europe.demon.co.uk
http://www.sanguinarius.org
Give blood as an act of love.

Way Too Personal
http://www.waytoopersonal.com
Wild and woolly adventures in Internet dating.

Weddings in the Real World
http://www.theknot.com
http://www.nearlywed.com
Prepare to jump the broom – or untie the knot: http://www.divorcesource.com

Tips for Dating

Emotional Cripples

Religion

If you haven't yet signed up with a religious sect or are unhappy with the one passed down by your folks, here's your opportunity to survey the field at your own pace. Most are open to newcomers, though certain rules and conditions may apply. For a reasonably complete and unbiased breakdown of faith dealerships, try:

BeliefNet http://www.beliefnet.com
Comparative Religion http://www.academicinfo.net/religindex.html/
Religious Tolerance http://www.religioustolerance.org

But don't expect such an easy ride from those demanding proof:

Atheism http://atheism.miningco.com
Christian Burner http://www.christianburner.com
The Secular Web http://www.infidels.org

Anglicans Online
http://anglicansonline.org
A gentle catapult into the Church of England worldwide.

Avatar Search
http://www.AvatarSearch.com
Search the occult Net for spiritual guidance and lottery tips.

The Bible Gateway
http://bible.gospelcom.net
Set your table with the Good Book.

The British Druid Order
http://www.druidorder.demon.co.uk
Dance around Stonehenge, make potions and meet fellow wizards.

BuddhaNet
http://www.buddhanet.net
Take a ride on the wheel of dharma and download the Diamond Sutra.

**Catholic Church –
God's One and Only Church**
http://www.truecatholic.org
More troops armed with the truth.

Catholic Online
http://www.catholic.org
Saints, Angels, shopping, discussion
and a portal to the online territory
occupied by Catholics.

Celebrity Atheist List
http://www.celebatheists.com
Big names you won't spot in Heaven.

Cheesy Jesus
http://www.cheesyjesus.com
http://www.ship-of-fools.com/Gadgets/
Buy gadgets to bring you closer to God

Chick
http://chick.com
Hardcore Christian pornography.

Christian Answers
http://christiananswers.net
Movies and computer games reviewed and hard questions answered, by Christians who know what's good for you and your family.

Christians v Muslims
http://debate.org.uk
http://www.rim.org/muslim/islam.htm/
http://members.aol.com/AllahIslam/
http://www.answering-islam.org
http://www.muslim-answers.org
http://www.biblicalchristianity.freeserve.co.uk
Put your faith on the line.

Christian Naturists
http://home.vistapnt.com/markm/
Frolic with other Christian funseekers, the way God intended.

Church of England
http://www.church-of-england.org
The home of Anglicanism online. Presbyterians should head north of the border at Church of Scotland (http://www.churchofscotland.org.uk).

Church of the Subgenius
http://www.subgenius.com
Find the truth through slackness.

CrossSearch
http://www.crosssearch.com
Set sail through safe waters to find Christian groups of all denominations.

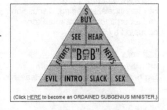

Crosswalk
http://www.crosswalk.com
Catch up with the latest on Jesus.

Demon Possession Handbook
http://diskbooks.org/hs.html/
Train for a job with the Watcher's Council.

Free Deliverance
http://www.demonbuster.com
Use Jesus's teachings to cast out demons, wage spiritual warfare and overcome bipolar disorder, depression, addiction, obesity and other modern ailments.

The Greatest Truth Ever Revealed
http://www.sevenseals.com
Revelations from survivors of the Waco siege.

The Hindu Universe
http://www.hindunet.org
Hindu dharma – the philosophy, culture and customs.

The Holy See
http://www.vatican.va
Official hideout of the pope and his posse.

Islamic Gateway
http://www.ummah.net
http://www.musalman.com
http://www.fatwa-online.com
Get down with Muhammed (*sallallahu `alaihi wa sallam*).

Jah Rastafari
http://www.webcom.com/nattyreb/rastafari/everlasting.html/
A packed site devoted to worshipping Haile Selassie as the living god.

Jesus, a Historical Reconstruction
http://www.concentric.net/~Mullerb/
Getting to the truth about the man from Nazareth.

Jesus of the Week
http://www.jesusoftheweek.com
The original Mr Nice Guy in 52 coy poses per year. Catch him winking at: http://www.winkingjesus.com

The Miraculous Winking Jesus

On April 23rd 1996, this picture of Jesus Christ miraculously winked at me. This experience has changed my life. Over six hundred and thirty thousand people have come to witness this miracle. Many people have had a lot to say about their experience. If you are fortunate enough to witness this image of Jesus Christ wink, please tell your friends and family about this miracle!
- Rev. Jonathan C. Chance (Internet Field Missionary)

[Jesus winked at me!] [Jesus did not wink at me!]

Winking Jesus   Super Store   Reflections   Donate   Contact

Latter Day Designs Vinyl Figures
http://www.lehi.com/vin1.html/
Action figures from The Book of Mormon.

Miracles Page
http://www.mcn.org/1/miracles/
Spooky signs that point towards a cosmic conspiracy.

The 93 Current
http://www.93current.de
The magick of Aleister Crowley. Do more of what thou wilt at An Introduction to Crowley Studies (http://www.maroney.org/Crowley Intro/) and The Works of Aleister Crowley (http://netropic.speakeasy.org/crowley/index.cg/i/).

Not Proud
http://www.notproud.com
Confess your most entertaining sins.

OrishaNet
http://www.seanet.com/Users/efunmoyiwa/
Learn about the Cuban religion of Santeria and consult with Oshun, Ifá and Elegba.

The Pagan Library
http://www.paganlibrary.com
Pagan and Wiccan texts and other information on the mysteries of the Craft.

Peyote Way Church of God
http://www.peyoteway.org
Unless you're Native American or live in select southern US states, you stand to be locked up for finding God through the psychedelic cactus. Otherwise, feel free to fry your brain; just don't drive home from church.

Prophecy and Current Events
http://www.aplus-software.com/thglory/
http://www.prophezine.com
You'll never guess who's coming to dinner. Don't bother cooking, though; he's supposed to be a real whiz with food.

Religious Frauds
http://religiousfrauds.50megs.com
Esteemed reptile slayer David Icke sniffs out Christian cons.

Roy Taylor Ministries
http://www.roytaylorministries.com
"American Pie" is God's song and other examples of questionable hermeneutics.

Saint John Coltrane African Orthodox Church
http://www.saintjohncoltrane.org
Branch of the One Holy Catholic and Apostolic Church whose patron saint is the great jazz saxophonist.

Satinism 101
http://www.satanism101.com
Enter this address and go straight to Hell:
http://www.what-the-hell-is-hell.com
http://www.virtualhell.org

Religion

Shamanism
http://deoxy.org/shaman.htm/
Entheogens, plant sacraments and other ecstatic vehicles.

Ship of Fools: the Magazine of Christian Unrest
http://ship-of-fools.com
The lighter side of Christianity.

Sikh Museum
http://www.sikhmuseum.org
The teachings and history of the main religion of the Punjabi region of India.

Skeptics Annotated Bible
http://www.skepticsannotatedbible.com
Contends that the Good Book is a misnomer.

Spirit Web
http://www.spiritweb.com
Pass the joss-sticks, stroke some crystals, get in touch with your past lives and hitch a ride on a passing UFO.

Stories of the Dreaming
http://www.dreamtime.net.au
Selection of enchanting bedtime stories in text, video and audio that explain creation from an Aboriginal perspective. Don't believe in creation? Go tell it to the jury: http://www.talkorigins.org

Totally Jewish
http://www.totallyjewish.com
http://www.maven.co.il
http://judaism.about.com
http://aish.com
Spiritual guidance and community portals for the chosen people (http://www.chosen-people.com) and curious goyim. More good mozel at JewishNet (http://www.jewishnet.co.uk).

24 Hour Church of Elvis
http://www.churchofelvis.com
No spiritual advice here, just the gift shop.

Universal Life Church
http://ulc.org
Become a self-ordained minister.

The Vodou Page
http://members.aol.com/racine125/
Learn how to convene with the loas.

The Witches' Voice
http://www.witchvox.com
http://www.witchesweb.com
Expresses a burning desire to correct misinformation about witchcraft,
a legally recognized religion in the US since 1985.

Zen
http://www.do-not-zzz.com
Take a five-minute course in meditation.

Science

To keep abreast of science news and developments stop by
Scitech, which aggregates stories from the leading scientific
media:
Scitech Daily Review http://www.scitechdaily.com

Or go straight to one of the many science journals:
Archeology http://www.archaeology.org
Beyond 2000 http://www.beyond2000.com
British Medical Journal http://www.bmj.com
Bulletin of Atomic Scientists http://www.bullatomsci.org
Discover http://www.discover.com
Discovery Channel http://www.discovery.com
Earth Times http://www.earthtimes.org
Edge http://www.edge.org
Highwire Press http://highwire.stanford.edu

Science

The Lancet http://www.thelancet.com
National Geographic http://www.nationalgeographic.com
New Scientist http://www.newscientist.com
Popular Mechanics http://www.popularmechanics.com
Popular Science http://www.popsci.com
Science à GoGo http://www.scienceagogo.com
Science Magazine http://www.sciencemag.org
Science News http://www.sciencenews.org
Scientific American http://www.scientificamerican.com
The Scientist http://www.the-scientist.com
SciQuest http://www.sciquest.com
Skeptical Inquirer http://www.csicop.org/si/
Technology Review http://www.techreview.com

Looking for a something specific or a range of sites within a strand? Try browsing or searching a directory:

About Science http://home.about.com/science/
Hypography http://www.hypography.com
Open Directory http://dmoz.org/Science/
SciSeek http://www.sciseek.com
Treasure Troves of Science http://www.treasure-troves.com
Yahoo http://dir.yahoo.com/science/

Albert Einstein Online
http://www.
westegg.com/
einstein/
In essence an Albert
Einstein portal, with
links to biographies,
quotes, articles and
essays, photos and
other pages related to
Time magazine's Man
of the Century.

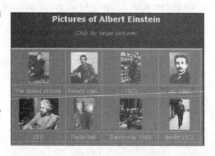

Pictures of Albert Einstein
(Click for larger pictures)

The oldest picture · Patent clerk · 1930 · ca. 1900
1931 · Radio talk · Barcelona, 1923 · Berlin 1922

Amusement Park Physics
http://www.learner.org/exhibits/parkphysics/
If your kid has absolutely no interest in potential and kinetic energy, send them to this fantastic site for the coolest science lesson on the Web and give them the chance to design their own rollercoaster.

AnthroNet
http://www.anthro.net
Gateway to the world of anthropology, archaeology and other social sciences.

Biology
http://mindquest.net/biology/
Vast life-science portal, with highlighted study guides, quizzes and exams for students.

Bizarre Stuff You Can Make in Your Kitchen
http://freeweb.pdq.net/headstrong/
A really fun archive of classic home science experiments from the 1930s to the 1960s. Brings out the Magnus Pike in everyone.

The Braintainment Center
http://www.brain.com
http://www.mensa.org
http://www.iqtest.com
http://www.mind-gear.com
http://www.mindmedia.com
Start with a test that says you're not so bright, then prove it by buying loads of self-improvement gear. Short on brains? Try:
http://www.brains4zombies.com

Bunny Survival Tests
http://www.pcola.gulf.net/~irving/bunnies/
Determining whether marshmallow bunnies can survive lasers, flames, hot tubs, coyotes, radiation and oxygen deprivation. For more rabbit "science", go to The Bunnies Strike Back (http://marks. networktel.net).

Chemistry.org.uk
http://www.liv.ac.uk/Chemistry/Links/link.html/
The chemistry section of the WWW Virtual Library has some 8500 links

to chemistry sites. Advanced chemists should check out ChemWeb (http://www.chemweb.com) and its Available Chemical Directory of 278,000 compounds (you need to subscribe to gain access).

The Constants and Equations Pages
http://tcaep.co.uk
A great reference resource for students of maths and sciences: trigonometric identities, Avogadro's Number, SI units and other memorization headaches.

Cool Robot of the Week
http://ranier.hq.nasa.gov/telerobotics_page/coolrobots.html/
Clever ways to get machines to do our dirty work. For a directory of simulators, combat comps, clubs and DIY bots, direct your agent to: http://www.robotcafe.com

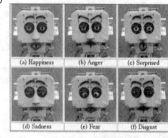

(a) Happiness (b) Anger (c) Surprised
(d) Sadness (e) Fear (f) Disgust

Documentation and Diagrams of the Atomic Bomb
http://serendipity.magnet.ch/more/atomic.html/
Let's hope this doesn't fall into the wrong hands; imagine the effect on your neighbourhood: http://www.pbs.org/wgbh/amex/bomb/sfeature/mapablast.html/

Gray's Anatomy Online
http://www.bartleby.com/107/
The complete edition of the essential anatomical text.

History of Mathematics
http://www-groups.dcs.st-andrews.ac.uk/~history/
The life and times of various bright sparks with numbers.

HotAir – Annals of Improbable Research
http://www.improbable.com
Science gone too far, or around the bend. Includes the Ig Nobel awards for achievements that cannot, or should not, be reproduced.

How Stuff Works

http://www.howstuffworks.com

Unravel the mysterious machinations behind all sorts of stuff from Christmas to cruise missiles.

Institute of Physics

http://www.iop.org

Fast, well-designed physics portal. For articles like "The Industrial Physicist Who Has it All", check out PhysicsWeb (http://physicsweb.org).

Interactive Frog Dissection

http://teach.virginia.edu/go/frog/

Pin down a frog, grab your scalpel and follow the pictures.

The Lab

http://www.abc.net.au/science/

ABC science news and program info with Q&As from Aussie pop-science superstar, Dr Karl Kruszelnicki.

MadSciNet: 24-hour Exploding Laboratory

http://www.madsci.org

Collective of more than a hundred scientific smarty-pantses set up specifically to answer your dumb questions. More geniuses for hire at:
http://www.ducksbreath.com
http://www.wsu.edu/DrUniverse/
http://www.sciam.com/askexpert/
http://www.sciencenet.org.uk

MIT Media Labs

http://www.media.mit.edu

If you've read *Being Digital* or any of Nicholas Negroponte's *Wired* columns, you'll know he has some pretty tall ideas about our electronic future. Here's where he gets them.

Museum of Dirt

http://www.planet.com/dirtweb/dirt.html/

Celebrity dirt of an entirely different nature.

Science

National Inventors Hall of Fame
http://www.invent.org
Homepage of a museum based in Akron, Ohio dedicated to the world's most important inventors. Includes short biographies and pictures of luminaries like Thomas Edison, Enrico Fermi and Louis Pasteur. For more modern inventions, go to Inventions And Technologies (http://www.inventions-tech.com/epanel.htm/), and for questionable inventions see Patently Absurd! (http://www.patent.freeserve.co.uk).

Netsurfer Science
http://www.netsurf.com/nss/
Subscribe to receive weekly bulletins on science and technology sites.

Nobel e-Museum
http://www.nobel.se
Read all about Nobel Prize winners.

Rocketry Online
http://www.rocketryonline.com
Take on NASA at its own game.

Skeptics Society
http://www.skeptic.com
http://www.csicop.org
Don't try to pull a swift one on this crowd.

Strange Science: The Rocky Road to Modern Palentology and Biology
http://www.turnpike.net/~mscott/
A great site exploring the fallout of science's paradigm wars.

Time Travel
http://freespace.virgin.net/steve.preston/
"We discuss many of the common objections to time travel and we show that these objections are without foundation."

USGS National Earthquake Info Center
http://gldss7.cr.usgs.gov
http://www.gps.caltech.edu/~polet/recofd.html/
Stats and maps of the most recent quakes worldwide.

Virtual Autopsy 2

http://www.le.ac.uk/pathology/teach/va2/

Definitely not for the squeamish, this site gives you the opportunity to fish around the insides of eight cadavers and try to determine the cause of death from their case histories.

Volcano World

http://volcano.und.nodak.edu

Monitor the latest eruptions, see photos of every major volcano in the world, and virtually tour a Hawaiian smoky without choking on sulphur fumes.

VoltNet

http://www.voltnet.com

Celebrate the power of electricity by blowing things up. For more exploding objects, see Fun With Surge Generators (http://www.netcomuk.co.uk/~wwl/surge.html/).

WebElements

http://www.webelements.com
http://www.chemsoc.org/viselements/

Click on an element in the periodic table and suss it out in depth. Now crosscheck its comic book reference: http://www.uky.edu/Projects/Chemcomics/ and recite its poem: http://www.superdeluxe.com/elemental/

Weird Science and Mad Scientists

http://www.eskimo.com/~billb/weird.html/
http://www.student.nada.kth.se/~nv91-asa/mad.html/

Free energy, Tesla, anti-gravity, aura, cold fusion, parapsychology and other strange scientific projects and theories.

Why Files
http://whyfiles.news.wisc.edu
Entertaining reports on the science behind current news.

BizRate
http://www.bizrate.com
Shopping sites rated and reviewed. More can be found at
PopularShops.com (http://www.popularshops.com).

Bottom Dollar
http://www.bottomdollar.com
One of the biggest comparison engines or shopping bots: enter a product name or keyword here and it'll return a listing of prices and availability across a range of retailers. Of course, a bargain finder is only as good as its sources, so the best ones scour a broad range of sites. For more deals, try: Dealtime (http://www.dealtime.com), Even Better (http://www.evenbetter.com), Shop Genie (http://www.shopgenie.com), ShopSmart (http://www.shopsmart.com) and Value Mad (http://www.valuemad.com).

Buy.co.uk
http://www.buy.co.uk/Personal/Calculators/
Price and service comparisons of mobile phones, credit cards, electricity, water and gas suppliers. For more info on mobile phone and utilities supplies try uSwitch (http://www.uswitch.com).

Buyersview
http://www.buyersview.co.uk
Similar in some senses to Productopia (see opposite) and other shopping review sites in that it houses consumer reviews and rankings of shopping sites. But it also has added features like Get Me the Manager, an online complaints service, and Abandoned Trolley, which aims to discover why potential online shoppers decided to go elsewhere.

Catalog World

http://www.catalogworld.com

If you're unconvinced by online shopping and would prefer it on paper, drive your postie crazy by ordering every catalogue in the world. For even more junk mail, try Buyers' Index (http://www.buyersindex.com), Catalogs2Go (http://www.catalogs2go.com) and Catalog Site (http://www.catalogsite.com).

Consumer World

http://www.consumerworld.org

Not all of the information here may be appropriate because it's an American site, but this should be an automatic bookmark for anyone intending to do any shopping either on- or offline. Aside from the comparison engines, bargain listings and product reviews, it has alerts on the latest scams and annoying marketing practices.

iWant

http://www.iwant.com

You've been to eBay, Amazon and just about every Internet garage sale you could get to and still can't find what you're after. Try placing a want ad here and see what happens.

LetsBuyIt.com

http://www.letsbuyit.com

This site uses collaborative buying power to clinch lower prices for its members across Europe.

PriceWatch

http://www.pricewatch.com

If you're after computer products, this shopping bot is one of the best comparison engines on the Web. Also try Shopper.com (http://www.shopper.com).

Productopia

http://www.productopia.com

The most thorough collection of buying guides, customer opinions, ratings and links to external reviews. More consumer advice is available at: Amazon (http://www.amazon.co.uk), Consumer Review (http://www.consumerreview.com), Deja (http://www.deja.com), Dooyoo (http://www.dooyoo.com), Epinions (http://www.epinions.com), eSmarts (http://www.esmarts.com), Product Review Net (http://www.productreview.net) and Rateitall.com (http://www.rateitall.com). Of course, there's always Which? (hhtp://www.which.net) for trustworthy consumer advice.

ShittyGift.com
http://www.shitty-gift.com

Like any provincial high street but magnified a million times, the Internet is a minefield of tack and bad ideas. This site is a reminder that taste and bandwidth don't always go hand in hand.

ShopSmart
http://www.shopsmart.com

UK directory of shopping sites. Since it's impossible to be complete, if you can't find what you're after here, try: Buyers' Guide (http://www.buyersguide.to), eDirectory (http://www.edirectory.com), Internet Shopper (http://www.internetshopper.com), My Taxi (http://www.mytaxi.co.uk), No Bags (http://www.nobags.com), Shopfind (http://www.shopfind.com), Shop Finger (http://www.shopfinger.com), UK Shopping (http://www.ukshopping.com) and UK Shop Search (http://www.ukshopsearch.com).

Ybag
http://www.ybag.co.uk

Type in your shopping request here and they will approach several different merchants looking for the best price. Similar services can be found at Buyers' Edge (http://www.buyeredge.com) and myGeek (http://www.mygeek.com).

Silver Surfers

ARP/O50
http://www.arp.org.uk
News, information and forums from the Association of Retired and Persons Over 50.

BBC Health: Health at 50
http://www.bbc.co.uk/health/50plus/
Easily among the best of the BBC sites, largely because – unlike most of the Beeb's pages – it's not dependent on Auntie's programming. The advice is honest and trustworthy and there are no bells or whistles.

Better Government For Older People
http://www.bettergovernmentforolderpeople.gov.uk
Unfortunately, this governmental site is as dull, tedious and cumbersome as its domain name.

FiftyOn
http://www.fiftyon.co.uk
A portal for 50-pluses, with its best and most laudable feature being the advice and vacancies database it maintains for older job seekers.

Hell's Geriatrics
http://www.hellsgeriatrics.com
Grow old disgracefully.

I Don't Feel 50
http://www.idf50.co.uk
A fun, irreverent site run by Graham Andrews, with topics like "Is Age Concern too Old?" and "Mind the Generation Gap".

National U3A UK
http://www.u3a.org.uk
Continuing adult education from the Third Age Trust and the University of the Third Age.

Silver Surfers

Retirement Matters
http://www.retirement-matters.co.uk
Online magazine specializing in news, reviews and information for over-50s.

Saga Magazine
http://www.saga.co.uk/magazine/
Homepage of the magazine for over 50s, with content from the current issue, although there is no archive of past articles.

See How They Grow
http://www.seehowtheygrow.com
A guide to grandparenting, with chat boards, advice and plenty of stories about little monsters.

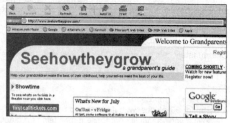

Senior Site
http://www.
seniorsite.com
American online
community for grown-ups, with Pat Boone as the entertainment correspondent and an excellent section on protecting yourself against "senior scams".

Seniority.co.uk
http://www.seniority.co.uk
Like all online communities, this one for senior citizens is only as good as its contributors. While some of Seniority is hit-and-miss, it does have an impressive community spirit.

SeniorsSearch
http://www.seniorssearch.com
Search engine dedicated to resources for silver surfers.

Third Age
http://www.thirdage.com
This American online magazine for older women may look like some ter-

rible advert for feminine hygiene products, but underneath the terrible design is an informative, friendly e-zine.

Write a Senior Citizen
http://www.writeseniors.com
Penpals for seniors.

Space

If you have more than a passing interest in space, skip the popular science mags (p.273) and newswires (p.222), and go straight to the source:
British National Space Centre
http://www. bnsc.gov.uk
European Space Agency
http://www.esrin.esa.it
NASA http://www.nasa.gov

Or try any of these specialist space ports:
About Space http://space.about.com
Amateur Astronomy Magazine http://www.amateurastronomy.com
Astronomy.com http://www.astronomy.com
Astronomy Now http://www.astronomynow.com
Explorezone http://explorezone.com
Human Spaceflight http://spaceflight.nasa.gov
Jet Propulsion Lab http://www.jpl.nasa.gov
Planetary Society http://planetary.org
Sky & Telescope Magazine http://www.skypub.com
Space.com http://www.space.com
Space Daily http://www.spacedaily.com
SpaceRef http://www.spaceref.com
SpaceScience http://www.spacescience.com
Universe Today http://www.universetoday.com

Alien Bases on Earth
http://www.earth-today.com
See, in great detail, where the Gods have parked their chariots.

Alien Scalpel
http://www.alienscalpel.com
Protect yourself against abduction.

Area 51
http://www.terraserver.com/Area51.asp/
Inspect the first public satellite photos of the infamous no-fly zone.

Artemis Project
http://www.asi.org
Join a queue to go to the moon.

AstroCapella
http://www2.smart.net/~ksmale/astrocappella/idea.html/
Learn astronomy through great tunes such as "Doppler Shifting" and "Habitable Zone".

Astronomy Picture of the Day
http://antwrp.gsfc.nasa.gov/apod/astropix.html/
Enjoy a daily helping of outer space served up by a gourmet astrochef.

Auroral Activity
http://www.sec.noaa.gov/pmap/
Instantly see the current extent and position of the auroral oval above each pole.

**Auroras:
Paintings in the Sky**
http://www.exploratorium.edu/learning_studio/auroras/
http://www.alaskascience.com/aurora.htm/
If you're ever lucky enough

to see the Aurora during a solar storm, you'll never take the night sky for granted again. The Exploratorium does a commendable job in explaining a polar phenomenon that very few people understand. Except maybe these champs: http://www.haarp.alaska.edu

Bad Astronomy
http://www.badastronomy.com
Ditch your lifetime's supply of space misconceptions and clichés.

Chandra X-Ray
www.chandra.harvard.edu
Telescope's-eye view of black holes and supernovas.

Clickworkers
http://clickworkers.arc.nasa.gov
Wangle a NASA job onto your résumé by counting craters on Mars.

Comets & Meteor Showers
http://comets.amsmeteors.org
Be on the lookout for falling rocks.

Darksky
http://www.darksky.org
Join the campaign against wanton street lighting. You'll see why in the gallery.

Deep Cold
http://www.deepcold.com
Artistic mockups of chic space racers that never left the hangar.

Earth Viewer
http://www.fourmilab.ch/earthview/
View the Earth in space and time.

Eclipse Cam
http://eclipse.span.ch/liveshow.htm/
You don't even need a special box designed by your science teacher to view this site.

Space

Galactic Information Service
http://home.c2i.net/galactic/torealf/
"Here you will find information about the technology of the spacepeople. UFO pictures. Spacelanguage and pictures from other dimensions/planets".

Geocentricity
http://www.biblicalastronomer.org
Dedicated to proving the sun revolves around the earth.

Heavens Above
http://www.heavens-above.com
Correctly identify nearby satellites and space stations.

Hubblesite
http://hubble.stsci.edu
Intergalactic snapshots fresh from the Hubble telescope.

Hypothetical Planets
http://seds.lpl.arizona.edu/nineplanets/nineplanets/hypo.html/
Paul Schylter's history of planets that have vanished or perhaps existed only in the minds of pre-Hubble scientists.

Inconstant Moon
http://www.inconstantmoon.com
http://www.spacescience.co.uk
Click on a date and see what's showing on the Moon.

International Star Registry
http://www.starregistry.co.uk
Raise your flag in outer space.

Mars Home Page
http://mpfwww.jpl.nasa.gov
Get a bit more red dirt live from NASA's space safari before you stake out your first plot at http://www.marsshop.com. For the latest news, see: http://www.marsnews.com

Mars Society UK
http://www.marssociety.org.uk
British chapter of an organization dedicated to get humans to visit Mars.

The Martian Archives
http://www.infocom.com/~thomil/
Prepare yourself for the coming global superstorm.

MrEclipse
http://www.mreclipse.com
Dabble in the occultations.

Net Telescopes
http://www.telescope.org/rti/
http://denali.physics.uiowa.edu
Probe deep space by sending requests to remote telescopes.

The Nine Planets
http://www.ex.ac.uk/Mirrors/nineplanets/
Bill Arnett's impressive multimedia tour of our solar system.

Retro Aerospace
http://www.retro.com
Recycling simpler, sturdier rockets to make space travel more accessible to the common man.

Rocket Guy
http://www.rocketguy.com/rocket.html/
The homepage of Brian Walker who plans to shoot himself thirty miles into the atmosphere in May 2002. Wish him luck.

Scope Reviews
http://www.scopereviews.com
Read first, buy later – or maybe build your own:
http://www.atmjournal.com

Seti@home
http://setiathome.ssl.berkeley.edu
http://setifaq.org
Donate your processing resources to the non-lunatic end of the search

for extraterrestrial intelligence by downloading a screensaver that analyses data from the Arecibo Radio Telescope. Progress reports at:
http://www.seti.org
http://planetary.org
http://seti.uws.edu.au

Solar System Simulator
http://space.jpl.nasa.gov
Shift camp around the solar system until you find the best view.

Space Adventures
http://www.spaceadventures.com
If you've got $20 million lying around you could become the next Dennis Tito. For the more modest of means, this site offers zero gravity flights and personalized spacesuits just in case.

Space Calendar
http://www.jpl.nasa.gov/calendar/
Guide to upcoming anniversaries, rocket launches, meteor showers, eclipses, asteroid and planet viewings and other happenings in the intergalactic calendar.

Space Weather
http://www.spaceweather.com
http://www.windows.ucar.edu/spaceweather/
Monitor the influence of solar activity on the Earth's magnetic field.

SpaceWeather.com
Science news and information about the Sun-Earth environment.

SPACE WEATHER
Current Conditions

Solar Wind
velocity: **337.0 km/s**
density: **6.6 protons/cm³**
explanation | more data
Updated: Today at 1006 UT

What's Up in Space -- 2 Jul 2001
Subscribe to Space Weather News!

QUIET SUN: The Sun is sprinkled with a half-dozen small sunspots today, but none pose a threat for powerful flares. Forecasters expect solar activity to remain low for the next 48 hours.

Star Stuff
http://www.starstuff.com
Beginner's guides to astronomy for kids.

Sport

For live calls, scores, tables, draws, teams, injuries and corruption inquiries across major sports, try the newspaper sites (p.222), breaking news services (p.225) or sporting specialists like:

SkySports http://www.skysports.com

Sport365 http://www.sport365.com

Sportal (INT) http://www.sportal.com

Sporting Life
http://www.sporting-life.com

Sports.com (Euro)
http://sports.com

Total Sports http://www.total-sports.com

But if your interest even slightly borders on obsession you'll find far more satisfaction on the pages of something more one-eyed. For clubs and fan sites, drill down through Yahoo and the Open Directory. They won't carry everything, but what you'll find will lead you to the right forces:

Open Directory http://dmoz.org/Sports/

Yahoo Sports http://dir.yahoo.com/recreation/sports/

If you can't get to the telly or are looking for Webcasts of that crucial Ryman's League derby, check Sport On Air (http://www.sportonair.com) for listings of streaming audio coverage of sport on the Web.

American Football

NFL
http://www.nfl.com
http://www.nfluth.com
Media schedules, chats, news, player profiles, stats and streaming highlight videos from the National Football League's past and current seasons.

Sport

Athletics

The Athletics Site
http://www.athletix.net
Almost everything you could want to know about athletics – other than how to run as fast as Maurice Greene.

Aussie Rules

Australian Football League
http://www.afl.com.au
Men in tight shorts playing aerial ping-pong.

Baseball

Major League Baseball
http://www.mlb.com
Home of the second most boring sport on earth.

The Baseball Archive
http://www.baseball1.com
The most outrageous complete statistical analysis of sport anywhere. For more lunatic scholarship, see Big Bad Baseball (http://www.bigbadbaseball.com).

Basketball

NBA.com
http://www.nba.com
Pro basketball news, picks, player profiles, analyses, results, schedules and highlight videos.

Boxing

Seconds Out
http://www.secondsout.com
With its merger with Boxing News, this site is effectively a pugilism portal, linking up to just about everything related to the sweet science.

Cricket

Click Cricket
http://www.clickcricket.com
This site may be a bit heavy on coverage of cricket in the Indian sub-continent, but it's one of the few cricket sites that feature tips and advice on playing the game.

Cricinfo
http://www.cricinfo.com
Perhaps a bit like cricket itself this site is a bit creaky and not exactly flashy, but it has all the news and information anyone who hasn't memorised *Wisden* could ever need – from Test level down to local leagues.

Don Bradman bowled by Bill Bowes for a duck in his first Test innings at Melbourne (2nd Test)

334 Not Out
http://www.334notout.com
The "Bodyline Series", the exploits of Donald Bradman and the rest of the history of the Ashes are enshrined at this fun site, along with current news.

Wisden
http://www.wisden.com
Inevitably the voice and Bible of the cricket establishment hasn't yet embraced the potential of the Net. Its current site is a mere shadow of the book, but a revamp is promised.

Cycling

Cycling News
http://www.cyclingnews.com
Tour de force coverage of the Tour De France.

Darts

Toe the Oche
http://www.toetheoche.co.uk
Complete coverage of the professional darts scene, plus a campaign to bring *Bullseye* back to British TV screens.

Sport

Extreme Sports

Adventure Sports Directory
http://www.adventuredirectory.com
http://dmoz.org/Sports/Extreme_Sports/
For all that falls under the banner of "extreme sports" – from taking your
pushbike offroad to the sort of sheer recklessness that would get you
cut from a will. For something more flashy, check out
http://www.pie.com and http://expn.go.com.

Goals – Global Online Adventure Learning Site
http://www.goals.com
Chase adventurous lunatics like Mick Bird, who's circling the globe in a
canoe.

Fishing

Fishing Directories
http://www.thefishfinder.com
http://fishsearch.com
Trade tips and generally exaggerate about aquatic bloodsports.

Fitness

Abdominal Training
http://www.timbomb.net/ab/
Build "abs ripped liked ravioli".

Asimba
http://www.asimba.com
Log your training and nutrition regime online.

Football

Football Ground Guide
http://www.footballgroundguide.co.uk
Comprehensive guide to the homes of all 92 league clubs.

Football365

http://www.football365. co.uk
Everything you need to know about the Premiership and beyond. Not enough news? Try:

FA Premier http://www.fa-premier.com

Nationwide http://www.football.
nationwide.co.uk

One Football http://www.onefootball.com

Planet Football
http://www.planetfootball.com

Rivals Network http://www.rivals.net

Soccer Association http://www.soccerassociation.com

SoccerNet http://www.soccernet.com

When Saturday Comes http://www.wsc.co.uk

Soccerbase http://www.soccerbase.com
For game, club and player stats.

Team Talk

http://www.teamtalk.com
The latest news from every club in Britain constantly updated.

Golf

GolfWeb

http://www.golfweb.com
Unbeatable coverage of the American PGA. For European golf, try Europeantour.com (http://www.europeantour.com). For women's golf, your clubhouse of choice should be the LPGA site (http://www.lpga.com).

OnlineGolf

http://www.onlinegolf.co.uk
Very good all-round shopping site for clubs, shoes, fleeces and balls, plus tips for beginners and experts alike.

Gymnastics

International Gymnast
http://www.intlgymnast.com
Peerless news and views from the competitive gymnastics world. For
training tips and advice on routines, try Girls Gymnastics
(http://www.girlsgymnastics.com) or Gymnastics Routine Directory
(http://www.gym-routines.com).

Hockey

Fieldhockey.com
http://www.fieldhockey.com
Sticks and stuff.

Ice Hockey

The A to Z Encyclopaedia of Ice Hockey
http://www.azhockey.com
Complete coverage of ice hockey throughout the world. For results and
stats from the best league in the world, go to NHL.com
(http://www.nhl.com).

Ice Skating

SkateWeb
http://www.frogsonice.com/skateweb/
News, pics and bios of your favourite stars on ice.

Technical Figure Skating
http://www.nsn.org/eakhome/skating/kevinnew/
Figure-eights, Hammil Camels, Triple toe-loops and more.

Martial Arts

Martial Arts Network
http://www.martial-arts-network.com
All you need to become the next Chuck Norris or Jet Li.

Motorsport

World Motorsport Index
http://www.worldmotorsport.com
Start here for your gasoline-induced pleasure. More revs at Auto Sport (http://www.autosport.com). For more specific pleasures, try:

Atlas F1
http://www.atlasf1.com
Extensive coverage of Formula 1.

Indy Car Racing
http://www.indyracingleague.com
All the news from the Brickyard.

Monster Truck Racing
http://www.ushra.com/m_trucks.html/
Put a pinch of chewing tobacco between your cheek and gum and watch Grave Digger and cohorts squash some bugs.

Motograndprix.com
http://www.motograndprix.com
Just about every motorcycle event in the world is covered here.

NASCAR
http://www.nascar.com
Dixie's favourite stock cars.

World Rallying
http://www.worldrally.net
Small cars sliding into trees and skidding in the mud.

Rugby

Planet Rugby
http://www.planet-rugby.com
http://www.rleague.com
http://www.ozleague.com
http://www.scrum.com

http://www.rugbyheaven.com
Up-to-the-minute coverage of hard men trotting in and out of the blood bin, plus columnists, a historical archive, rules and a shop.

Sailing

Sailing Index
http://www.smartguide.com
http://www.madforsailing.com
Everything seaworthy: from swapping yachts to choosing a GPS.

Skiing

SkiCentral
http://www.skicentral.com
http://www.skiclub.co.uk
Indexes thousands of ski-related sites covering such things as snow reports, resort cams, snowboard gear, accommodation and coming events in resorts across the world. For snowboarding, see:
http://www.soltv.com
http://www.boardtheworld.com.au
http://www.twsnow.com
http://www.board-it.com

Snooker

SnookerNet
http://www.snookernet.com
All the news from the bays, plus masterclasses from Terry Griffiths.

Statistics

Stats
http://www.stats.com
Pig out to an overflowing trough of US sport statistics.

Surfing

Swell
http://www.swell.com
Unquestionably the best surfing site on the Web, with a magazine, shop, numerous Webcams and free surfing forecasts for the entire world which you can have emailed out – alerting you when a killer wave is headed to your local break.

World Surfing

http://www.goan.com/surflink.html/
Every day's like Big Wednesday. For daily breaks and Aussie seaboard cams, see: http://www.coastalwatch.com

Swimming

Swimmersworld.com
http://www.swimmersworld.com
Coverage of the competitive swimming scene.

WebSwim
http://www.webswim.com
The FAQ of the rec.sport.swimming newsgroup, with information on training, suits, etc.

Tennis

Tennis.com
http://www.tennis.com
All the news from the pros, plus instructional sections, racquet and shoe reviews, pro endorsements and fitness tips.

Wrestling

For the official line, go to WWF (http://www.wwf.com), but for the unofficial line and the bottom line, try:

Sport

You call that a sport?

British Minigolf Association
http://members.aol.com/MiniGolf98/

You won't be laughing when you find out that tournament prize money can reach $100,000.

Canadian Amateur Tug of War Association
http:// www.tugofwar.ca

You're just pulling my leg.

Disc Golf World
http://www.discgolfworld.com

The latest news from the frisbee golf scene, plus all the "drivers" and "putters" you'll ever need.

International Beltsander Drag Racing Association
http://www.beltsander-races.com

All the news and highlights from the fast-paced, laugh-in-the-face-of-death world of beltsander drag racing.

PaintBall.com
http://www.paintball.com

All the information you need to make life hell for the groom-to-be.

World Elephant Polo Association
http://elephantpolo.com

How is it that a team from Iceland is the best in the world?

The DDT Digest
http://www.ddtdigest.com

Great wrestling zine, with the history of blading, the downfall of the WCW in pictures, vintage programmes and other crucial tidbits of wrestling ephemera.

1Wrestling.com
http://www.1wrestling.com

For coverage of the grappling world beyond the WWF and for the most influential coverage of the big boys, this should be your first wrestling bookmark. For more news, check out Wrestle Line (http://www.wrestleline.com).

Solie's Vintage Wrestling
http://members.aol.com/Solie/
Do you remember grappling before Vince McMahon's delusions of grandeur or do you have no idea who Kerry Von Erich, Magnum TA or Bruno Sammartino are? Either way you need to visit this shrine to the squared circle's old school.

Telecoms

The Big Number
http://www.numberchange.org
Having trouble getting to grips with the ever-changing telephone exchanges? Try this official site or UK STD Dialing Codes (http://www.brainstorm.co.uk/utils/std-codes.html/).

Campaign for Unmetered Telecommunications
http://www.unmetered.org.uk
http://www.telecom.eu.org
Rail against the call-charging system that's making Europe an Internet backwater.

Directory Enquiries
http://www.bt.co.uk/phonenetuk/
BT's directory enquiries site. For other British phone searches, try Numbercheck (http://www.numbercheck.co.uk), 192.com (http://www.192.com), Thomson Directories (http://www.thomweb.co.uk), UK Phone Book (http://www.ukphonebook.com) and the Yellow Pages (http://www.yell.co.uk).

Free Fax Services
http://www.tpc.int
Transmit faxes via the Internet free.

Telecoms

Efax
http://www.efax.com
http://www.j2.com
Free up a phone line by receiving your faxes by email.

Letterpost
http://www.letterpost.com
Buy a stamp. Type a message. Have it posted.

MobileWorld
http://www.mobileworld.org
http://www.unwin.co.uk/phonez.html/
Assorted info on mobile phones and cellular networks.

The Payphone Project
http://www.payphone-project.com
An utterly bizarre site devoted to that near-extinct dinosaur of 20th century technology, the payphone. Includes payphone news, history of the payphone, photos and numbers. For more payphone numbers, try the Pay Phone Directory (http://www.payphone-directory.org).

Postcode Pages
http://www.grcdi.nl/linkspc.htm/
Find a postcode in almost any country.

Reverse Phone Directory
http://www.reversephonedirectory.com
Key in a US phone number to find its owner. To find a UK location see:
http://www.warwick.ac.uk/cgi-bin/Phones/nng/

SMS Text Messages
http://www.quios.com
http://www.mtnsms.com
Send free text messages to mobile phones worldwide.

Splash Mobile
http://www.SplashMobile.com
Ring tones, logos, games and other essential accessories for your mobile. The site pays fees to the MCPS, so you can rest assured that the composer of the *Knight Rider* theme will get his just royalties. Other ring tone sites:

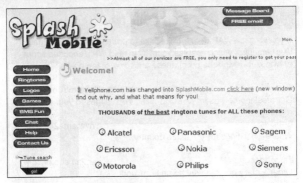

Jippii! http://www.jippii.co.uk

Mobilerings http://www.mobilerings.co.uk

Mobile Tones http://www.mobiletones.com

Monstermob http://www.monstermob.com

Phunky Phones http://www.phunkyphones.com

Ringtones Online http://www.ringtones.co.uk

Your Mobile http://www.yourmobile.com

The Telegraph Office
http://fohnix.metronet.com/~nmcewen/tel_off.html/
http://www.navyrelics.com/tribute/bellsys/
Trip through the history of wired communications from Morse telegraphy to the Bell System.

UK.Telecom FAQ
http://www.gbnet.net/net/uk-telecom/
Satisfy your curiosity about the British phone network.

UK Telecom Tariff Comparisons
http://www.magsys.co.uk/telecom/
Compare the prices of leading landline phone service providers for free, but if you want business rate comparisons or to view the results in spreadsheet format you've got to subscribe. For mobile phone rates, try

WAP Sites

If you've got a WAP phone or just like to pretend that you do (get a WAP emulator which enables your PC to read WML encoded script at http://updev.phone.com), these are some of the best sites:

Ananova www.ananova.com/alerts/list.html/bodytext/
Get breaking news sent as customized WAP pages to your phone.

Ents24 www.ents24.co.uk
What's-on listings for the entire country.

Jamshoes wap.jamshoes.com
Order a curry on your way home from work.

Mail2Wap http://www.mail2wap.com
Collect your POP3 mail on a WAP phone.

Mobile WAP www.mobilewap.com
The largest WAP search engine.

Railtrack www.railtrack.co.uk/wap/
Why talk to an operator at the National Rail Enquiries line when you can have the info zapped to your phone instead?

Unmissable TV www.unmissabletv.com/txw/wap.wml/
Plan your evening's sofa surfing while on the Tube home.

WAP-A-Result www.waparesult.com
Up-to-the-minute sports scores.

uSwitch (http://www.uswitch.com/Mobiles/) or Buy.co.uk (http://www.buy.co.uk/Personal/Calculators/mobiles.asp/).

What Does Your Phone Number Spell?
http://www.phonespell.org
Enter your phone number to see what it spells. The reverse lookup might help you choose a number.

World Time & Dialing Codes
http://www.whitepages.com.au/wp/search/time.html/
International dialing info from anywhere to anywhere, including current times and area codes.

Television

Most TV stations maintain excellent sites with all kinds of extras such as live sports coverage and documentary follow-ups. We won't need to give you their addresses because they'll be flashing them at you at every opportunity. In any case, you'll find them all at: http://www.tvshow.com

For personalized listings, perhaps delivered by email, try your local Yahoo or:
http://www.uk-tv-guide.com
http://www.cableguide.co.uk
http://www.unmissabletv.com
http://www.ananova.com/tv

The best of these, however, might be: Digiguide (http://www.digiguide.co.uk) which is a customizable listings database that covers terrestrial, cable, digital and satellite. You download the site's free software, tell the program which region you live in or whether you have cable or digital and then download the next two week's worth of listings.

To be notified when something's on:

Spyonit http://www.spyonit.com

asSeenonScreen
http://www.asseenonscreen.com
Buy stuff you've seen on TV or in movies.

Bigglethwaite.com

http://www.bigglethwaite.com

With its comprehensive links page to UK TV Websites, this is a good place to start any search.

Broadcast.com

http://www.broadcast.com/television/

With Yahoo's broadcast site, you can watch local US stations to your heart's delight.

Drew's Script-O-Rama

http://www.script-o-rama.com/snazzy/tvscript.html/

A huge set of links to an astonishing array of predominantly American television scripts and episode transcripts. Also try Daily Script (http://www.dailyscript.com) and Simply Scripts (http://www.simplyscripts.com).

Epguides

http://epguides.com

If you're serious about TV – really, really serious – this site is your holy grail. Containing complete episode guides for over 1700 shows (mostly American) which are linked to the Internet Movie Database for cross-referencing, this is an amazing research tool for academics, journalists, enthusiasts and general freaks. For similar coverage of Britcoms, try TV Comedy Resources (http://www.phill.co.uk), or Hu's Episode Guides (http://www.episodeguides.com) and Mighty Big TV (http://www.mightybigtv.com).

Jump The Shark

http://www.jumptheshark.com

Named after that episode in *Happy Days* when Fonzie ski-jumped over a shark, starting the show's inexorable downward spiral, this brilliant site is dedicated to documenting the moment when your favourite programme goes south. Signals of impending doom include same-character-different-actor,

puberty, "A very special..." and the presence of Ted McGinley (aka Jefferson on *Married With Children*).

Live TV
http://www.comfm.fr/live/tv/
Tune into live video feeds from hundreds of real world television stations. To record US cable shows and play them back in Real Video (court case pending) see: http://www.recordtv.com

Sausagenet
http://www.sausagenet.co.uk
Tribute to cult and vintage television shows that babysat for Generation X. It has a reviews section (covering video and DVD releases of old programmes) and downloadable sound files, but is most useful as a portal for retro TV enthusiasts.

Sitcoms Online
http://www.sitcomsonline.com
Very US-focused, but if you're looking for any information on a Yankee comedy, this is the first place to look. There are also games, discussions and polls that are fun for any comedy enthusiast regardless of nationality.

Skyride
http://www.skyride.co.uk
An interesting history of Rupert Murdoch's efforts to bring satellite television to the UK. Check out Independent TeleWeb (http://www.itw.org.uk) for similar coverage of independent commercial broadcasting.

Soap City
http://www.soapcity.com
http://members.tripod.com/~TheSoapBox/
http://www.soapweb.co.uk (UK)
http://www.soapdigest.com
Keep up with who's doing what to whom, who they told and who shouldn't find out in the surreal world of soap fiction.

Television Commercials
http://www.televisioncommercials.com
If you can't get enough of them on TV, then point your browser here

immediately and search a mindblowing database of over 30,000 adverts. Other ports of call: Ad Slogans (http://www.adslogans.co.uk), Ad Critic (http://www.adcritic.com), Commercial Archive (http://www.commercialarchive.com), Digi Reels (http://www.digireels.co.uk) and UK Television Adverts (http://www.westwood.u-net.com/ads/).

Test Card Circle
http://www.testcardcircle.org.uk
The homepage of Test Card Circle, an organization of enthusiasts of the music that accompanied the test card sequences that reigned over British TV in the dark days before cable.

The 30 Second Candidate
http://www.pbs.org/30secondcandidate/
A fascinating history of the political TV spot from PBS, America's answer to the BBC.

Transdiffusion
http://www.transdiffusion.org
A truly fantastic resource for anyone interested in the history of British broadcasting, this site hosts the archives of the Transdiffusion Organisation, which is dedicated to preserving the history of radio and TV in the UK. Included are screen grabs from TV coverage of historical moments, jingles, theme tunes, in-depth articles on various aspects of broadcasting history and course notes for students and teachers.

TV Ark
http://www.tv-ark.co.uk
With its focus on arcana and minutiae, this online museum of British television is one for true believers. Mostly downloadable sound and video files of station identifications and theme tunes at the moment, but videos and information are promised in the future.

TV Cream
http://tv.cream.org
This is everything the Web is meant to be all about: tons of useless knowledge and remembrances by people who should know better. This one features naff telly from the '60s, '70s and '80s, photos of Henry Kelly, station idents from a time when "digital" meant an LCD watch and maths lessons with Lesley Judd. For less tongue-in-cheek cover

Regional TV archives

With big media companies like Carlton and Granada dominating ITV, the halcyon days of regional broadcasting are almost gone. However, since television breeds lunacy like no other medium, there are a number of enthusiasts throughout the country dedicated to preserving the memory of low production values, terrible clothes and hopeless segues.

ATV Unofficial Web Site
http://members.nbci.com/atvnetwork/atvhome.htm/
A tribute to the sadly departed Midlands broadcaster.

Border Television Area
http://www.bordertvarea.co.uk
Comprehensive archive of ITV in the North.

Harlech House of Graphics
http://freespace.virgin.net/farcical.films/
Thirty years of ITV in the West and Wales.

ITV Southern England
http://members.tripod.co.uk/Southern_TV/
Independent telly from the South since 1958.

Television Southwest
http://www.television-southwest.co.uk
Dedicated to ITV in the West Country.

Tyne Tees Logo Page
http://www.durge.org/~bods/tv/tynetees/
A wry look at the North East's independent station.

age of the same territory, try Classic Television (http://www.classic television.com), Spud TV (http://www.spudtv.com) for an American perspective or Whirligig (http://www.whirligig-tv.co.uk) for a trip back to the 1950s.

TV Eyes
http://www.tveyes.com
Informs you when your search term is mentioned on TV.

TV Go Home
http://www.tvgohome.com
Onion-style parodies of *The Radio Times*.

TV Party
http://www.tvparty.com
Irreverent, hilarious and more fun than a barrel of Keith Chegwins, this American site is the hall of fame that the medium truly deserves. Included are an amazing archive of uncensored out-takes, frighteningly in-depth articles about all manner of televisual ephemera and pull-no-punches features on programmes.

TV Show
http://www.tvshow.com
Everything TV – from schedules of every station worldwide and links to just about every show ever made to the technical aspects of production and broadcasting. Start all your TV-related searches here.

TV Tickets
http://www.tvtickets.com
Secure your chance to clap on cue.

VCR Repair Instructions
http://www.fixer.com
How to take a VCR apart and then get all the little bits back in so it fits easier into the bin.

VCR Repair Instruction

TV Programmes

The Web would be nothing without people who have obsessions that transcend rational thought, and television is particularly well-served by fanaticism. Here are some of the best sites devoted to a single show.

Angelic Slayer   http://www.angelicslayer.com
Run by a teenage fan from Arizona, this rather amazing site devoted to *Buffy The Vampire Slayer* and *Angel* has attracted over two million hits.

Corrie Net   http://www.corrie.net
This Coronation Street archive has everything everyone could ever want to know about Ken Barlow and Hilda Ogden.

Erinsborough.com   http://www.erinsborough.com
Catch up with all the gossip from Ramsay Street.

Frank Butcher's Philosophical Car Lot   http://geocities.com/SunsetStrip/Stadium/1123/page1.html/
RealAudio clips of *EastEnders*' philosopher-king.

Friends Place   http://www.friendsplace.com
Every script of every episode ever. But if you have that much spare time it might make you wish you had some of your own.

Jupiter Mining   http://www.jupitermining.com
Homepage of the *Red Dwarf* fan club.

Thrift Funnel   http://www.koekie.org.uk/funnel/
Site devoted to the warped comedy and media terrorism of Chris Morris.

Virtue TV
http://www.virtuetv.com
If you're one of the lucky few with broadband access, this virtual chan-

nel features independent short films, an archive of music concerts and sports footage.

Who Would You Kill?
http://www.whowouldyoukill.com
So who would you toss into Dawson's Creek?

Calendarzone
http://www.calendarzone.com
Calendar links and, believe it or not, calzone recipes.

DateReminder
http://www.datereminder.co.uk
http://www.cvp.com/freemind/
Remind yourself by email.

The Death Clock
http://www.deathclock.com
Get ready to book your final taxi.

Heroes of Horology
http://www.shadow.net/~bobt/heroes/heroes.htm/
A picture gallery of history's greatest timekeepers.

Horology – The Index
http://www.horology.com
This text-heavy portal to all things pertaining to the science of time-keeping includes information on collecting timepieces, email addresses of "cyber-horologists" and links to horological organisations.

International Earth Rotation Service
http://hpiers.obspm.fr
Ever felt like your bed's spinning? The truth is even scarier.

iPing (US)
http://www.iping.com
Arrange free telephone reminders for one or many.

Martian Time
http://members.nbci.com/mars_ultor/mars/calendar.htm/
Learn exactly when the little green men will be coming.

Metric Time
http://www.billcollins.com.au/bc/mt/
Decimalized excuses for being late.

Online Planners
http://www.dailydrill.com
http://www.appoint.net
http://www.when.com
http://www.visto.com
Maintain your planner online. Excite, Yahoo, MSN, and Netscape offer similar things.

Time and Date
http://www.timeanddate.com
http://www.smh.com.au/media/wtc/smhwtc.html/
Instantly tell the time in your choice of cities. Keep your PC clock aligned with a time synchronizer: http://www.eecis.udel.edu/~ntp/software.html

Time Cave
http://www.timecave.com
Schedule an email to be sent at a specific time in the future.

Time Cube
http://www.timecube.com
Disprove God through the simultaneous 4-day Time Cube.

US National Debt Clock
http://www.brillig.com/debt_clock/
Watch your children's future slip away.

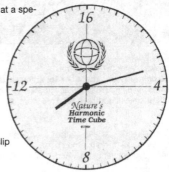

USNO Master Clock Time
http://tycho.usno.navy.mil/what.html/
Compute the local apparent sidereal time in your part of the world or listen to a live broadcast of the USNO Master Clock announcer. Get your computer's clock set by modem at:
http://tycho.usno.navy.mil/modem_time.html/

End of the Line
http://www.vcom.cwc.net
Site devoted to the faded (and rusting) glory of withdrawn locomotives lying on the scrap heap.

Loco Watch
http://www.locowatch.com
This detailed news magazine for enthusiasts of both modern and historical railways includes regular updates on which locomotives are being serviced, news and listings of rail tours, photos and resources for spotters.

Mike Wright's Roaring Forties Web Site
http://www.d-m-hall.demon.co.uk
Site boasting twenty Real Audio files of Class 40 diesel locomotives in full song.

Steamy Affairs

Railway preservation may not have the hippest image in the world, but steam engines are enjoying a renaissance throughout the world. The UK currently boasts around 430 miles of track (more than the London Underground) used by the country's 1200 steam engines. Here are a few sites devoted to historical railways both in Britain and abroad.

Richard Leonard's Steam Locomotive Archive
http://members.aol.com/rlsteam/
Nostalgia-sodden photos of North American railroads in the '50s.

Mainline Steam Tours Index
http://www.march.demon.co.uk/tours
Listings of steam locomotive journeys in the UK.

Steam Dreams
http://www.steamdreams.co.uk
The Cathedrals Express

Team Central
http://www.steamcentral.com
Steam locomotion from an American perspective.

UK Heritage Railways
http://ukhrail.uel.ac.uk
Guide to the UK's heritage railway scene.

Vintage Trains
http://www.vintagetrains.co.uk
A collection of steam engines preserved by the Birmingham Railway Museum Trust.

Rail Britain
http://www.railbritain.com
A big site aimed at both the traveller and the enthusiast, including

news, chat rooms, timetables, maps, rolling stock guides and fleet information. For similar – if less professional – coverage from a strictly enthusiast perspective, try http://www.gbrail.org.uk and http://www.railnet.org.uk.

Steam Locomotive
http://www.steamlocomotive.com

This impressive American site is a storehouse of information on steam trains geared towards the serious, tech-minded enthusiast. Includes detailed information on wheel arrangements, horsepower and hundreds of locomotives from the golden age of rail travel.

Track Bed
http://www.trackbed.com

An impressive site aiming to become the online authority on British rail history. The database includes comprehensive histories of the UK's main rail companies, routes, maps, an in-depth (100k) glossary and photos.

Train Orders
http://www.trainorders.com

Railway hobby site hosting lots of discussion groups, rail cams covering two Californian main lines, quizzes and an archive of over 1,000 loco photos.

Train Web
http://www.trainweb.org

This portal is a train spotter's paradise. In addition to a site catalogue cleverly organised as both white and yellow pages, Train Web hosts chat rooms, forums, photo collections, the Rail Search search engine and the ever-popular Railcams.com so you can catch the Flying Scotsman without ever leaving your armchair.

Travel

Whether you're seeking inspiration, planning an itinerary, shopping for a ticket or already mobile, there'll be a tool online worth throwing in your box. You can book flights, reserve hotel rooms, research your destination, monitor the weather, convert currencies, learn the lingo, locate an ATM, scan local newspapers, collect your mail from abroad, find a restaurant that suits your fussy tastes and plenty more. If you'd like to find first-hand experiences or travelling companions, hit the Usenet discussion archives at Google (http://groups.google.com) and join the appropriate newsgroup under the rec.travel or soc.culture hierarchies. As with all newsgroups, before you post a question, skim through the FAQs first:

Rec.Travel Library http://www.travel-library.com

Air Travel Handbook http://www.cs.cmu.edu/afs/cs/user/mkant/Public/Travel/airfare.html

You could also try consulting a volunteer "expert".

Abuzz http://www.abuzz.com/category/travel/

All Experts http://www.allexperts.com/travel/

Ask Me http://www.askme.com

Then see what the major guidebook publishers have to offer:

Fodors http://www.fodors.com

Frommer's http://www.frommers.com

Insiders http://www.insiders.com

Let's Go http://www.letsgo.com

Lonely Planet http://www.lonelyplanet.com

Michelin http://www.michelin-travel.com

Moon Travel http://www.moon.com

Rough Guides http://www.roughguides.com

Routard http://www.club-internet.fr/routard/

Robert Young Pelton http://www.comebackalive.com

Alternatively, check out online guides such as:

Beachtowel http://www.beachtowel.co.uk

CityVox http://www.cityvox.com

IExplore http://www.iexplore.com

Locals in the Know http://www.localsintheknow.com

World Travel Guide http://www.wtg-online.com

While it might seem like commercial suicide for the Rough

Guides to give away the full text of its guides to more than 10,000 destinations, the reality is that books are still more convenient, especially on the road when you need them most. If you'd like to order a guide or map online you'll also find plenty of opportunities either from the above publishers, the online bookshops (p.66), or from travel bookshops such as:

Adventurous Traveler http://www.atbook.com
Literate Traveler http://www.literatetraveller.com
Stanfords http://www.stanfords.co.uk

Many online travel agents also provide destination guides, which might include exclusive editorial peppered with chunks licensed from guidebooks linked out to further material on the Web. For example:

Away.com http://away.com
Escaperoutes http://www.escaperoutes.net
Travel Vision http://www.travelvision.com

The biggest problem with browsing the Web for regional information and travel tools is not in finding the sites, but wading through them. Take the following directories for example:

About Travel http://travel.about.com
Budget Travel http://www.budgettravel.com
Excite Travel http://travel.excite.com
Lycos Travel http://travel.lycos.com
Open Directory http://dmoz.org/Recreation/Travel/
My Travel Guide http://www.mytravelguide.com
Traveller Online http://www.travelleronline.com
World Travel Net http://www.world-travel-net.com
Trip Advisor (US) http://www.tripadvisor.com
Virtual Tourist http://www.vtourist.com
World Travel Guide http://www.travel-guide.com
Yahoo Directory http://www.yahoo.com/Recreation/Travel/
Yahoo Travel http://travel.yahoo.com

These are perfect if you want to browse through regions looking for ideas, or find a range of sites on one topic – health, for example. But if you're after something very specific, you might find it more efficient to use a search engine such as Google (see p.5). Keep adding search terms until you restrict the number of results to something manageable. If you'd like to coincide your vacation with a festival or event, go straight to:

What's on When http://www.whatsonwhen.com
What's Going On http://www.whatsgoingon.com

Or for entertainment, eating, and cultural events, a city guide:

Citysearch http://www.citysearch.com
Sidewalk http://www.sidewalk.com.au
Time Out http://www.timeout.co.uk
Wcities.com http://www.wcities.com
Yahoo Local http://local.yahoo.com
Zagat (Dining) http://www.zagat.com

If you're flexible, you might find a last-minute special. These Net exclusives are normally offered directly from the airline, hotel, and travel operator sites, which you'll find through Airlines.com (http://www.airlines.com) or Yahoo. There are also a few Web operators that specialize in late-notice and special Internet deals on flights, hotels, events, and so forth, such as:

Bargain Holidays http://www.bargainholidays.com
Best Fares http://www.bestfares.com
Lastminute.com http://www.lastminute.com
Lastminutetravel.com http://www.lastminutetravel.com
Smarter Living http://www.smarterliving.com
Travel Zoo http://www.travelzoo.com

Then there are the reverse-auction sites like Priceline.com where you bid on a destination and wait. You might strike up a good deal if you bid shrewdly and don't mind the somewhat draconian restrictions (see: http://www.angelfire.com/nt/priceline/).

Hotwire offers similar discounts on undisclosed airlines but names the price up front. If you're super-flexible, you could try Airhitch or a courier company:

Air Courier Assoc. http://www.aircourier.org
Airhitch http://www.airhitch.org
Hotwire http://www.hotwire.com
IAATC Air Courier http://www.courier.org
Priceline.com http://www.priceline.com

Booking a flight through one of the broad online ticketing systems isn't too hard either, but bargains are scarce. Unless you're spending someone else's money you'll want to sidestep the full fares offered on these major services:

Expedia http://www.expedia.co.uk
Travelocity http://www.travelocity.co.uk
Travel Select http://www.travelselect.co.uk

Although they list hundreds of airlines and millions of fares, the general consensus is that they're usually better for research, accommodation and travel tips than cheap fares and customer service. So if you think it's worth the effort, drop in and check which carriers haul your route, offer the best deals and still have seats available. You can then use their rates as a benchmark. Compare them with the fares on the airline sites and discount specialists such as:

Bargain Holidays http://www.bargainholidays.com
Cheap Flights http://www.cheapflights.com
Deckchair http://www.deckchair.com
Ebookers.com http://www.ebookers.com
Flight Centre http://www.flightcentre.com
1Travel.com http://www.1travel.com

Or compare the prices across several agencies simultaneously using these sites:

Farechase http://www.farechase.com
Hotwire http://www.hotwire.com

QiXO http://www.qixo.com
Sidestep http://www.sidestep.com

Finally, see if your travel agent can better the price. If the difference is only marginal, favour your agent. Then at least you'll have a human contact if something goes wrong. See how the online bookers rate at:

Gomez.com http://www.gomez.com

Maps and Atlases

You can generate road and airport maps for most cities worldwide, driving directions for North America and Europe, US traffic reports, world maps and more at:

MapBlast http://www.mapblast.com
MapQuestUK http://www.mapquest.co.uk
Expedia http://maps.expedia.com
Multimap http://www.multimap.com
Easymap http://www.easymap.co.uk
Mappy http://www.mappy.co.uk
Ordnance Survey http://www.ordsvy.gov.uk
Shell Geo Star Route Planner http://www.shellgeostar.com

To create UK or Australian street and road maps from postcodes or addresses, see:

Whereis (AUS) http://www.whereis.com.au
Streetmap (UK) http://www.streetmap.co.uk

If you require highly detailed US topographic maps, try:

TopoZone http://www.topozone.com

For more maps, geographical and GPS resources see:
http://geography.about.com
http://dmoz.org/Reference/Maps/

12Degrees
http://www.12degrees.com
Rope in a guidebook author to plan your adventure holiday.

A2Btravel.com (UK)
http://www.a2btravel.com
http://www.ferrybooker.com
http://www.ukonline.co.uk/content/travel.html/
Resources for getting into, around, and out of the UK, such as car-hire comparison, airport guides, train timetables and ferry booking.

Africam
http://www.africam.com
Sneak a peek at wild beasts going about their business.

The Africa Guide
http://www.africaguide.com
Good, general guides of a region that nearly all the major guide books and travel services ignore. Try also Africa Net (http://www.africanet.com).

Art of Travel
http://www.artoftravel.com
How to see the world on $25 a day.

ATM Locators
http://www.visa.com/pd/atm/
http://www.mastercard.com/atm/
Locate a bowser willing to replenish your wallet.

The Bathroom Diaries
http://www.thebathroomdiaries.com
One of the most essential sites on the Web: You're in Bamako, Mali when nature calls and you're after a good, clean Western style toilet, click here to find out the nearest one. A wireless version is promised soon, so you'll have to hang on until then.

Bed & Breakfast.com
http://www.bedandbreakfast.com
http://www.babs.com.au (AUS)
http://www.innsite.com
Secure your night's sleep worldwide.

Bugbog
http://www.bugbog.co.uk
Nice, compact, easy-to-navigate miniguides for people wanting to go somewhere a bit out of the ordinary. Good features include the best beaches in the world by month, and a destination finder giving you options like colourful culture, festivals and weather.

Canals & Waterways: Roots & Routes
http://www.canalroutes.org.uk
All you ever wanted to know about canal barging.

Caravan Sitefinder
http://caravan-sitefinder.co.uk
Where to hitch your rusting hulk of steel without looking like hippy scum. For places to pitch your tent, try Camp Sites (http://www.camp-sites.co.uk).

CIA World Factbook
http://www.odci.gov/cia/publications/pubs.html/
Vital stats on every country. For the score on living standards: http://www.undp.org

Concierge.com
http://www.concierge.com
Get packing with advice from *Traveler* magazine.

Danger Finder
http://www.comebackalive.com/df/
Adventure holidays that could last a lifetime.

Days Out
http://www.virgin.net/daysout/
You might not want to use their trains to get you there, but Virgin does at least provide an excellent service with this site, which is crammed with ideas for successful day trips. For more ideas, try About Britain (http://www.aboutbritain.com) and DaysOutUK (http://www.daysoutuk.com).

Digistreets
http://www.digistreets.com
Enter a London postcode in return for an instant photo of the address.

Easy Stay
http://www.easystay.co.uk
Useful database of B&Bs and hotels in Britain, covering all price ranges. For accommodation throughout the globe, try Travel Web (http://www.travelweb.com).

Electronic Embassy
http://www.embassy.org
Directory of foreign embassies in DC plus Web links where available. Search Yahoo for representation in other cities.

Eurotrip
http://www.eurotrip.com
http://www.ricksteves.com
Look out Europe, here you come.

Family Travel Files
http://www.thefamilytravelfiles.com
Look here for help on what to do when the little monsters start asking, "Are we there yet?" For more UK-specific destinations, try PlanIt4Kids (http://www.planit4kids.com).

Flight Arrivals & Departures
http://www.flightarrivals.com
Stay on top of takeoffs and touchdowns across North America.

FrequentFlier.com
http://frequentflier.com
The information here is definitely more useful for Americans, but it's nevertheless a great resource for frequent travellers after the best deal for their miles. See also Web Flyer (http://www.webflyer.com).

Gap Year
http://www.gapyear.com
Excellent site dedicated to students about to take a year out, with loads of travel tips and stories.

Global Freeloaders
http://www.globalfreeloaders.com
Take in a globetrotting dosser in exchange for some return hospitality.

HolidayComplaint.com
http://HolidayComplaint.com
Vent some steam about a disappointing holiday here, and read others' complaints before you book.

Hotel Discount
http://www.hoteldiscount.com
http://www.hotelnet.co.uk
http://www.hotelwiz.com
Book hotels around the world. For backpacker rates, try:
http://www.hostels.com

How far is it?
http://www.indo.com/distance/
Calculate the distance between any two cities.

IgoUgo
http://www.igougo.com
Packed full of travellers' photos and journals, this roughguides.com partner site offers candid firsthand information.

Incredible Adventures
http://www.incredible-adventures.com
Convert your cash into adrenaline.

plan a trip

Infiltration
http://www.infiltration.org
Confessions of a serial trespasser.

share experiences

International Home Exchange Network

earn rewards

http://www.homexchange.com
http://www.sunswap.com
http://www.homebase-hols.com
Trade your dreary digs for a palatial beach house.

International Student Travel Confederation
http://www.istc.org
Save money with an authentic international student card.

Journeywoman
http://www.journeywoman.com
Reporting in from the sister beaten track.

Mail2Web
http://www.mail2web.com
Collect and send your POP3 mail instantly from any Web browser. Faster than Hotmail.

Mungo Park
http://www.mungopark.com
If you'd rather New Year in Timbuktu than Times Square.

My Travel Rights
http://mytravelrights.com

Disgruntled? Maybe you'll be reimbursed.

No Shitting in the Toilet
http://www.noshit.com.au
Delighting in the oddities of low-budget travel.

The Original Tipping Page
http://www.tipping.org
Make fast friends with the bell-hop.

Railtrack
http://www.railtrack.co.uk
Depress yourself at the state of the country's railways by looking at
corporate reports or the timetable details. To book tickets online try The
Train Line (http://www.thetrainline.com), and for general public transport information try Public Transport Info (http://www.pti.org.uk).

Resorts Online
http://www.resortsonline.com
Your way through 3,000 resorts throughout the world categorized by
beach, golf, spa, ski, etc.

Roadside America
http://www.roadsideamerica.com
Strange attractions that loom between squished animals on US high-
ways.

Sahara Overland
http://www.sahara-overland.com
Leave the city in a cloud of dust.

Satellite and Aerial Imaging
http://www.terraserver.com
http://terra.nasa.gov
http://www.crworld.co.uk
http://www.photolib.noaa.gov
http://www.globexplorer.com
http://www.multimap.com (UK)
See why nine out of ten Martian honeymooners prefer your planet.

Subway Navigator
http://www.subwaynavigator.com
http://www.manhattanaddress.com
Estimate the travelling times between city stations worldwide, or find the right stop in NY.

Theme Parks of England
http://tpoe.virtualave.net
Reviews and info on all the major high G-force thrills to be had without leaving the country.

Tips4Trips
http://www.tips4trips.com
More than 1000 tips for the traveller, from packing to navigating customs on your way back home.

TNT Live!
http://www.tntmagazine.com
Survive London and venture onward with aid from expat streetmags, *TNT* and *Southern Cross*.

Tourism Offices Worldwide
http://www.towd.com
Write to the local tourist office. They might send you a brochure. For even more propaganda, try Official Travel Info (http://www.official travelinfo.com).

Traffic and Road Conditions
http://www.accutraffic.com
http://traffic.yahoo.com
Live traffic and weather updates across the US.

Travel and Health Warnings
http://www.dfat.gov.au (Aus)
http://www.fco.gov.uk (UK)
http://travel.state.gov (US)
Don't ignore these bulletins if you're planning to visit a potential hotspot or health risk, but seek a second opinion before postponing your adventure. If you're off on business, try a professional advisory such as Kroll: http://www.krollworldwide.com

Travel Doctor

http://www.tmvc.com.au
http://www.cdc.gov/travel/
http://www.masta.org
http://www.travelhealth.co.uk
http://www.who.int

Brace yourself against the bugs eagerly awaiting your arrival. For a list of travel medicine clinics worldwide, see http://www.tripprep.com, and for more travel health information and a WAP service, try Medicine Planet (http://www.medicineplanet.com).

Traveldonkey

http://www.traveldonkey.co.uk

Big database of travel reviews written by ordinary people, not travel journalists on press junkets. The reviews are hooked up to maps and links to other sites. For more adventurous travelogues, try Virtual Tourist (http://www.virtualtourist.com).

Travelmag

http://www.travelmag.co.uk

Several intimate travel reflections monthly.

Travel News Organisation

http://www.travel-news.org

Independent travel news, holiday ideas and bargains for British travellers. For more, point your browser to eTravel (http://www.etravel.org).

Travel Paperwork

http://www.travelpaperwork.com

Sort out the red tape before you hit the border.

Travlang

http://www.travlang.com

Add another language to your repertoire.

Unclaimed Baggage

http://www.unclaimedbaggage.com

You lose it; they sell it.

UK Passport Agency
http://www.ukpa.gov.uk
Speed up your passport application at this streamlined site.

Underbelly
http://www.underbelly.com
Short, sharp, shocked guides to the places tourists rarely ever see.

Universal Currency Converter
http://www.xe.net/cc/
Convert Finnish Markkas into Central African Francs on the fly.

Vindigo
http://www.vindigo
Is Vindigo the future of travel guides? Download its Palm Pilot or
AvantGo city guides and decide for yourself.

Visit Britain
http://www.visitbritain.com
http://www.uktravel.com
Understand the British way of doing things.

Walkabout
http://www.walkabout.com.au
Get the lowdown on the land down under.

WebFlyer
http://www.webflyer.com
Keep tabs on frequent flier schemes.

What Cruise
http://www.whatcruise.co.uk
Great ways to spend your kids' inheritance money, plus a section on
last-minute deals if you're feeling guilty.

What's on When?
http://www.whatsonwhen.com
http://www.whatsgoingon.com
Annoyed you've missed *Thaipusam* or the *Turning of the Bones* yet
again? Get your dates right here.

World Heritage Listing
http://www.unesco.org/whc/
Plan your itinerary around international treasures.

Weather

Most news sites report the weather but it's rarely up-to-the-minute. For that you need to go directly to your local weather bureau or a specialist weather reporting service. For five-day forecasts, charts, storm warnings, allergy reports and satellite photos for thousands of cities worldwide, try:

Accuweather http://www.accuweather.com
CNN Weather http://www.cnn.com/WEATHER/
Intellicast http://www.intellicast.com
Online Weather http://www.onlineweather.com
Weather Centre http://www.weather-centre.co.uk
Weather Channel http://www.weather.com
Weathernet http://www.weathernet.com
Weather Organizer http://www.weather.org
Yahoo Weather http://weather.yahoo.com

Weather

For more intricate and timely detail, particularly outside the USA, drop by the Met Office: http://www.metoffice.gov.uk

For amateur observations and the fanatical extremes of weather watching, scan these specialist portals:

About Weather http://weather.about.com

Daniel's Weather Radar Page http://danielwxradar.tripod.com

European Centre for Medium Range Weather Forecasts
http://www.ecmwf.int

Open Directory http://dmoz.org/News/Weather/

The Very Useful UK Weather Page http://www.maalla.co.uk/uk-weather/

The Weather Resource http://www.nxdc.com/weather/

UM Weather http://cirrus.sprl.umich.edu/wxnet/

WMO Members http://www.wmo.ch/web-en/member.html/

Aviation Digital Data Service
http://adds.awc-kc.noaa.gov
If you're flying to the US, this pilot-orientated site will tell you if you need to pack extra sickbags.

Climate Ark
http://www.climateark.org
Fret about coming changes in the weather.

Hurricane Hunters
http://www.hurricanehunters.com
The homepage of the 53rd Weather Reconnaissance Squadron features photographs taken from the eye of the storm.

National Environmental Satellite and Data Information Service
http://www.nesdis.noaa.gov
Based in the US, this global headquarters of the world's weather trainspotters.

Ocean Weather
http://www.oceanweather.com
http://www.ssec.wisc.edu/data/sst.html/
Chart the swells and temperatures across the seven seas.

Paul's Weather Satellite and Waffle Page
http://www.hayes06.freeserve.co.uk
Learn how to build your own weather satellite and meet other climate
fanatics.

Snoweye
http://www.snoweye.com
http://www.snow-forecast.com
Spy on thousands of ski resorts worldwide through strategically hidden
cameras – or simply have the forecasts beamed directly to your WAP
phone.

Space Weather
http://www.spaceweather.com
Monitor the effect of solar activity on the earth's atmosphere.

Tornado and Storm Research Organisation
http://www.torro.org.uk
If you're into twisters,
this site will spin you
right round, baby, right
round.

Weather Images
http://www.weather
images.org
Depress yourself with
images from Bondi
Beach, and then cheer
yourself up with the
page of weather humour.

WeatherPlanner
http://www.weather-
planner.com
Plan your washing
around a long-term forecast.

Weather Software
http://weather.hypermart.net/software.html/
Stick out a wet thumb from the safety of your swivel chair.

Weather

Focused Forecasts

Tired of imprecise regional forecasts? Do you need to know exactly what time of day it will be safe to mow your lawn? Try these sites (most of which have been set up by enthusiasts) offering weather reports right down to your postcode:

Bablake Weather Station
http://bws.users.netlink.co.uk
In-depth forecasts for the Midlands.

BBC Online Weather Centre
http://www.bbc.co.uk/weather/
Forecasts for your postcode.

Meteorological Data From Sussex
http://cpesw3.mols.sussex.ac.uk/es/meteo/
Let the Uni of Sussex help you out.

North West England Weather Site
http://www.argonet.co.uk/users/jim.matt/
From Crewe to Lancaster.

Scottish Weather Information
http://www.geo.ed.ac.uk/home/scotland/scotweather.html/
North of the Border.

Stoke-On-Trent Weather Station
http://www.coyney.demon.co.uk
How specific do you want?

Wild Weather
http://www.wildweather.com
http://australiasevereweather.com
http://www.storm-track.org
http://www.nssl.noaa.gov
Set your course into the eye of the storm.

World Climate
http://www.worldclimate.com
http://www.weatherbase.com
Off to Irkutzk next August? Here's what weather to expect.

World Meteorological Organization
http://www.wmo.ch
UN division that monitors global climate.

Webcams

Africam
http://www.africam.com
Go on a (virtual) safari without even leaving your armchair.

The Amazing Cooler Cam
http://www.coolercam.com
As if your workplace wasn't boring enough, watch Americans get drinks from the office water cooler.

Beer Lover Cam
http://www.beerlovercam.com
Watch a couple of guys agonize over whether to grab a can of Bud or just go for the Miller.

Earth Cam
http://www.earthcam.com
Links to a vast array of Webcams, usefully organized into categories and subcategories including Traffic, Arts & Entertainment, Metro, Weird

and more. Also check Allcam (http://www.allcam.com), Webcam
Central (http://www.camcentral.com), Webcam World
(http://www.webcamworld.com) and Webviews (http://www.
webviews.co.uk).

Electrolux Real Fridge Cam
http://www.electrolux.com/node230.asp/
Discover once and for all whether the light stays on or off when you
close the door.

Fly on the Wall
http://www.flyonthewall.com
A portal dedicated to Webcams and streaming video footage of movie
premieres and showbiz parties, as well as Times Square, spacecraft
landings and, umm, guinea pigs.

Jennicam
http://www.jennicam.org
The most celebrated webcam of 'em all. The enormous success of
Jennicam is partially responsible for that most loathsome aspect of
contemporary culture: reality television. But if you want to see where the
phenomenon started, log on, pay your membership fee and watch Jenni
get drunk and snog strangers ... provided you're an adult.

Pavement Terror
http://www.backfire.co.uk
As if you needed more reason not to trust White Van Man, former delivery man Howard Stone has posted streaming videos of pedestrian horror when his van backfires.

Steve's Ant Farm
http://www.stevesantfarm.com
Watch blurry black punctuation marks build tunnels.

Wearcam
http://www.wearcam.org
Your one-stop shop for information on "photoborgs" and wearable
computers.

Weird

Absurd.org
http://www.absurd.org
Please do not adjust your set.

Aetherius Society
http://www.aetherius.org
Continue the legacy of the late Sir Dr George King, Primary Terrestrial Mental Channel of the Interplanetary Council.

Aliens and Soul Abduction
http://www.cia.com.au/brough/
Fact: spooky space dudes are stealing our souls. The Bible wouldn't lie: http://aliensin thebible.com

American Pie and the Armageddon Prophecy
http://www.roytaylorministries.com
How Madonna testified against the descendants of Israel all the way to number one. But what tragedy awaits her: http://www.geocities.com/Athens/Atrium/3933/madonna.htm/

Animal Mating Zone
http://www.matings.co.uk
Hardcore sex: the type you only get to see in wildlife documentaries.

Brother Ellis Society
http://www.freespeech.org/besna/besna.html/
Appease God by eating unwanted pets. No details spared. In complete contrast to: http://www.jesusveg.com

Build a Better Batsuit
http://www.geocities.com/thebatguy_99/
Take off on a caped crusade.

Christian Guide to Small Arms
http://www.frii.com/~gosplow/cgsa.html/
"He that hath no sword, let him sell his garment and buy one – Luke 22:36. It's not just your right; it's your duty, darnit.

Circlemakers
http://www.circlemakers.org
Create crop circles to amuse New Agers and the press.

A Citizen from Hell
http://www.amightywind.com/hell/citizenhell.htm/
If Hell sounds this bad, you don't want to go there.

Clonaid
http://www.clonaid.com
Thanks to the Raelians, we now know all life on earth was created in extraterrestrial laboratories. Here's where you can buy genuine cloned human livestock for the kitchen table. Ready as soon as the lab's finished.

Corpses for Sale
http://distefano.com
Brighten up your guestroom or spoil your pet with a life-sized chew-toy.

The Darwin Awards
http://www.officialdarwinawards.com
http://www.darwinawards.com
Each year the Darwin Award goes to the person who drops off the census register in the most spectacular fashion. Here's where to read about the runners-up and er ... winners.

Derm Cinema
http://www.skinema.com
Know your celebrity skin conditions. But would you recognize them under a gas mask? http://www.geocities.com/TimesSquare/Alley/8207/

Dolphin Society
http://www.dolphinsociety.org
Driftnet-eating submarines rescue humans who've shape-shifted into dolphins.

Dr MegaVolt
http://www.drmegavolt.com
The Doc sure sparked right up when they switched on the power, but could he cut in the big league? http://www3.bc.sympatico.ca/lightningsurvivor/

English Rose Press
http://www.englishrosepress.com
Diana sends her love from Heaven.

Fetish Map
http://www.deviantdesires.com/map/map.html/
Join the dots between piggy-players, fursuitters, inflators, crush freaks and where you're standing now.

Flatulence Filter
http://flatulence-filter.com
Because life wasn't meant to be a gas.

Fortean Times
http://www.forteantimes.com
Updates from the print monthly that takes the investigation of strange phenomena more seriously than itself. See also http://www.parascope.com and http://www.bizarremag.com.

Freaks, Geeks, & Weirdness on the Web
http://www.rosemarywest.com/guide/
http://www.the-strange.com
http://www.student.nada.kth.se/~nv91-asa/
Make that three big sacks of assorted nuts, please.

Future Horizons
http://www.futurehorizons.net
Snap off more than your fair share through solid-state circuitry.

Weird

Gallery of the Absurd
http://www.absurdgallery.com
Strange ways to sell strange stuff.

Great Joy In Great Tribulation
http://www.dccsa.com/greatjoy/
Biblical proof that Prince Chuck is the Antichrist and key dates leading
to the end of the world. For more enlightenment, including how to
debug the pyramids, see: http://members.aol.com/larrypahl/lpahl.htm/

God Channel
http://www.godchannel.com
Relay requests to God via His official Internet channel.

I Can Eat Glass Project
http://hcs.harvard.edu/~igp/glass.html/
Deter excess foreign suitors and carpet dealers with the only words you
know in their language.

Illuminati News
http://www.illuminati-news.com
Storm into secret societies and thump your fist on the table.

I Love Leather Pants
http://www.geocities.com/westhollywood/heights/2828/
Don't expect to get André out of his skintight black trousers.

International Ghost Hunters Society
http://www.ghostweb.com
http://www.ghostresearch.org
They never give up the ghost. Nab your own with:
http://www.maui.net/~emf/TriFieldNat.html/

Itz Fun Tew Be Dat Kandie Kid
http://www.angelfire.com/ma/talulaQ/kandie.html/
Mothers – don't let your babies grow up to be ravers.

Kaol's Ol' Sinkin' Hole
http://www.geocities.com/SoHo/8090/
What's sexier than sinking in quicksand? Nothing, says Kaol, except

perhaps being gassed, drowned, strangled or blown out into space:
http://www.fortunecity.com/lavendar/mockingbird/472/

Mind Control Forum
http://mindcontrolforum.com
http://www.mindcontrolmanual.com
http://www.psychops.com
http://www.raven1.net
Unpick Big Brother's evil scheme and then put it to work on the dance-floor.

Mozart's Musikalisches Würfelspeil
http://sunsite.univie.ac.at/Mozart/dice/
Compose a minuet as you play Monopoly.

Mudboy
http://www.mudboyuk.com
Some get their kicks from muddy boots.

Museum of Non-Primate Art
http://www.monpa.com
Become an aficionado of moggy masterpieces.

A Mathematical Survey of the English Language
http://www.geocities.com/garywaterbury/
Plot your future through simple arithmetic.

Myrla's Korner
http://myrla.tripod.com
Thank goodness the ancient felinoid Ka'ats from planet Zimmorrah have Myrna. Otherwise no one would take them seriously.

Neuticles
http://www.neuticles.com
Pick your pet's pocket but leave his dignity intact.

News of the Weird
http://www.nine.org/notw/
http://www.thisistrue.com
http://www.weirdlist.com
Dotty clippings from the world press.

Nibiruan Council
http://www.nibiruancouncil.com
Stock your bar to welcome the heroic Starseeds, Walkins, and Lightworkers from the Battlestar Nibiru, who will finally usher in the fifth dimensional reality.

Non-escalating Verbal Self Defence
http://www.taxi1010.com
Fight insults by acting insane.

PhobiaList
http://phobialist.com
So much to fear, it's scary.

Planetary Activation Organization
http://www.paoweb.com
Prevent inter-dimensional dark forces from dominating our galaxy by ganging up with the Galactic Federation of Light.

Poop in a Box
http://www.poopinabox.com
Express your gratitude with a gift-wrapped "loaf".

Professional Paranoid
http://www.proparanoid.com
For when no one else will believe you.

Reincarnation.org
http://www.reincarnation-org.com
Stash your loot with this crowd, then come back to collect it in your next life.

Reptoids
http://www.reptoids.com
Was that an alien or merely the subterranean descendant of a dinosaur?

Rocket Guy
http://www.rocketguy.com
Brian's about to launch himself into space. Bye-bye, Brian.

The Sacred Geometry Stories of Jesus Christ
http://www.jesus8880.com
How to decode the big J's mathematical word puzzle.

Scrambled Eggs
http://www.callnetuk.com/home/busted/
Nothing a swift kick in the groin won't fix.

Sensoterapia
http://www.sensoterapia.com.co
Master the sex secret you'll never see revealed in this month's *Cleo*.

Sightings
http://www.sightings.com
Fishy newsbreaks from talk radio truthfer-ret Jeff Rense. For more real life X-file blather, tune into: http://www.artbell.com

Sulabh International Museum of Toilets
http://www.sulabhtoiletmuseum.org
Follow the evolution of the ablution at the world's leading exhibition of bathroom businessware. No need to take it sitting down: http://www.restrooms.org

Terry J Hokanson lives under the Mafia
http://www.geocities.com/terry_tune/
Mild mannered inventor speaks out against the crime syndicate that controls his life through government hypnotists.

Things My Girlfriend and I Have Argued About
http://homepage.ntlworld.com/mil.millington/things.html/
Add this page to that list.

Time Travel Devices
http://home.inreach.com/dov/tt.htm/

Step back to a time that common sense forgot.

Toe Amputation Project
http://www.bme.freeq.com/spc/
toecutter.htm/
No big deal. He still has a couple left.

Toilet-train Your Cat
http://www.karawynn.net/mishacat/
http://susandennis.com
How to point pusskins at the porcelain.

Trapped Angels
http://www.cyberspaceorbit.com/
april.html/
Leading authorities point to evidence that angels may be alien frauds. Backed up at http://www.mt.net/~watcher/

WearCam
http://www.wearcam.org
Steve has a Netcam fixed to his head. You see what he sees. But that won't stop him having fun.

Why I will never have a girlfriend
http://www.nothingisreal.com/girlfriend/
Derived from first principles, and confirmed by his nickname.

World Database of Happiness
http://www.eur.nl/fsw/research/happiness/
Discover where people are happiest and statistically what they mean by that.

Xenophobic Persecution in the UK
http://www.five.org.uk
If you're below British standards the MI5 will punish you by TV.

ZetaTalk
http://www.zetatalk.com
Nancy's guests today are those elusive aliens that frolic in the autumn mist at the bottom of her garden.

ROUGH GUIDES: Travel

100 Essential

CDs *Eight titles, one name*

ROUGH GUIDES

Sorted

ROUGH
GUIDES